W9-BZR-093

Building a Data Warehouse for Decision Support

Second Edition

Vidette Poe
Patricia Klauer
and
Stephen Brobst

To join a Prentice Hall PTR Internet mailing list,
point to: http://www.prenhall.com/mail_lists/

Prentice Hall PTR
Upper Saddle River, NJ 07458

Library of Congress Cataloging-In-Publication Data

Poe, Vidette.
Building a data warehouse for decision support / Vidette Poe, Patricia Klauer, and Stephen Brobst. — [2nd ed.]
p. cm.
Includes bibliographical references and index.
ISBN 0-13-769639-6
1 Decision support systems. 2. Data warehousing. I. Klauer, Patricia. II. Brobst, Stephen. III. Title.
T58.62.P63 1997
658.4'038—dc21 97-29161
CIP

Acquisitions editor: Mark Taub
Cover designer: Design Source
Cover director: Jerry Votta
Manufacturing buyer: Alexis R. Heydt
Compositor/Production services: Pine Tree Composition, Inc.

Prentice-Hall, Inc.
A Simon & Schuster Company
Upper Saddle River, New Jersey 07458

Prentice Hall books are widely used by corporations and government agencies for training, marketing, and resale. The publisher offers discounts on this book when ordered in bulk quantities.
For more information contact:
Phone: 800-382-3419
FAX: 201-236-7141
email: corpsales@prenhall.com
or write:
Corporate Sales Department
Prentice Hall PTR
One Lake Street
Upper Saddle River, New Jersey 07458

Printed in the United States of America
10 9 8 7 6 5 4 3 2 1

ISBN: 0-13-769639-9

Prentice Hall International (UK) Limited, *London*
Prentice Hall of Australia Pty. Limited, *Sydney*
Prentice Hall Canada, Inc., *Toronto*
Prentice Hall Hispanoamericana, S.A., *Mexico*
Prentice Hall of India Private Limited, *New Delhi*
Prentice Hall of Japan, Inc., *Tokyo*
Simon & Schuster Asia Pte. Ltd., *Singapore*
Editora Prentice Hall do Brasil, Ltda., *Rio de Janeiro*

To Frederick, for his unceasing compassion and commitment
—VP

To my mother, Gloria Neese
—PK

To Hilda, Crystal, and Saphira
—SB

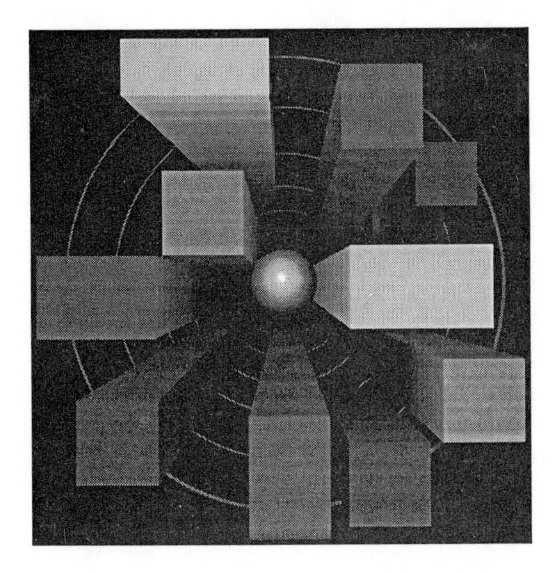

CONTENTS

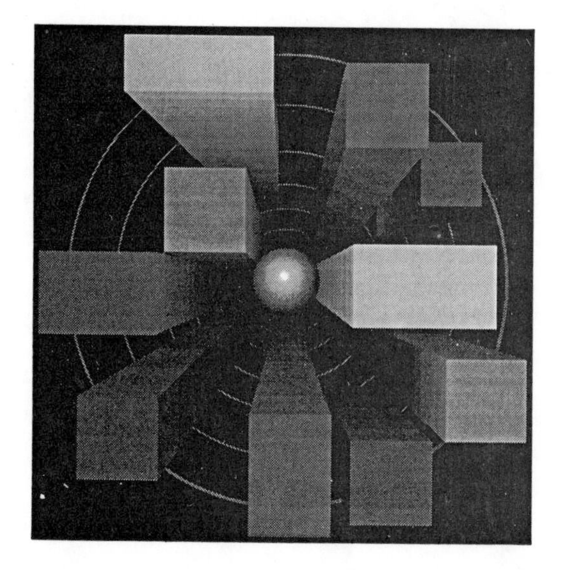

PREFACE

It has been almost two years since the first edition *of Building a Data Warehouse for Decision Support* was written. In that time, the marketplace for data warehouse related products has changed dramatically. The database vendors are providing new capabilities to handle large volumes of data efficiently, as well as indexing strategies to retrieve data more efficiently and quickly. Data integration and conversion tools have improved. There has been an explosion of sophisticated, well-developed multidimensional front-end tools to enable end users to access the data they need to do their jobs. Network and data management products have emerged. Decision support environments have become more sophisticated and the sizes of the databases are growing increasingly larger.

While the products and technologies surrounding and complementing data warehouse implementation have become much more refined, the process of actually building a data warehouse has not significantly changed. You must still plan and scope your project well, work with end users to gather requirements, design the database for On Line Analytical Processing (OLAP) processing, and move through all the appropriate stages of the life cycle for the development of your data warehouse to be successful.

Certainly, with the experience accumulated over the last few years, there is a better understanding of where the problems will arise in the life cycle and what aspects of building a warehouse will generally become obstacles within an organization and how to overcome them. Additionally, we have found more suitable techniques for gathering requirements.

As consultants actively working in the decision support arena, we are more convinced than ever that the success of a data warehouse is built not on specific technologies or platforms, but on finding the appropriate solution to the business users' needs. New technologies are too often used as panaceas within corporations, negating the very real necessity of clearly identifying the business needs and finding workable solutions to address those needs. Decision support systems are unique in that they are developed solely to enable end users to access data to make better decisions, thereby leveraging both resources—the considerable business knowledge of the end user and the data. For this reason, a successful decision support system requires more interaction with business users than ever before. It is not a specific technology that makes a data warehouse successful, but an understanding of the business objective and the end users' needs, and working together toward an appropriate solution.

Interestingly, although thousands of data warehouses have been deployed over the last several years, the integration of data for use in a data warehouse is still being routinely ignored within most corporations. Data is still relegated to the "don't ask, don't tell" policy; better not to notice its inconsistencies or address the nuances of meaning of the data that is being merged and loaded into the database.

The ability to view consistent data across business units or divisions within a corporation is one of the most valuable outcomes of a data warehouse, and often one of the primary reasons the warehouse is being implemented. Yet the majority of companies, even many of those with decision support systems actively being used, still do not have a synthesized view of their data because they have not gone through the process of analyzing and integrating the different characteristics of their source data, such as data names, definitions, data types and sizes, and business rules.

This reluctance to address the area of data integration and to develop the enterprise architecture and procedures to actively manage data as a leverageable resource is one of the largest holes that we see in the development of decision support systems. Consequently, it can have a profound effect on the overall success of the ongoing data warehouse development within a company.

To provide information to address the issue of data integration, we have added Chapter 8, "Data Integration," and Chapter 12, "Managing Metadata." We have consolidated many of the issues addressed throughout the book into Chapter 4, "Critical Success Factors." We have also added three new case studies to this edition.

The authors and contributors to the second edition of this book are some of the best people in the decision support arena, those having extensive, hands-on experience in creating data warehousing solutions. The primary authors of this second edition, Vidette Poe, Patricia Klauer, and Stephen Brobst, are experts in their respective fields. Vidette Poe's specialty is corporatewide data warehouse data architectures and associated infrastructures and hands-on project management for data warehouse implementations. Patricia Klauer specializes in designing architecture, infrastructures, and organizational structures for enterprisewide integration and management of data. Stephen Brobst specializes in the construction of data warehouses in high-end parallel processing environments. Other contributors provided case studies from within their own industries or companies.

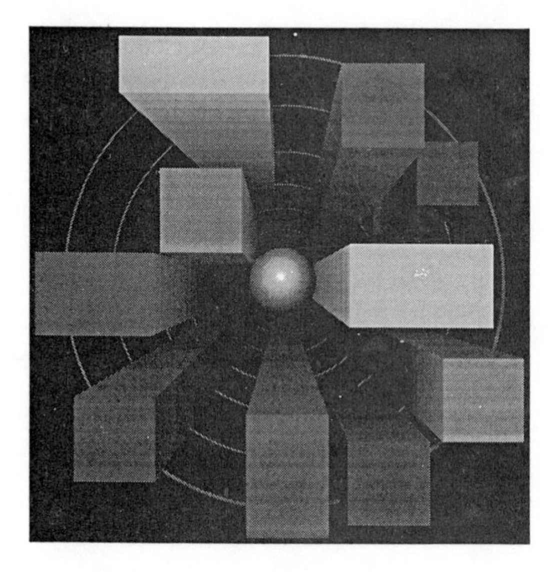

PREFACE TO THE FIRST EDITION

Many corporations are actively looking for new technologies that will assist them in becoming more profitable and competitive. Gaining competitive advantage requires that companies accelerate their decision making process so that they can respond quickly to change. One key to this accelerated decision making is having the right information, at the right time, easily accessible.

Currently, data exists within the corporate business systems that can provide this decision-making information. However, in most companies, this data is spread across multiple systems, platforms, and locations creating issues of data integrity and making access in a timely fashion next to impossible.

A data warehouse for decision support developed within an architected environment is designed specifically to supply this critical information to decision makers.

Advances in technology now make the development of a data warehouse providing credible and timely decision support information feasible. These technologies include:

- Open client server architectures
- Advanced techniques to replicate, refresh, and update data
- Tools to extract, transform, and load data from multiple, heterogeneous sources
- Databases specifically designed to handle very high volumes of data
- Front-end data access and analysis software with extensive functionality

This book is about building a data warehouse for decision support in an architected environment. It is being written to provide practical and realistic guidelines for your data warehouse development project so that you can move forward in a knowledgeable and informed manner. It will clarify the aspects of development that are critical to success and those that are not. "Tips from the Trenches" will furnish practical tips, ideas, and ways to approach development that have been learned over the course of several data warehouse projects.

This book will provide a good understanding of the technical issues involved in building a data warehouse for decision support including:

- The life cycle for building decision support systems
- Data warehouse architectures

- Planning the data warehouse
- Gathering requirements from users and transforming them into a database schema
- Database design for a data warehouse
- The data access environment—successfully using the data warehouse

The primary focus of this book is on the actual development of a data warehouse. The intended audience are the members of a project team whose task is to make the data warehouse work. This includes a broad range of data processing and business professionals including:

- Project Managers
- Data modelers and database designers
- DBAs
- Programmers and analysts
- System and data architects
- Users

This book presumes some understanding or experience with building systems in general, and a knowledge of relational database technology for the technical discussions.

Some aspects of this book may be too technical for users. However, it will provide them with a strong understanding of what a data warehouse is, how it is developed, the kinks in the development cycle, and why it may take a little longer than was first imagined. I would encourage users to read it.

This book was written to be both comprehensive and easy to understand. In an effort to convey as much as possible about data warehouse development, the chapters are structured to move through the data warehouse development life cycle as closely as possible to actual development.

This book covers the fundamental development issues you will need to address to build your data warehouse. Because of time constraints, other important issues, for instance, data replication technologies and the technicalities surrounding the scheduled update to the warehouse, have not been discussed in depth. Perhaps as more data warehouses are developed, you will find informative articles on these subjects that will assist you.

A well-architected and designed data warehouse can, in fact, furnish your company with the decision support information it needs in a competitive market. Finding solutions to the technical issues surrounding the data warehouse, its integration into current system architectures, and successfully making all of the necessary components—the data transformation tools, the heterogeneous platforms and databases, the communications, networking and data replication technologies—work together to make these systems interesting and challenging to develop. This book will provide information to assist you with this challenge.

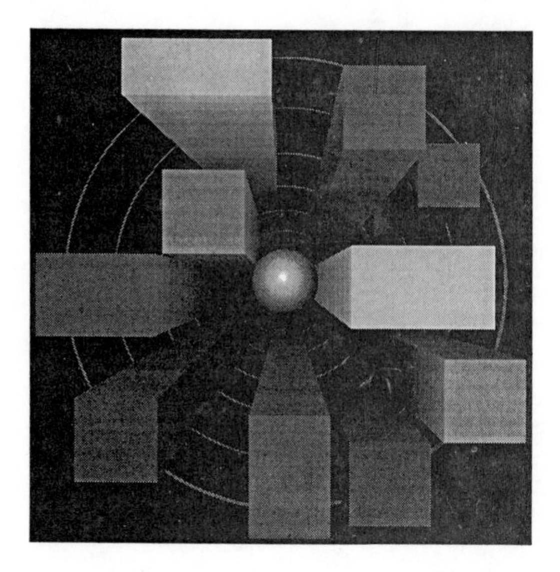

ACKNOWLEDGMENTS

Many talented people assisted with the development of this edition of *Building a Data Warehouse for Decision Support.* Thank you to my co-authors and all of the case study contributors for their work and perseverence in getting the job done.

Many thanks to Mark Taub, our wonderful editor at Prentice Hall. I would like to acknowledge and thank my family for their unconditional support over the last year. A special kind of thanks to the three little guys at home—you keep me smiling. Finally, to the women who have worked and studied with me for many years and are changing the face of business and the technical arts, I salute you with this book.

—Vidette Poe

I would not be writing this if it weren't for my mentor, who taught me how to be myself by challenging me to be more than I ever dreamed I could. I would like to thank Andy Martin for his uncompromising grace under fire, wearing every day another face of love.

—Patricia Klauer

Thanks to Andy Holman and Owen Robertson of Tanning Technology Corporation for their input and review in developing the chapter on critical success factors.

—Stephen Brobst

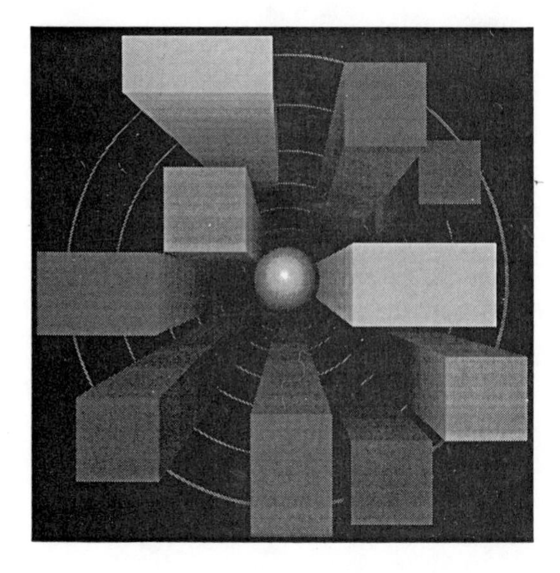

ABOUT THE AUTHORS

Vidette Poe

Vidette Poe (*warebs@aol.com*) is President of Strategic Business Solutions, Inc. Vidette has focused on data-related technologies, including data architecture, data integration, relational database design and development, and data administration strategies, for 10 years.

Vidette's specialty is developing enterprisewide data architectures and strategies for decision support systems, hands-on management of project teams through data warehouse development and implementation, and setting up infrastructures to support data-focused decision support environments. Vidette has experience developing data warehouses, Operational Data Stores, and related business strategies for the retail, financial, manufacturing, pharmaceutical, and agricultural industries.

Vidette is the author of the first edition of *Building a Data Warehouse for Decision Support,* published by Prentice Hall in 1996.

Patricia Klauer

Patricia Klauer (*pklauer@aol.com*), a co-founder of Manage Data Inc., has developed strategies to support data integration, distribution, and management for enterprisewide applications for the last 10 years. She specializes in assisting large organizations in designing the infrastructures, architecture, organizational structure, and procedures to support enterprisewide intelligent information management.

Patricia has designed integrated databases and data warehouses for a variety of strategic On Line Transaction Processing (OLTP) and Decision Support (DSS) applications including Risk Management, Market Analysis, Financial Instrument, and Client Relationship Management Systems.

Stephen Brobst

Stephen Brobst (*sabrobst@jj.lcs.mit.edu*) is a Senior Consultant at Tanning Technology Corporation. He also is a founder and Managing Partner of Strategic Technologies & Systems. His specialization is the construction of data warehouse solutions for Fortune 500 companies in the United States and internationally. Stephen performed his graduate work in Computer Science at the Massachusetts Institute of Technology where his Master's and Ph.D. research focused on high-performance parallel processing. He also completed an M.B.A. with joint course and thesis work at the Harvard Business School and the MIT Sloan School of Management.

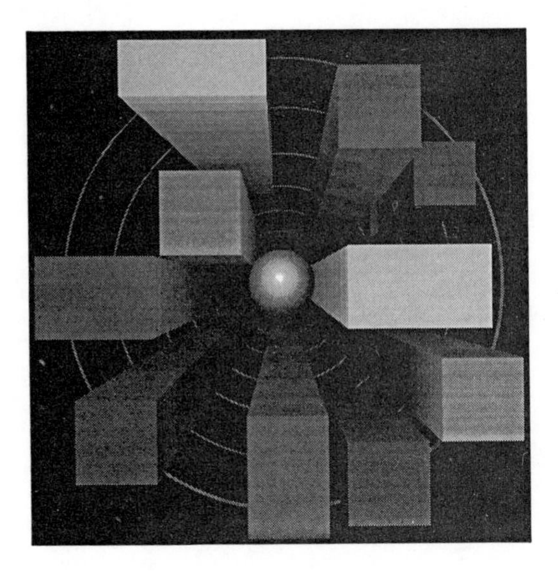

Other Contributors to This Book

Anne Meyers

Anne Meyers is the Executive Director of Decision Support Systems at Anthem Blue Cross & Blue Shield, Cincinnati, Ohio. Anne assisted with the development of the case study "Ongoing Data Warehouse Development at Anthem Blue Cross & Blue Shield."

Debora Stranaghan

Debora Stranaghan, Implementation Services Manager at British Columbia Hydro, was responsible for the case study "Selecting a Front End to the Data Warehouse."

Chip Kelly

Chip Kelly is Program Manager for Web Enablement at SAS Institute. Chip is responsible for providing technical consultation on the Internet and Web enablement as it relates to SAS software. His experience at SAS Institute includes over 13 years in both technical and management areas developing the Institute's market position, and most recently on implementation opportunities within the Internet and intranet markets.

Chip earned a B.S. degree in forestry from Rutgers University and holds an M.S. degree in genetics from North Carolina State University. Chip is co-author with Chap Gleason of the Environmental Protection Agency (EPA) of the case study "EPA Intranet Helps Policymakers Protect the Environment."

Jim O'Reilly

Jim O'Reilly (joreilly@corvu.com) is the Vice President of Sales for CorVu Corporation, a provider of end-user-based business intelligence, balanced scorecarding, and predictive OLAP products. With a technical background in database architectures, and over five years' experience consulting with companies in strategic data warehouse implementations, Jim has a broad base of experience with decision support systems. Prior to CorVu Jim was the Director of Sales for Prodea Software Corporation before its acquisition by Platinum technology, inc. Jim reviewed the first edition of *Building a Data Warehouse for Decision Support* and modified Chapter 2, "Understanding Terms and Technology" for this edition.

Judith Vanderkay

Judith A. Vanderkay, Senior Consultant at Rogers Communications Inc., assisted in the development of the case study "Selecting a Front End to the Data Warehouse."

Laura Reeves

Laura L. Reeves (ReevesLL@AOL.com) is co-founder and principal of StarSoft Solutions, Inc., a leading provider of data warehouse and decision support services. Her experience includes developing global project plans, business requirements documents, Business Dimensional Models, logical and physical database designs, DSS applications, and supporting production rollout of data warehouses. She previously held consulting management positions for MicroStategy, Inc. and Metaphor, Inc Laura authored Chapter 10, "Successful Data Access" in the first edition of *Building a Data Warehouse for Decision Support.*

Linda Bronstein

Linda Bronstein is the Chief Actuary at Anthem Blue Cross & Blue Shield in Cincinnati, Ohio. Linda assisted with the development of the case study "Ongoing Data Warehouse Development at Anthem Blue Cross & Blue Shield."

Mark Johnson

Mark I. Johnson is the President and CEO of InER-G Solutions, Ltd., and internationally recognized as a leader in the information technologies industry. He is a lecturer and writer on the subject of data warehousing and business intelligence information systems with over 15 years of systems engineering and integration experience. Mark's leadership abilities include facilitation, presentation, and conflict resolution and his experience includes retail, manufacturing, telecommunications, financial, and consumer products decison support systems. Mark provided technical information for the case study "Moving through the Obstacles to Implementation."

Mark Thompson

Mark Thompson is responsible for developing a market-based forecasting and planning system to effectively drive the sales/operations planning process and facilitating marketing and sales measurements for Hoffman Engineering. He oversees the design and implementation of the marketing information system that provides users information for improved decision making. In addition, he is responsible for conducting market research, developing market trend analysis, and industry/competitor profiles.

Mark began his career as a CPA. He then joined Northwest Airlines where he assumed a variety of posts including Director of Market Planning and Director of Financial Planning. Prior to joining Hoffman, Mark was Vice President of Corporate Planning at Dain Bosworth. Mark has an M.B.A. in marketing from the University of Minnesota. He received his B.A. degree from Concordia College with majors in accounting and organization communications. Mark co-authored the case study "Moving through the Obstacles to Implementation."

Building a Data Warehouse for Decision Support

Second Edition

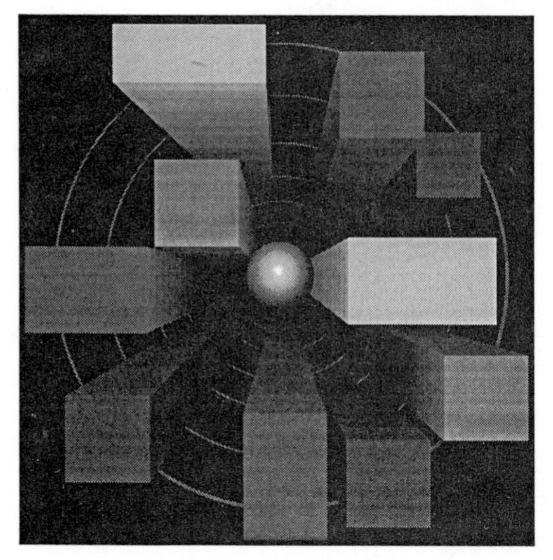

Chapter 1

Let's Start with the Basics

WHAT IS A DECISION SUPPORT SYSTEM?

A decision support system is a system that provides information to users so that they can analyze a situation and make decisions. Put another way, a decision support system provides information to assist employees in making decisions and doing their jobs more effectively. This decision making can be long-term strategic decision making, such as analyzing buying patterns over several years to develop a new product or service or perhaps to introduce a product into a new European or Far Eastern location. Decision making could also be short term and tactical in nature, such as reviewing and changing recommended order quantities for a particular product. The systems providing this information so that employees are better equipped to make more informed decisions are decision support systems.

UNDERSTANDING OPERATIONAL VERSUS ANALYTICAL PROCESSING

When you hear people talking about operational processing, they are referring to the systems that run the day-to-day business of a company. These will often be on-line transaction systems, which are updated continually throughout the day. For instance, if someone buys a printer from your computer store, the operational system will subtract one from the number of printers on hand at your site. As printers continue to sell throughout the day, the operational systems will consistently subtract from (or make additions to, in the case of shipment receipts) the inventory. When the inventory reaches a specific level, these operational systems may automatically generate a purchase order for more stock from the supplier. This is an example of operational processing which handles the day-to-day operations of the business.

Analytical systems are systems that provide information used for analyzing a problem or situation. Analytical processing is primarily done through comparisons, or by analyzing patterns and trends. For instance, an analytical system might show you how a specific brand of printer is selling throughout different parts of the United States, and also how that specific brand is selling since it was first introduced into your stores. Comparing sales between the different territories within the United States can provide a certain type of analytical information, while scanning historical information will show you how the product is selling over time.

Analytical databases do not hold up-to-the-minute information but hold information *as of a specific point in time.* This makes perfect sense for a system that is providing information being used for comparisons and trends. Comparisons require a stable number *to compare to.* For instance, it is possible to ascertain that June's sales of printers were substantially lower than the previous three months because monthly sales figures are available for comparison. Sales figures for printers *as of month end* were stored in the database. It's possible to monitor printer sales *as of* the preceding day, the preceding week, the preceding month, or year (or other period), if that is the level of information being held in the analytical database.

Trying to find out how sales of laptops and printers compare, for example, would be quite difficult if up-to-the-minute information was constantly changing the data in the database. This is the reason that analytical databases hold information *as of a specific point in time.*

Information that is as of a certain point in time is also called *a snapshot of data.* For example, if your analytical database holds a *snapshot* of sales information as of midnight each night, you will know that any day you look at the figures you will be seeing information as of midnight of the previous day. This way, daily, weekly, monthly, or yearly comparison will make sense, since you will always have a consistent value with which to compare.

Analyzing data patterns and trends over time often requires large volumes of historical data. You may wish to analyze, for instance, how your customer base has been changing over time. Several years of data would be useful for such analysis, providing information on the demographics of your client base. Certainly, being aware that more women are buying computers and software than ever before and understanding their buying patterns and trends would provide substantial information for changes in advertising and associated products. Another example may need 12 months of historical data to monitor sales volumes for the phase out of one product with the concurrent marketing and introduction of a comparable new product.

The idea that the data in an operational system is volatile and the data in an analytical system is nonvolatile directly relates to the different functionality of operational and analytical systems. The operational systems, which are running the daily business, have data that is changing constantly, as the previous inventory example indicates. This operational data is highly volatile. However, the data in the analytical database is a snapshot of data that will not change, as illustrated by the amount recorded as of midnight of the previous day.

Although data in an operational database may be changing throughout the day as business progresses, data in an analytical database will stay consistent and the database will be updated according to a predefined schedule.

An analytical database is most commonly designed as a *read-only database*. With a read-only database, users can look at the information, perhaps manipulate it in various ways on their desktops, but they can't change the value of the data in the database. A read-only database makes sense for analytical processing. Would you want the sales information as of a certain date to be changed at the discretion of the person in the department next to yours? Of course not. The only updates to the analytical database will be done according to its predefined schedule.

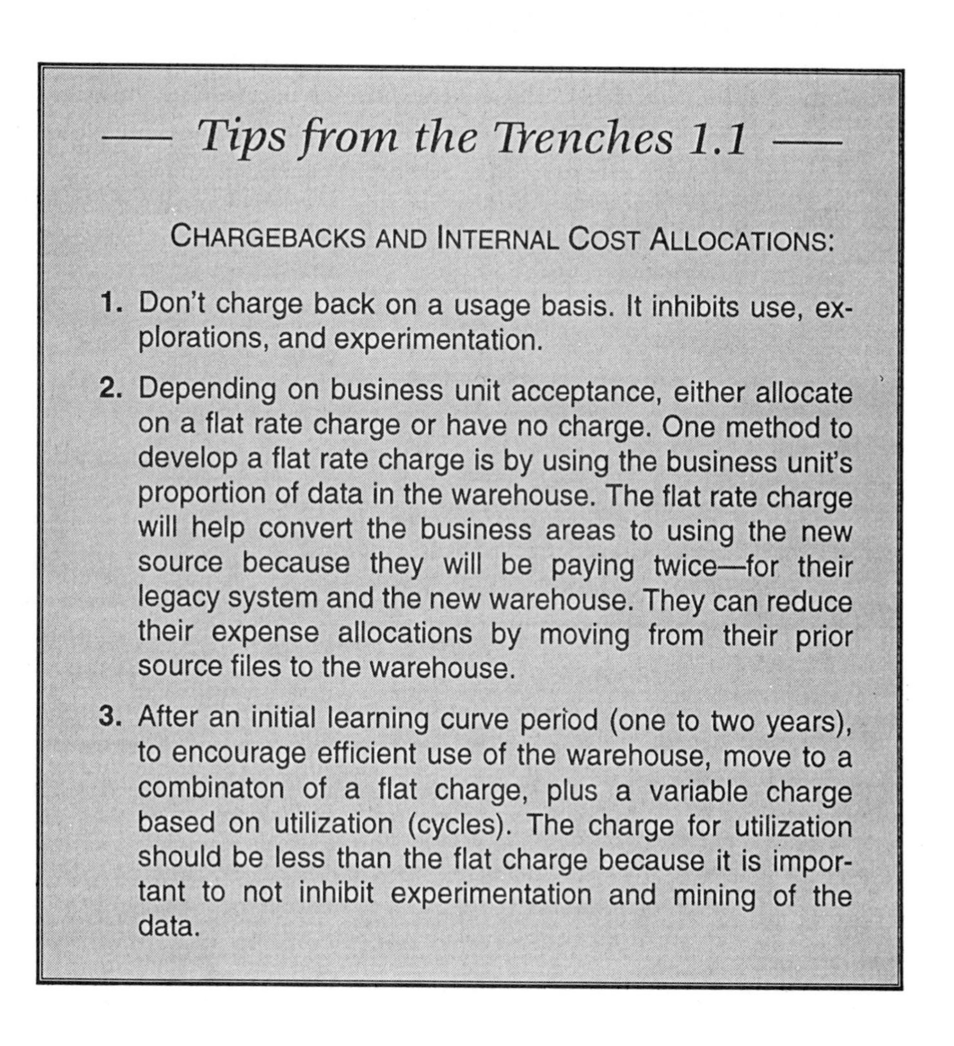

— Tips from the Trenches 1.1 —

CHARGEBACKS AND INTERNAL COST ALLOCATIONS:

1. Don't charge back on a usage basis. It inhibits use, explorations, and experimentation.
2. Depending on business unit acceptance, either allocate on a flat rate charge or have no charge. One method to develop a flat rate charge is by using the business unit's proportion of data in the warehouse. The flat rate charge will help convert the business areas to using the new source because they will be paying twice—for their legacy system and the new warehouse. They can reduce their expense allocations by moving from their prior source files to the warehouse.
3. After an initial learning curve period (one to two years), to encourage efficient use of the warehouse, move to a combinaton of a flat charge, plus a variable charge based on utilization (cycles). The charge for utilization should be less than the flat charge because it is important to not inhibit experimentation and mining of the data.

Another characteristic that distinguishes an operational system from an analytical system is the *design of the database*. An operational system is often designed to take in data, make changes to existing data, reconcile amounts, keep track of transactions, run reports, maintain data integrity, and manage transactions as quickly as possible. An analytical system is not designed to do any of those things. An analytical database is designed for large volumes of read-only data, providing information that will be used in making decisions. Thus, the design of an analytical database differs significantly from that of an operational database.

WHAT IS A DATA WAREHOUSE?

The concept of the data warehouse is often misunderstood. To minimize confusion, we have chosen to define a data warehouse as a read-only analytical database *that is used as the foundation of a decision support system.* Throughout the remainder of this book, the terms analytical database and data warehouse will be interchangeable and synonymous, having all of the characteristics we have discussed thus far.

SUMMARY

In this chapter, you should have learned the following:

- A decision support system provides information to assist employees in making decisions and doing their jobs more effectively.
- Decision support systems can be used for short-term tactical decision making, such as the movement of inventory on a weekly basis, or for long-term strategic decision making, such as the introduction of a product or service into a new market.
- Operational systems are systems which run the day-to-day business of a company.
- Analytical databases provide information that is used for analyzing a problem or situation. Analytical processing is primarily done through comparisons, or by analyzing patterns and trends.

- Analytical databases do not hold up-to-the-minute information but hold information as of a specific point in time. This is also called a snapshot of data.
- Analytical databases are often quite large because analyzing patterns and trends often requires large volumes of historical data.
- Analytical databases are usually read-only. They cannot be updated on-line by users and will only be updated systematically, according to a predefined schedule.
- A data warehouse is an analytical database that is used as the foundation of a decision support system.

Case Study 1

Ongoing Data Warehouse Development at Anthem Blue Cross & Blue Shield

by Linda Bronstein and Anne Meyers,
Anthem Blue Cross & Blue Shield, and Vidette Poe

ANTHEM BLUE CROSS & BLUE SHIELD

Our first data warehouse case study is from Anthem Blue Cross & Blue Shield. Anthem is a good example because its experiences in building and maintaining a data warehouse exhibit characteristics found in an overwhelming number of corporations that are building data warehouses. These shared characteristics include

- The creation of predecessor systems that develop new skills and provide experience that directly transfers to the later development of the data warehouse.
- A user community that is spread across a continuum of sophisticated power users, mid-level users, and casual users.
- Ongoing decision support development.

Anthem also has two characteristics that are not as prevalent among corporations but have added significantly to its success:

- It had, and continues to have, strong sponsor support for development from the initial planning throughout its life cycle. This strong sponsorship for the data warehouse ensured continued support of the data warehouse as a high priority, strategic project.
- Project managers and technical personnel responsible for providing information to clients and users have been working with the data warehouse since its beginning several years ago and continue to do so through its various stages of change and development.

A CORPORATE OVERVIEW

Anthem Blue Cross & Blue Shield, an Ohio-based company, is a financially secure provider of quality health-care benefits serving over 2 million participants.

Over the past five years, Anthem has reorganized and developed a concise business strategy to reposition itself as a managed care company and to focus on its financial strength, diversification, marketing, organization, and operations. Anthem has developed a number of information management systems to support this business strategy, including a data warehouse for decision support.

MEETING THE NEED FOR INFORMATION—PREDECESSOR SYSTEMS

A merger in 1984 required bringing together data from 18 distinct systems for financial analysis. Anthem felt it was "drowning in data"; 90 percent of reporting analysis time was spent in collecting data from the various systems before analysis could be done. Customers and management wanted and needed more information, but analysts could provide only minimal information at a high cost within the desired time frames.

In 1988 and 1989, Anthem designed the Corporate Financial & Statistical System, a predecessor to the data warehouse. Created to provide information and simplify reporting, it was a flat file extraction of selected corporate financial and statistical information. Batch SAS and COBOL programs were written against the file for reporting. Soon thereafter, a DB2 pilot project that extracted and summarized information was undertaken to do ad hoc reporting, but Anthem found that the table sizes (17+ million rows) made response times prohibitive for ad hoc reporting.

In a continuing effort to become more efficient so that more time could be spent on analyzing and producing valuable information for business decisions, plans for a data warehouse were developed. The data warehouse was started in October 1990 and took 18 months to build.

The scope of the first project included the Financial and Actuarial subject areas, including claims, membership, and premium data. The source information was stored in flat files and IMS. A platform comparison project was done, with Teradata MPP becoming the target platform.

In the Beginning

At its inception, the knowledge base of the developers on the data warehouse development team included limited experience with DB2, some data modeling, and a fairly strong knowledge of structured life-cycle development techniques. At the beginning of development, in 1990, Anthem did not have specific front-end tool expertise. Skill sets and tools specific to decision support processing were scarce.

Gathering Data Requirements

Data requirements for the data warehouse were gathered through a series of

Joint Application Development (JAD) sessions. Fast paced to get momentum moving, these JAD sessions were used to gather, organize, and order information requirements from multiple functional areas. Using their experience with structured methodologies, Anthem did process modeling first, decomposing functional areas and finding the decision support data useful for each high-level process. This provided a clearer understanding for JAD attendees of the overlap in data between processes and how much of the desired data was the same (although called something different) and provided a forum for "if you could have any data, what would be?"

The information gathered during requirements gathering was modeled using an Entity Relationship Diagram (ERD). This was beneficial for presenting a pictorial way to represent the logical flow and relationships of the business. The initial JAD sessions were held for the Vice President and director levels, with a second round for managers.

Infrastructures

Infrastructures for the data warehouse were developed over the years as the project developed. No specific "infrastructure project" was undertaken to ascertain what structures to put into place. Rather, as technology and business requirements became apparent, appropriate structures were identified and implemented. For example, the business requirements of large volumes of detail accessible for timely ad hoc reporting were determined to require the power of a Massively Parallel Processing (MPP) platform, which in this case was Teradata. Like many other companies, Anthem moved from mainframe to a client-server environment. The introduction of Local Area Networks (LAN), gateways, communications, training, and front-end tool infrastructures were driven by other projects. These infrastructures were then available for use in the data warehouse environment.

User Reaction to Initial Development

The initial users of the Anthem data warehouse were a group of 20 to 30 business analysts who had been providing SAS reporting to the various business units inside the company. These were sophisticated users, who were used to the mainframe and data sets, knew the data, and took three days of SQL training. These users used a mainframe TSO screen, then logged into Teradata, which provided an on-line SQL and batch query capability.

Although the initial reaction to the data warehouse was quite positive, it took several months before even technical users began using the warehouse actively. The movement from standard reporting technologies using flat files to relational decision support technologies encompassed a broad learning curve. Additionally, the paradigm shift from high data acquisition time to high data analysis time was quite a jump. Few of the initial users had an understanding of the valuable processing power now available to them with the introduction of the data warehouse for decision support.

The User Community

Three distinctly different levels of users have emerged over the course of the last three years at Anthem. A similar user continuum has evolved in many organizations developing decision support systems and requires thoughtful management and deployment of front-end data access tools.

The levels of users at Anthem included

- The power users (the technically sophisticated analysts described above).
- The mid-level users who develop ad hoc queries using parameters. These users were also trained on the data model. For this level of user, Anthem introduced GQL from Andyne Corporation, which allowed access to Teradata, thus bypassing the complexity of the mainframe for mid-level users.
- The novice or casual users, who are most comfortable in a point and click environment, where icons kick off predefined queries. Over the last few years, Visual Basic front-end applications were also developed and maintained to accommodate this level of user.

Currently, the data warehouse at Anthem has about 400 users, which is about 10 percent of the employees having access to the platform. It is available to every strategic business unit, and almost all the divisions within the corporate services area use it.

BUILDING ON THE WAREHOUSE

The first pass of the data warehouse covered 85 to 90 percent of their decision support data needs in 1992. Data was held at the detail level, which encompassed all the components of a transaction. Development of the data warehouse included setting up a dedicated staff of Programmers, DBAs, System and Business Analysts, Training and User Support Personnel. Expansion of the warehouse has been ongoing and includes:

- Adding data from additional source systems.
- Creating summarization tables to meet specific business needs.
- Creating front-end data access applications.
- Ongoing training.

- Establishing a help desk to assist users using the warehouse, as well as to provide a springboard for surfacing data integrity problems and resolutions. It was also used as a communication vehicle for user alerts, hardware downtime, and so on.
- Providing ongoing in-house marketing: A status report describing new capabilities within the data warehouse as well as new ideas for its use is published every month.
- Forming a Data Warehouse Key Users Group to identify strategic issues and associated future data needs within the business units.

WHAT THE FUTURE HOLDS

The decision support environment at Anthem continues to evolve. These are considered strategic systems having ongoing funding and support at the CEO level. Development over the next year includes

- Reviewing the data transformation tools on the market to automate processing that is currently done with COBOL transformation programs.
- Modifying the methods of chargeback for data warehouse usage.
- Reengineering the front-end source systems and business models and modifying subsequent sources for the warehouse.
- Modifying summary tables for reengineered processes.
- Enhancing data warehouse administration.
- Modifying the logical and physical models for integrated health delivery systems.

20/20 HINDSIGHT

When reviewing the development and evolution of the data warehouse at Anthem, we asked the following questions:

1. What aspects of building the data warehouse were on track and went well?
   - Meeting the 18-month time line.
   - Using a dedicated development team.
   - User input in the development process.
   - Choice of target platform.
2. What would you do differently?
   - Put more emphasis on the difference between flat file and relational capabilities in the training program.
   - Market the capabilities of the data warehouse more actively.
   - Set better expectations of what the data warehouse can and cannot do.

- Consider nationally recognized data naming and format standards.

3. Are there issues that must be continually tended to?
   - User training.
   - Data integrity.
   - Source system changes.

4. What advice would you give to another company that is just beginning its warehouse development?
   - Get support and involvement from your end-user sponsor.

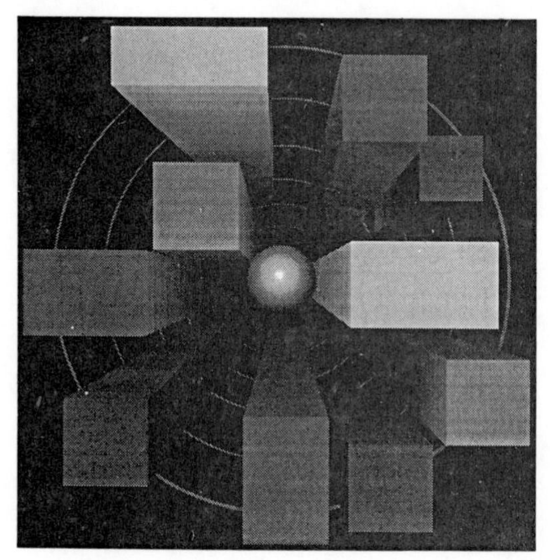

Chapter 2

Understanding Terms and Technology

Embarking on a decision support project means familiarizing yourself with many new technologies and technical terms. This chapter will define those that are pertinent to the development of a data warehouse for decision support. Some of the terms have entire chapters devoted to them; others are more common terms used throughout the book. This chapter will provide an overview of key concepts used in the remainder of this book.

ANALYTICAL PROCESSING

Analytical processing (also called informational or decision support processing) is that processing done to support strategic and management decision making. Data used in analytical processing is often historical in nature, permitting users to analyze trends and patterns with a large amount of data over wide ranges of time. Analytical processing systems are customarily read-only and do not permit the data to be updated by users as do operational systems.

OPERATIONAL PROCESSING

Operational processing refers to systems that run the day-to-day business for companies. The emphasis of these systems is to support business functionality by processing transactions accurately and efficiently and is also often referred to as "mission-critical" application processing. Common examples of this type of processing are order entry, manufacturing scheduling, and general ledger.

DECISION SUPPORT SYSTEMS

A *decision support system* is a system which provides information to users so they can analyze a situation and make decisions. Put another way, a decision support system provides information to assist employees in making decisions and thereby, doing their jobs more effectively. This decision making can be long-term strategic decision making, such as analyzing buying patterns over several years to develop a new product or service, or perhaps to introduce a product into a new European or Far Eastern location. Decision making could also be short term and tactical in nature, such as reviewing and changing recommended order quantities for a particular product.

DATA WAREHOUSE

A *data warehouse* is an analytical database that is used as the foundation of a decision support system. It is designed for large volumes of read-only data, providing intuitive access to information that will be used in making decisions. A data warehouse is created as an ongoing commitment by the organization to ensure the appropriate data is available to the appropriate end user at the appropriate time.

DATA MART

A *data mart*, often referred to as a subject-oriented data warehouse, represents a subset of the data warehouse comprised of relevant data for a particular business function (e.g., marketing, sales, finance, etc.). Similar to the data warehouse, data marts may contain data stored at various levels of granularity, depending on the end-user functions and business requirements. Many times, users of the data mart may require a lower level of detail data. Therefore, data marts can often be larger than originally scoped in the overall data warehouse design.

Organizations may choose to begin their corporate data warehouse project with a small pilot project for a specific subject area (business function). In so doing, those organizations have taken a bottom-up approach to the implementation of a decision support environment—and they have essentially created both a data mart and their first data warehouse simultaneously.

ENVIRONMENT FOR DATA ACCESS

In the world of data warehousing, the *environment for data access* includes the front-end (defined shortly) data-access tools and technologies allowing users to easily access the data, the training that must take place for users to use these tools and technologies, the implementation of metadata, and the training to navigate through the metadata. An improper environment, or ill-conceived architecture, for data access will generally cause the data warehouse project to fail.

ARCHITECTURE

An *architecture* is a set of rules or structures providing a framework for the overall design of a system or product. There are networking architectures, client-server architectures, architectures for specific products, as well as many others. A *data architecture* provides this framework by identifying and understanding how the data will move throughout the system and how it will be used within the corporation. The *data architecture for a data warehouse* has as a primary component a read-only database used for decision support. Figure 2–1 shows one possible data warehouse data architecture.

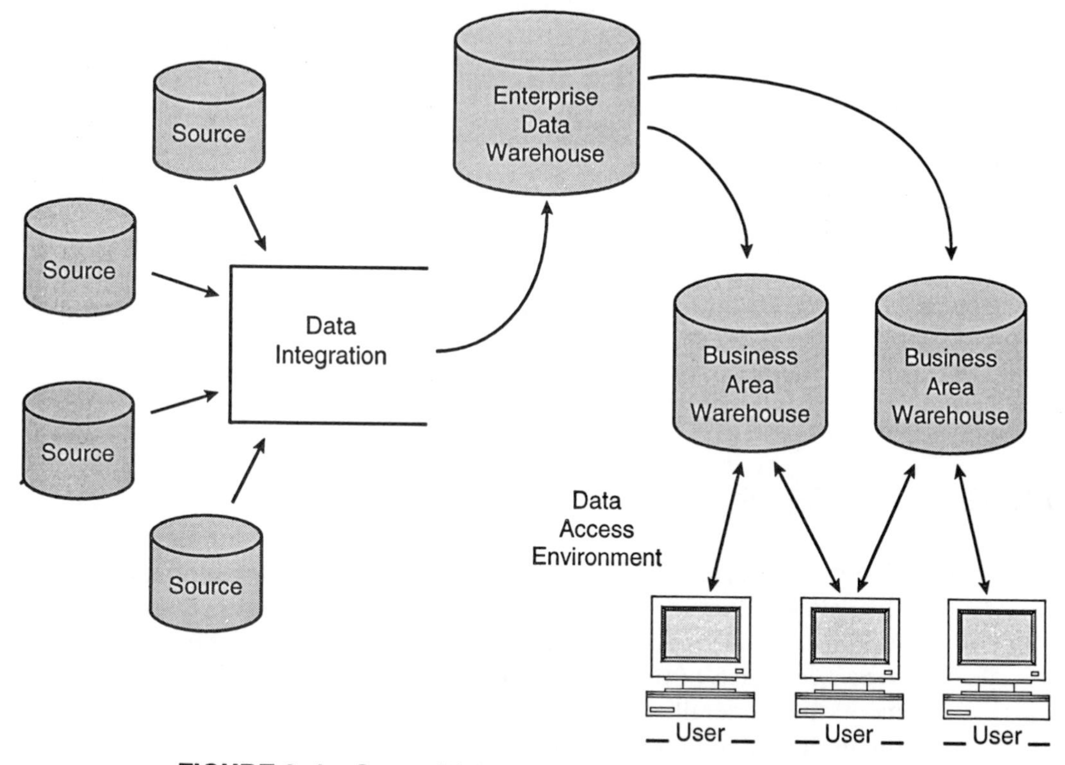

FIGURE 2–1 One valid data warehouse architecture.

TECHNICAL INFRASTRUCTURES

Technical infrastructures are closely related to architecture and are the technologies, platforms, databases, gateways, and other components necessary to make the architecture functional within the corporation. See Figure 2-2 for examples of technical infrastructures. For the purposes of this book, technical training is also considered a technical infrastructure.

SOURCE AND TARGET DATA

Source data is the data in the various operational databases, files, segments, (and so on, depending on your legacy system platforms) that run the day-to-day business. The data will be extracted from the source (day-to-day processing) systems and migrated/converted to the data warehouse. Source data can also come from outside the corporation through, for instance, companies specializing in providing data to corporations. The *target data* is the data that goes into the fields within the data warehouse database. For example, the source data may be your current IMS, DB2, and VSAM operational data, while your target may be DB2 (or any other relational or multidimensional database being used for your data warehouse) (see Figure 2-3).

LEVELS OF USERS

There is a broad spectrum of types of end users who will be leveraging the data warehouse. Levels of users can be categorized as the *novice* or *casual user, the business analyst,* the *power user,* and the *application developer.* Each of these levels of users may have different data requirements and generally require different data access methods. Additionally, the use and need for metadata differs substantially for each of these levels of users.

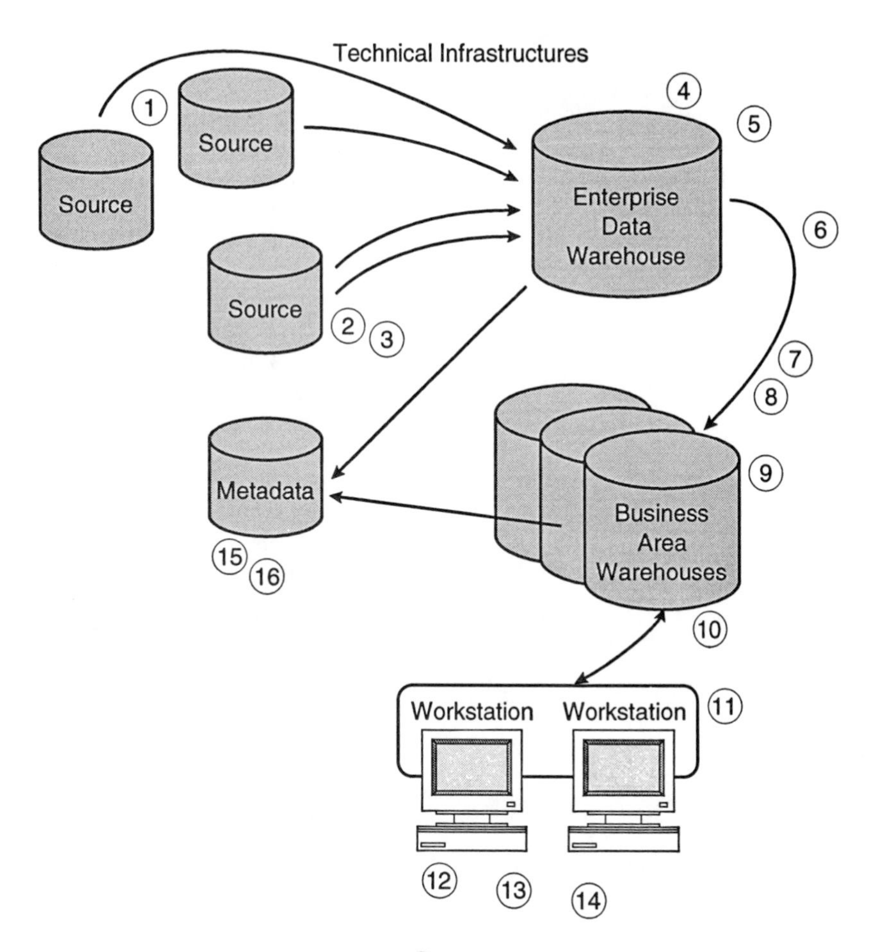

1. Decision Support Education
2. Data Transformation Tool Selection
3. Data Transformation Tool Training
4. Database, Platforms in Place
5. Database, Platform Expertise
6. Gateway Selection
7. Data Replication Strategies
8. Replication Tool Selection
9. Expertise in Data Warehouse Database Design
10. Database, Platforms in Place
11. Network, Communications in Place
12. Workstations, Software Installed
13. Data Access Tool Selection
14. Data Access User Training
15. Metadata Access
16. Metadata Navigation Training

FIGURE 2–2 Example of technical infrastructures in a data warehouse architecture.

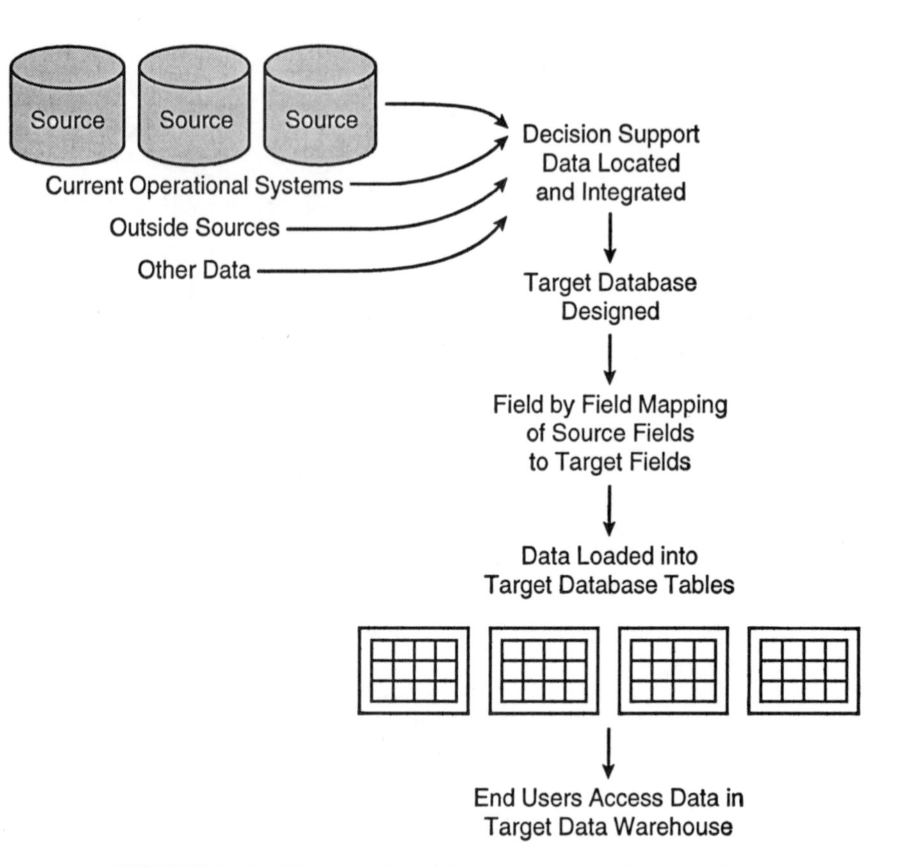

FIGURE 2–3 The relationship of source and target data.

CLASSES OF TOOLS

Data access/query tools provide a graphical user interface to the data warehouse. The user will interact directly with the table structures, sometimes with a layer of abstraction to allow him or her to assign business names to the different tables and columns.

Report writers may also provide a layer of abstraction that allows the assigning of business names to the different columns and tables. These tools provide extensive formatting capabilities to allow the recreation of a report to look a specific way.

Multidimensional Database Management Systems (MDBMSs) provide advanced metric support with extensive slice and dice capabilities. MDBMSs, now generally referred to as MOLAP (Multidimensional

Online Analytical Processing [OLAP]) typically support a specific subject area within the context of a data warehouse implementation.

Advanced decision support tools provide advanced multidimensional analysis directly against the relational database management system. These tools are often driven off shared metadata and support advanced metrics, extensive slice and dice, and drilling capabilities. ROLAP (Relational OLAP), DOLAP (Desk-top OLAP), and hybrid OLAP are examples of names given to describe architectures associated with advanced decision support tools.

Executive Information Systems (EISs) provide a structured, big button interface to predefined reports that provide highly summarized top-line information about the business. In addition, these systems present a high level of user friendliness and intuitiveness, thereby providing advanced functionality while shielding the users from the complexity of the underlying systems or data structures.

DECISION SUPPORT SYSTEM (DSS) APPLICATIONS

A *DSS application* is a collection of one or more predefined reports, analyses, or data navigation paths. These are developed in advance by an application developer or a power user. A specific predefined report can generate many unique variations simply by changing the constraints. These applications are usually developed using powerful data access tools rather than a third- or fourth-generation language.

DATA INTEGRATION

Within the data warehouse environment, *data integration* is the process by which the source data's characteristics are changed prior to loading the data into the data warehouse. Typically, data integration is done when data is extracted from the operational systems and may encompass integrating dissimilar data types, changing codes, and reconciling data definitions. Data integration is generally done by a data analyst.

SYNONYMS

Synonyms are data elements that have different names but have the same meaning or represent the same business fact.

HOMONYMS

Homonyms are data elements that have the same name but represent different business facts.

ANALOGS

Analogs are data elements that have "equivalent" meaning. Analogous data elements often appear to be synonyms but have shades of differences in meaning which are significant to the business understanding of the data.

DATA TRANSFORMATION

Data transformation is the process by which data in the data warehouse is turned into information which can then be accessed by the end-user community. Data transformation uses the data structures and data content of the data warehouse and transforms these into usable, value-added information by allowing the data to be formatted, summarized, and/or viewed in specific ways. Data transformation is generally accomplished through the functionality of your front-end data access tool or application.

DATA CONVERSION TOOLS

Data conversion tools are software designed to automate the process of extracting data from heterogeneous sources (databases, files, segments, etc.), mapping the source data to target data, generating the code to convert or manipulate the data, creating DDL (Data Definition Language), and loading the data into the target database. Some conversion tools have all of these features; some do not. Others, in addition, have the capacity to update the new target database on a scheduled basis. Figure 2-4 explains the general functionality of conversion technology.

MIDDLEWARE TOOLS

Due to the growing confusion surrounding the definition of this term in the marketplace, it will generally not be used in this book. One generally accepted, yet still controversial, description of middleware tools is that they are data conversion tools. However, since the advent of three-tier client server architectures, the term has been overused and should always be defined within the context of the conversation. When the term is used, always ask for a clarification of meaning.

METADATA

Metadata is "data about data" and provides information about the data structures and the relationships between the data structures within or between databases. In a data warehouse environment, there are two types of metadata. The first is data integration metadata encompassing the metadata associated with data from the source systems to the data

User
- Creates source skeletons
- Creates target skeletons
- Creates conversion skeletons
- Performs source-to-target field mapping

↓

Data Conversion Software
- Extracts data
- Generates table DDL
- Generate data conversion programs
- Generates programs to populate tables
- Holds metadata

FIGURE 2–4 Generic data conversion functionality.

warehouse. These may include the original source system name, data types, and source to target conversions.

The second type of metadata, transformation metadata, map data from the warehouse to the end user's front-end tool and will usually include business names and hierarchies. Transformation metadata may also be called DSS metadata. Data warehousing projects tend to reveal an organization's internal need to better analyze and manage both types of metadata.

STAR SCHEMA

A *star schema* is a specific type of database design used to support analytical processing. It has a specific set of denormalized tables. A star schema contains two types of tables: *fact tables* and *dimension tables.* Fact tables contain the quantitative or factual data about a business—the information being queried. Dimension tables are smaller and hold descriptive data that reflect the dimensions of a business. SQL queries then use predefined and user-defined join paths between the fact and dimension tables within the star schema, with constraints on the data to return selected information.

HIERARCHIES

Business *hierarchies* describe organizational structure and logical parent-child relationships within the data. An example would be store to district to region structures for managing a retail business. The typical data warehouse will have many hierarchies throughout the dimensions with many levels of calculated or stored aggregate values across the dimensions and hierarchies.

GRANULARITY

Granularity is the level of detail within the data warehouse and is one of the principal design issues in data warehouse development. Highly granular data provides a great deal of detailed information and subsequently a large volume of data. For instance, a high granularity level can provide a list of all the transactions in your checking account for the month and could answer the question, "Was there a debit to my account on June 5th?" Less granular data provide less detailed data, more levels of summary, and less data volume. Coarser data would not have that level of detail available but can provide an answer to, "What were the monthly (or yearly) balances on my account for the last three years?" (given the information for three years was available). Granularity levels directly affect the size of the database and the types of analysis that the database can support. One incorrect presupposition of most data warehouse projects is that the warehouse must store all detailed data with few stored aggregates.

DATABASE GATEWAY

A *database gateway* is a product that allows data to pass smoothly between heterogeneous databases or systems. Gateways can involve connections between different networks, different communications protocols, and different representations of data. For example, in the data warehouse environment where much of the legacy data resides on a mainframe, a gateway provides the connectivity required to access data from the mainframe to be used with other types of databases running on a different operating system.

MEGABYTES, GIGABYTES, AND TERABYTES

A *megabyte (MB)* is a unit of measurement of computer memory or data storage capacity equal to 1,048,576 bytes. A *gigabyte (GB)* equals 1,073,741,824 bytes or 1,024 megabytes. A *terabyte (TB)* equals 1,099,511,627,776 bytes or 1,024 gigabytes.

DECISION SUPPORT DEVELOPMENT CYCLE

The life cycle of decision support system development includes the following phases: planning, gathering data requirements, data analysis and modeling, physical database design and development, data mapping, populating the data warehouse, automating the data management process, creating the starter set of reports, data validation, and testing, training, and rollout.

SUMMARY

In this chapter, you should have learned the following:

- Data warehouse and decision support related definitions that provide many of the underlying concepts necessary to understand the remainder of this book.

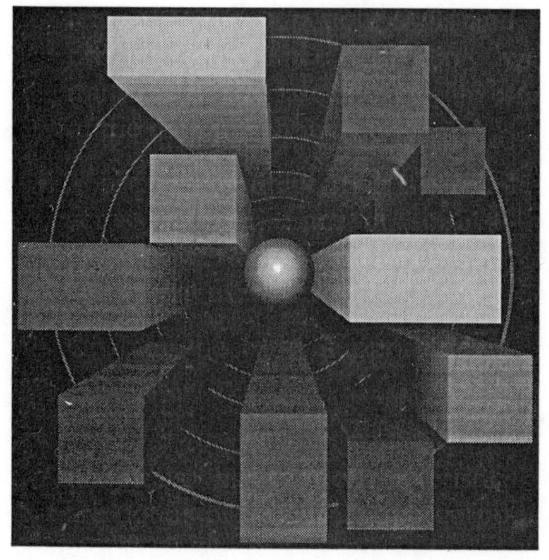

Chapter 3

UNDERSTANDING ARCHITECTURE AND INFRASTRUCTURES

THE TASK AT HAND

Setting the scene: A recent, well-publicized change in corporate direction has put a strong focus on customer profiling and market segmentation within your corporation. In an effort to get the customer information to the people who need it, a data warehouse is being developed. You have been assigned as the project manager and tasked with building a data warehouse for the marketing department of your multimillion dollar company.

The programmer in the cubicle next to yours says, "What's the big deal? All you have to do is put the data into a different database and slap an easy-to-use front end on it."

You find out the actuarial department has its own small "data warehouse" that they created last year that has a great front end. In fact, they use it in client presentations to show how easily they can get information on any client account at the click of a mouse!

You know there is no enterprise data model in the corporation. Everything you read says to start from the enterprise data model. Will you have to go through all the work of creating an enterprise data model to build the warehouse?

In a conversation about decision support systems, you are shocked when someone from the database group says, "We've got half a dozen different decision support systems in production right now."

Talking with the co-worker responsible for the recent corporatewide front-end tool survey, you find out there are dozens of companies marketing their products as the data warehouse front-end solution.

A division of your company in New York has developed several warehouses that do both decision support and on-line transaction processing.

Telephone calls to different companies to gather information elicits the following facts: One company has been developing its data warehouse for the last 3 years, with the initial development taking 15 months. They now have 200 people using it on a daily basis. Another company built its data warehouse in 3 months and are starting their second version now. Both companies had at least one unsuccessful attempt at building a data warehouse.

Still confused about all the different ideas, opinions, definitions, and products associated with building a data warehouse? Is it possible that one company took 3 months and another took 15 months to build a warehouse? Why such a disparity? What, exactly, is going on here?

UNDERSTANDING DATA WAREHOUSE ARCHITECTURE

The first step in clarifying some of the misunderstandings surrounding the data warehouse is understanding data warehouse architecture. Let's review the definition of architecture. An *architecture* is a set of rules or structures providing a framework for the overall design of a system or product. There are networking architectures, client-server architectures, architectures for specific products, as well as many others. A *data architecture* provides a framework by identifying and understanding how data will move throughout the system and be utilized within the corporation. A *data warehouse architecture* has as a primary component a read-only database used for decision support.

An architecture, then, is the framework made up of rules or structures that the system will be built upon. The architecture for a data warehouse has its own characteristics that differentiate it from other systems.

THE CHARACTERISTICS OF DATA WAREHOUSE ARCHITECTURE

The basic architecture for a data warehouse is shown in Figure 3-1.

The distinguishing characteristics of data warehouse architecture are:

- Data is extracted from source systems, databases, and files.
- The data from the source systems is integrated before being loaded into the data warehouse.
- The data warehouse is a separate read-only database designed specifically for decision support.
- Users access the data warehouse via a front-end tool or application.

Data Is Extracted from Source Systems, Databases, or Files

The legacy systems within the company are customarily the predominant source of data for the data warehouse. Data fields identified as necessary for decision support processing will be extracted from these sys-

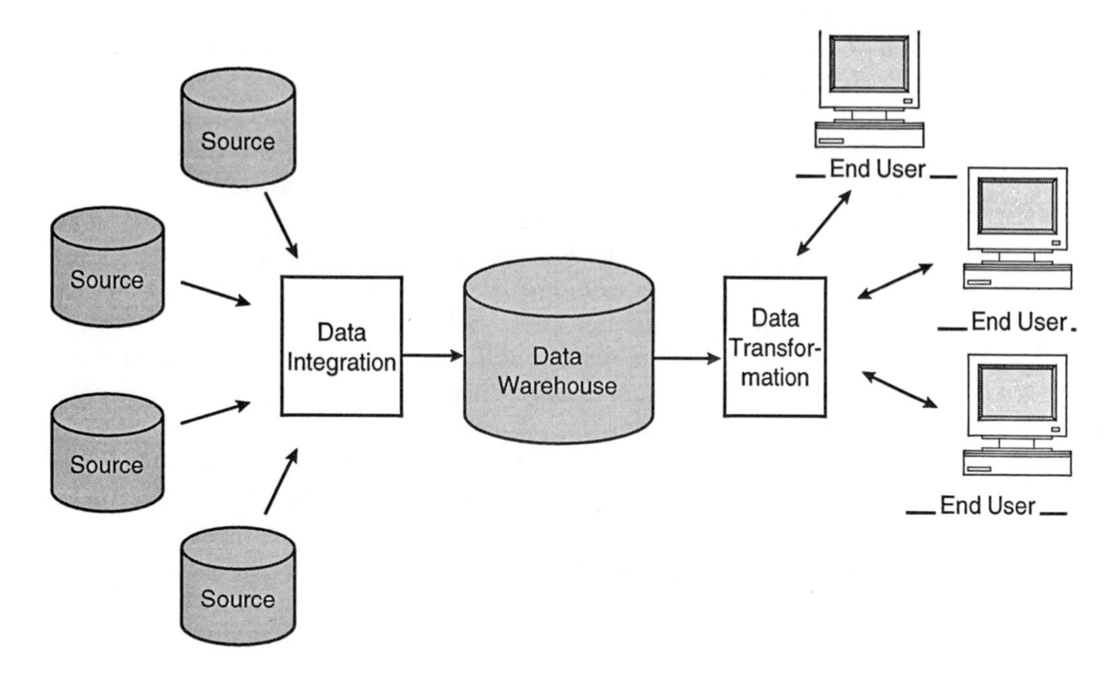

FIGURE 3–1 Data warehouse architectures: Generic data warehouse architecture.

tems. This may often entail extracting specific data fields from many different systems, databases, or files. Sometimes entire files may be extracted, if all the fields are necessary for decision support processing.

Other sources of data may be data that is bought from companies specializing in providing data, such as Metro Mail, A.C. Nielsen, or IRI. These sources of data may be in a variety of formats and on different mediums, so selective field extraction from the files may or may not be necessary.

In general, it is quite common within a data warehouse architecture for the data sources to be from multiple systems or applications. Source fields may come from different databases, different platforms, and in a variety of data types and formats.

The Data from the Source Systems Is Integrated before Being Loaded into the Data Warehouse

A significant component of data warehouse architecture is that the data from multiple sources are integrated before being loaded into the data warehouse. This is an important and often side-stepped characteristic of a data warehouse. If data is coming from multiple systems, databases, and platforms, some form of data integration will be necessary. For example, the product number being held in several different systems, in many corporations, has several different formats and sizes. In one system (within the same company) it may be a 9-digit code, in another an 11-digit field, while the third system automatically appends a product category code on the end for reporting purposes. Sound familiar? Of course it does, because there is a good chance these are the same types of data inconsistencies you are trying to deal with in your own corporate databases and applications. This data must go through an integration process before being loaded into the data warehouse. Refer to Chapter 8 for a thorough explanation of data integration.

The Data Warehouse Is a Separate Read-Only Database Designed Specifically for Decision Support

The operative words here are "read-only" and "designed for decision support." Inherent in the data warehouse architecture is the idea that operational and decision support processing is fundamentally different. Operational processing is running the day-to-day business operations of the corporation. Operational systems are often on-line transaction systems that take in, update, and store the core data that is running the corporate business systems. Decision support processing is providing, in an easy-to-understand format, analytical information to assist in making tactical and strategic business decisions within the corporation. These decision-making processes often require a range of historical data that is used for comparative analysis and allow for monitoring trends and information patterns over time.

The fundamental differences in functionality of operational and decision support systems require substantially different styles of database design. Operational databases are designed to store, update, and report on day-to-day business data with speed while decision support systems are designed to provide easy access to read-only historical and analytical information. One database design cannot efficiently provide both types of functionality. Hence, the separate read-only database is a primary component of the data warehouse architecture.

Users Access the Data Warehouse via a Front-End Tool or Application

In most data warehouse systems, the data access environment makes up another layer of the data warehouse architecture. This data access environment is comprised of the front-end tools, applications, training, and support necessary to provide useful and accessible decision support information from the data warehouse. In many cases, the core technologies for data access will be within a client-server environment, with the workstation as the client and the data warehouse as the server. There are, however, many variations of data access being used as more data warehouses are being implemented. The issues associated with the data access environment, the importance of the front end, and lack of knowledge about analytical analysis for decision support will be discussed extensively in Chapter 10. The data warehouse architecture will always include the data access environment that provides front-end data access to the users of the decision support data.

EXPANDING THE GENERIC DATA WAREHOUSE ARCHITECTURE

The data warehouse architecture described thus far contains the components which distinguish the data warehouse. This is considered a *generic data warehouse architecture.* Part of the task of building a data warehouse is to incorporate the primary constructs of the generic data warehouse architecture into your current system's architecture to fulfill your decision support processing needs.

It is important to understand that the constructs of the generic data warehouse architecture can be implemented within corporations in very sophisticated ways. A review of some data warehouse architectures that are currently being implemented in different companies will explain some variations on the generic data warehouse theme. For the first example, refer to Figure 3-2.

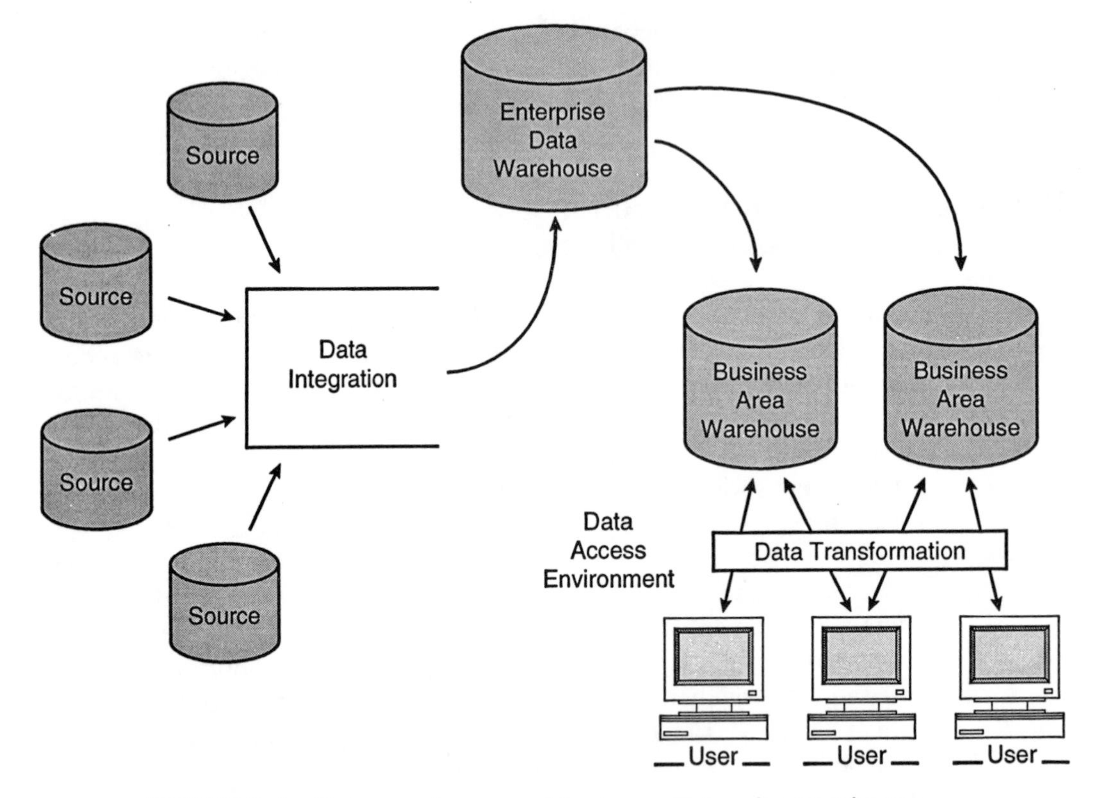

FIGURE 3–2 Data warehouse architectures: Enterprise warehouse feeding business area warehouses.

Figure 3-2 is a data warehouse architecture in which an enterprise data warehouse is loading data to business area warehouses. Why would a corporation implement this type of architecture for a data warehouse? There may be several reasons:

- To fulfill a strategic initiative requirement that all databases use the enterprise data model as their base.
- To separate the processes of source data integration from processes of database design and denormalization.
- To use the enterprise data warehouse as a consistent source for all source-to-target mappings for multiple business area warehouses.

The integration of a data warehouse architecture into your current system's architecture is not always as straightforward and simple as you would initially think. Current data processing system architectures are extremely sophisticated at some corporations (both by design and lack of design). In most corporations, there will be some type of constraints set in implementing the data warehouse architecture. These constraints can be a variety of technical, integration, strategic, or political considerations that introduce limitations as to how the data warehouse architecture can be implemented within your corporation.

Since an architecture is a set of rules or structures providing a framework for the overall design of a system or product, it cannot be separated from the data warehouse itself. The implementation of data warehouse architecture can be done in a variety of ways and can become quite complicated within a corporation. However, the basic constructs of the data warehouse architecture must be put into place. There is no right way to implement a data warehouse architecture. Additionally, there are different technical solutions in response to different corporate environments, constraints, and requirements.

In our example in Figure 3-2, the basic data warehouse architecture constructs are in place. Data is extracted from source systems, databases, and files. The data from the source systems is integrated before being loaded into the read-only enterprise data warehouse. This data is then restructured, redesigned, and loaded into separate read-only business area warehouses, which are used for decision support processing. Users access the data warehouse via a front-end tool or application. This is indeed a data warehouse architecture that has been modified to accommodate the strategic initiatives, the decision support requirements, and technical constraints of the company.

Part of building a data warehouse is a process of finding the correct technical solution to your decision support needs and creating a solid data warehouse architecture within the parameters you have to work with. One architecture is not better than another. Certainly, one architecture may be more difficult or time-consuming to develop than another. In most cases, however, the chosen data warehouse architecture implementation is the most appropriate technical solution based on the corporation's goals, architecture constraints, and decision support requirements.

Another data warehouse architecture implementation is shown in Figure 3-3.

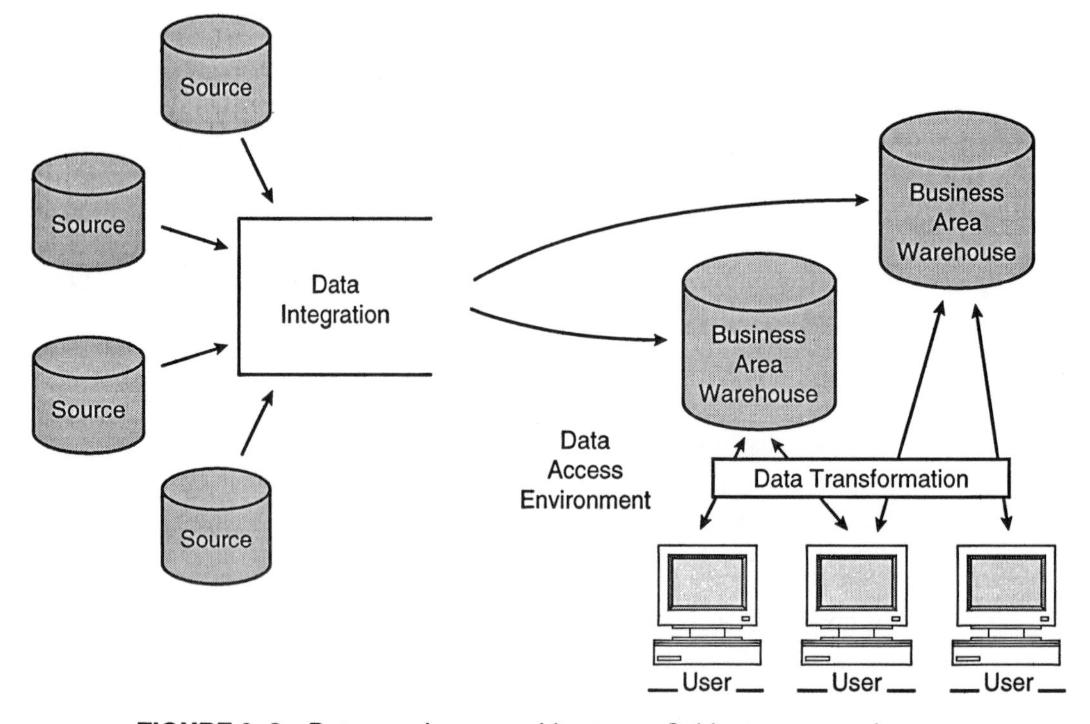

FIGURE 3–3 Data warehouse architectures: Subject area warehouses.

Figure 3-3 shows a data warehouse architecture in which the data is integrated and redesigned and then loaded into separate business area warehouses. Although this data warehouse architecture does not have one large database, it has all of the constructs that qualify it as a true data warehouse. Perhaps there are constraints associated with database size that this architecture implementation is accommodating.

Another real-life data warehouse architecture implementation is shown in Figure 3-4.

Figure 3-4 is a sophisticated architecture in which data is extracted from the source systems, goes through data integration, and is loaded into an integrated database, which is designed in third normal form. The information that is loaded from the source systems into the integrated database is read-only. However, other source data is being added to the database through an application that allows for name and address updates. Why would a corporation use this architecture? This company realized they needed integrated data to make their daily busi-

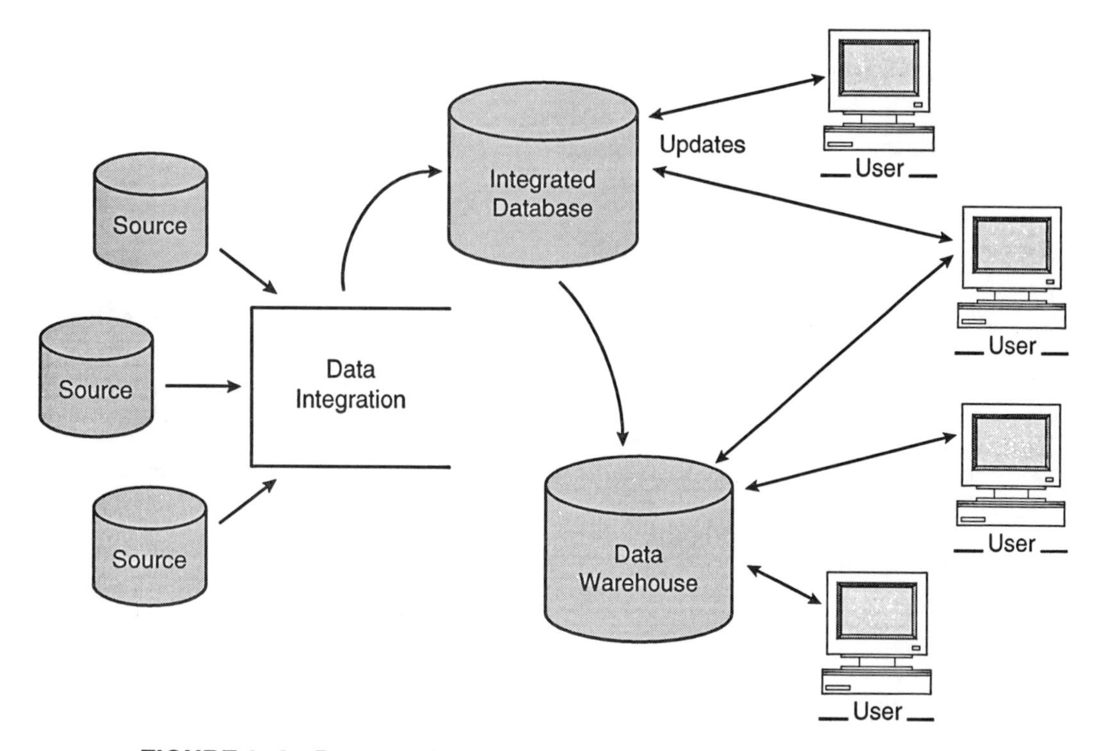

FIGURE 3–4 Data warehouse architectures: Integrated database feeding a data warehouse.

ness decisions because it was just too time and error intensive trying to get information from hundreds of applications. The issue of providing valuable, integrated information for making tactical decisions to run the business better was the first priority. Cleaning up and adding additional fields to the database was part of this process. Now this company is moving forward with a data warehouse for long-term strategic business decisions.

Using our definition of data warehouse architecture, is the integrated database shown in Figure 3-4, which is being used for daily tactical decision making, a data warehouse? Absolutely not. It does not have one of the primary components of the data warehouse architecture: a read-only database designed specifically for decision support. However, the data warehouse itself shown in Figure 3-5 has the primary characteristics of the data warehouse architecture.

There are options for loading the data warehouse in this architecture. One option would be to load the data from the integrated data-

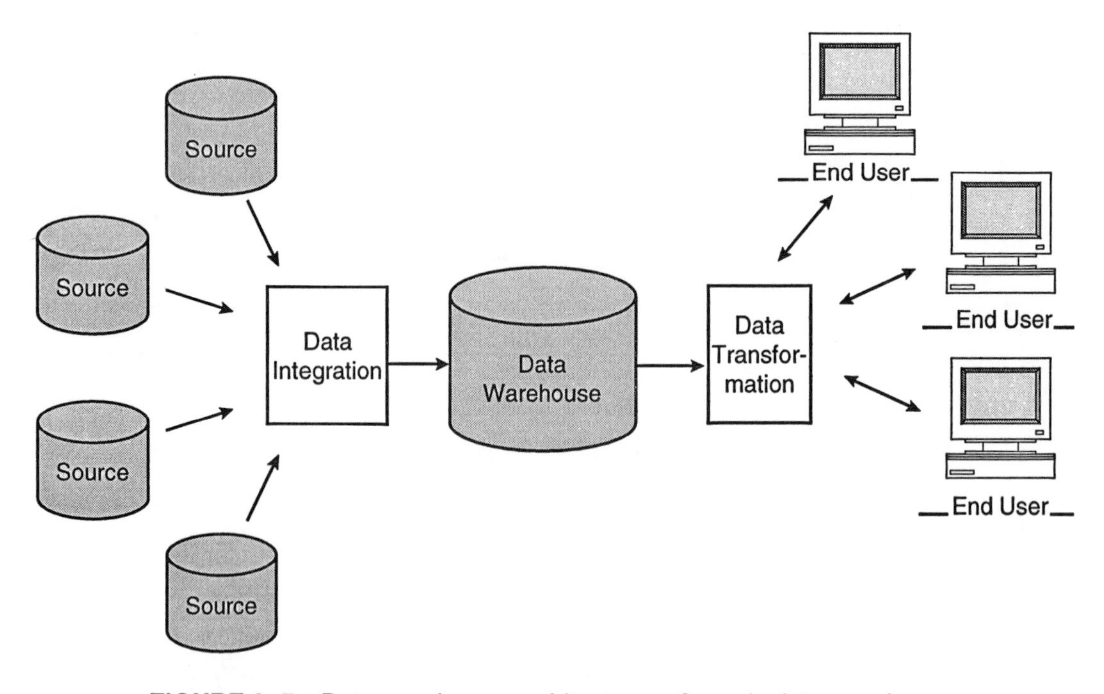

FIGURE 3–5 Data warehouse architectures: Generic data warehouse architecture.

base, knowing that the data has been through the cleansing and data integration process. The integrated database is in third normal form, so data loaded into the data warehouse would require redesign so the database can process decision support information effectively. Because this database has parts that are read-only while name and address fields are being entered by users, additional data cleansing programs would need to be part of the user update process to handle user input errors before being loaded into the integrated database.

UNDERSTANDING THE RELATIONSHIP OF ARCHITECTURE AND INFRASTRUCTURES

Technical infrastructures are closely related to architecture and are the technologies, platforms, databases, gateways, and other components necessary to support the chosen data warehouse architecture. For the purposes of this book, technical training is also considered a technical infrastructure. For example, technical infrastructures may include the choice and installation of the database, setting up the network, or choosing and installing the front-end tools. The architecture is a set of rules or structures that create a framework for development and implementation of a data warehouse. The technical infrastructures are the components that need to be in place for that architecture to perform.

Architecture and infrastructures are closely related. However, the same architecture may require different infrastructures depending upon the particular corporate environment. The following figures show the same data warehouse architecture being implemented using different infrastructures. Figure 3-5 shows the generic data warehouse architecture. Figures 3-6 and 3-7 show how the same architecture could be implemented with different infrastructures depending on the corporate environment, decision support needs, and system architecture.

In Figure 3-6, the company is a specialty insurance company that is building its first data warehouse. The source data is VSAM files off the

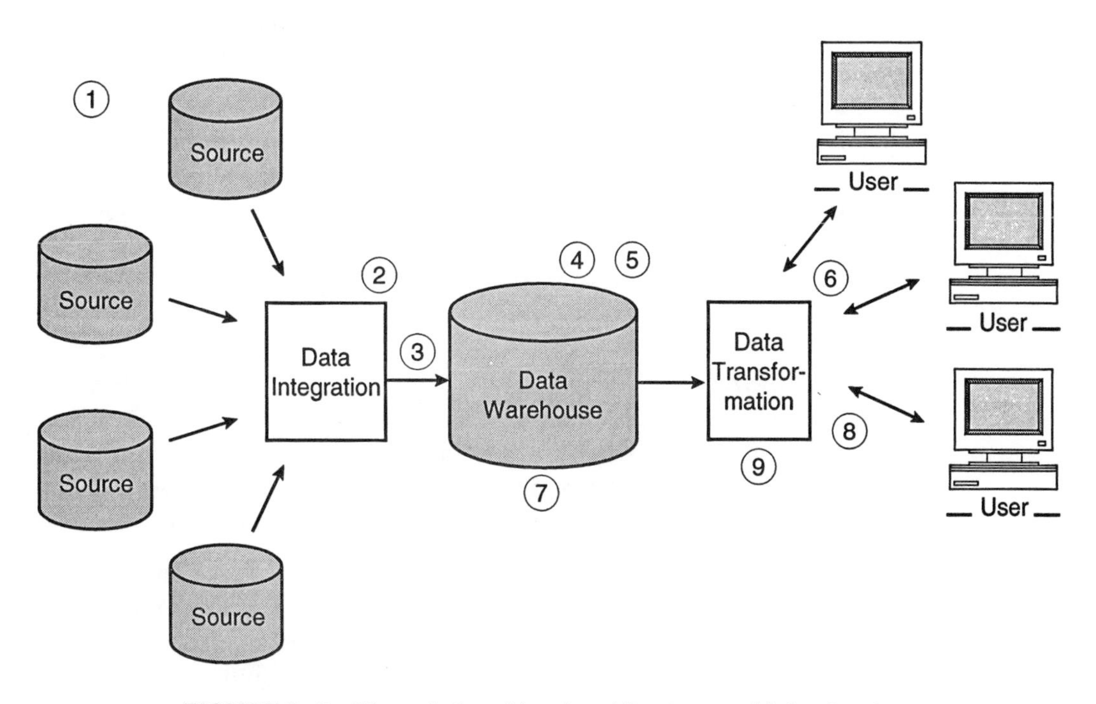

FIGURE 3–6 The relationship of architecture and infrastructures.

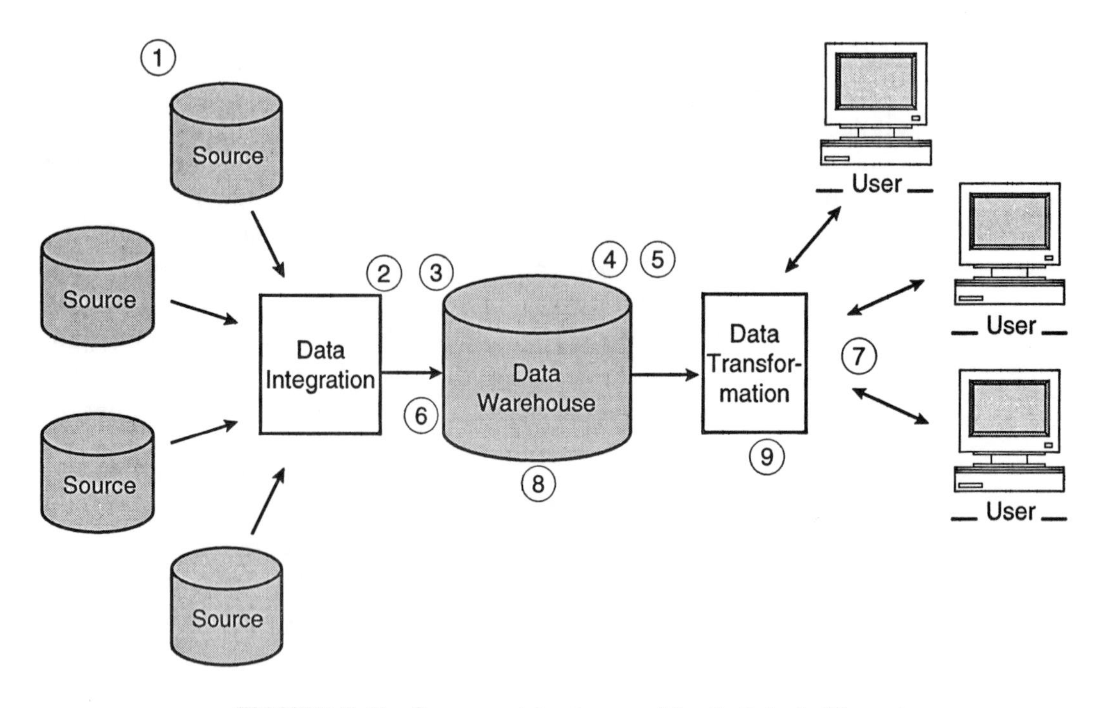

FIGURE 3–7 Same architecture as Fig. 3–6, but different infrastructures.

mainframe; the data warehouse target database is a relational database. Front-end tools are being used on workstations to provide data access to the new data warehouse. Figure 3-6 shows some of the infrastructures this company will implement to fulfill the goal of providing decision support information to its users.

The infrastructures for Figure 3-7 may be

1. *Training in decision support technology.* Training in decision support technology will describe what a data warehouse is, what it is used for, and how it is built. This is a necessary infrastructure for this company, which has no experience in decision support system's development. The audience will be the development project team.

2. *Training in relational database technology.* This company has always been a COBOL shop and has not yet had a reason to move into relational technology. The data warehouse will be its first attempt at building a relational system. Relational database training would be an important infrastructure at this company. A clear understanding of rela-

tional database design and the design characteristics particular to decision support processing will also be necessary.

3. *Data conversion tools.* Data conversion is being done programmatically and no data conversion tools will be bought to automate this process.

4. *Database Administrator (DBA) skills.* A consultant is being hired to assist the company in relational database design and administration. He or she will also act as a mentor to an in-house employee to ensure database knowledge is transferred to the company.

5. *The hardware and relational database are already purchased and the software is loaded.* This infrastructure is already in place.

6. *The local area network, communications, and workstations are set up.* This infrastructure is already in place.

7. *Gateway products are being reviewed for purchase.* The purchase, installation, and testing of the gateway is an infrastructure.

8. *Front-end software is being reviewed.* The original list of 15 front-end products is now down to 3 products that have been identified by Information Services (IS) and the users as options for data warehouse data access. Software purchases, installation, and training will be an infrastructure.

9. *Metadata navigation tools are being reviewed.* This infrastructure is being done in association with number 8. Some front-end tools provide metadata navigation functionality; many do not. A review of metadata tools enabling users to navigate through the data warehouse and understand the location and structure of the data is an important infrastructure.

As you can see, infrastructures are the software, the hardware, the training, and all of the other components providing the necessary support for the implementation of a data warehouse architecture. One aspect of developing a data warehouse in an architected environment is to take the time to find the best data warehouse data architecture for your particular environment. Another fundamental aspect of building a successful data warehouse is to identify the infrastructures that will be necessary to implement this chosen architecture. The implementation of infrastructures to support your data warehouse development and rollout will be a large percentage of the cost of building your decision support system.

In the next example, Figure 3-7, the same architecture is being implemented amidst different infrastructures. The source of data is DB2, IMS, VSAM, and an outside source. The target database is Sybase. Let's look at those infrastructures.

1. *Training in decision support technology.* Training in decision support technology will describe what a data warehouse is, what it is used for, and how it is built. This is a necessary infrastructure for this company, which has no experience in decision support systems development. The audience will be the development project team.

2. *Data conversion tool choice, purchase, and installation.* The data conversion tool was chosen as part of a corporatewide data architecture and infrastructure project. It is viewed as a strategic tool that will benefit several conversion or client-server projects being done within the company.

3. *Data conversion tool vendor training.* A three-day training course will provide the basic information necessary to make this tool usable in the corporate environment. Extra time is then added to the project plan to accommodate the learning curve as technicians get up to speed on the tool.

4. *New hardware and a new relational database have been chosen and installed.*

5. *Database administration and UNIX training have been scheduled.* This is an important infrastructure to begin to build a knowledge base on a new relational database, database-specific SQL, and in UNIX.

6. *DBA skills.* A consultant is being hired to assist the company in transferring current relational database knowledge to the new relational database. He or she will act as a mentor to the current DBAs about issues particular to the new database.

7. *The front end has been chosen.* An advanced decision support tool has been chosen, and an application developer has been trained on the tool.

8. *UNIX job-scheduling software.* Job-scheduling software has been located, purchased, and installed. In addition, two weeks of ven-

dor consulting has been purchased so the client site understands how to set up the scheduling process.

9. *Metadata access.* The metadata will be accessed via the company's new repository product. A separate project has been established to populate and implement the repository, define procedures, and develop the necessary user training for metadata navigation.

You can see that the infrastructures for the two corporations as depicted in Figures 3-6 and 3-7 are very different, although the architecture is the same. Time lines and budgets to implement these architectures and infrastructures could be significantly different. The first example is a bit simpler, easier to set up, and may be less costly.

ARCHITECTURE AND INFRASTRUCTURES AS A SEPARATE PROJECT

It is highly recommended that identifying data warehouse architecture and infrastructures be a separate project from the actual development of the data warehouse. It is not necessary to take a great deal of time working through the technical considerations necessary to understand the proper (or best choice) architecture for warehouse development. With some focused attention, recommendations on architecture and infrastructures can be done in a reasonable time.

It is not a good idea, however, to mix the analysis necessary for creating a solid data warehouse architecture into your data warehouse development project plan. Doing so may draw out your decision support development time lines to unacceptable dates. For example, how long will it take to get a specific piece of hardware purchased and installed? How about agreement on a front-end or data transformation tool? Many companies do not have corporate structures that provide quick and easy mechanisms for making these types of decisions and this will substantially affect your develoment time.

If you are developing the first data warehouse in your organization, chances are good that a data warehouse architecture has not been defined and the corresponding infrastructures are not set up. This puts you in a very difficult situation that will require you to clearly define the specific infrastructure needs for your project. Do this up front, as part of your planning process. Use the examples and diagrams in this chapter as a working task list to assist you in identifying the architecture and infrastructures you will need to implement so your project can be successful.

If there are several data warehouses under construction or being planned in your company, you will need an *enterprisewide data warehouse, data architecture, and infrastructure plan.*

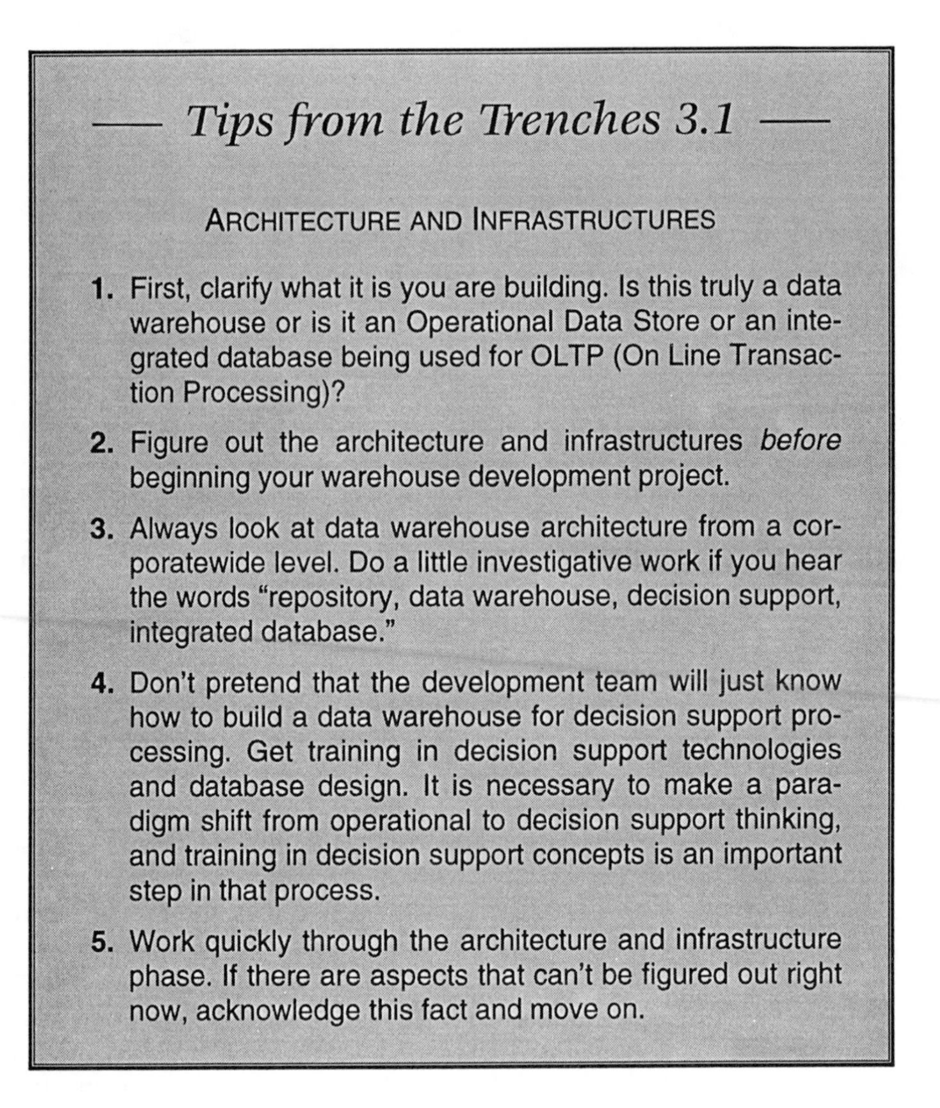

— *Tips from the Trenches 3.1* —

ARCHITECTURE AND INFRASTRUCTURES

1. First, clarify what it is you are building. Is this truly a data warehouse or is it an Operational Data Store or an integrated database being used for OLTP (On Line Transaction Processing)?
2. Figure out the architecture and infrastructures *before* beginning your warehouse development project.
3. Always look at data warehouse architecture from a corporatewide level. Do a little investigative work if you hear the words "repository, data warehouse, decision support, integrated database."
4. Don't pretend that the development team will just know how to build a data warehouse for decision support processing. Get training in decision support technologies and database design. It is necessary to make a paradigm shift from operational to decision support thinking, and training in decision support concepts is an important step in that process.
5. Work quickly through the architecture and infrastructure phase. If there are aspects that can't be figured out right now, acknowledge this fact and move on.

AND THE ANSWER IS . . .

Now let's go back to our original question. Is it possible for one company to take 15 months to build a warehouse when another company did it in 3 months? The answer: Absolutely! The question however, is: *What exactly is being built and what structures are needed to build it?*

Let's look, for example, at that small actuarial data warehouse being shown to potential customers. The data was dumped from a database, and a front end was created with a Graphical User Interface (GUI) development tool. No redesign was done to optimize the design for decision support processing. One reason it works so well is that the database has only a few thousand records, so response time is fast. If it were several million records, the design of the database would break down fairly quickly because it is designed for on-line transaction processing, not decision support processing. Additionally, the time it takes for data analysis, understanding decision support requirements, and integrating and cleaning up data was not necessary. Is this a decision support system? It is definitely being used for making decisions. From an architectural perspective, is this a data warehouse? No, because the database is actually designed for transactional processing (third normal form) and not for decision support processing. Additionally, the data has not been integrated.

The data warehouse architecture within your company may be implemented in a simple way using technologies that are already familiar to the development team. Or the architecture may require new platforms, new databases, integration tools, or a variety of other new technologies and skill sets. The data warehouse is often a company's first foray into the client-server environment. If this is so within your company, the learning curve may be part of the overall time it takes to build the data warehouse. It is the implementation of the architecture and infrastructures that most often increases the length of time and the cost associated with the development of a data warehouse.

Is it possible that one company took only 3 months while another company took 15 months to do development? Absolutely. Unless you understand the experience levels and skill sets of the developers, and the architecture and infrastructures that were implemented, the development time lines are not valid comparisons. The questions (once again) are: *What is being built and what structures were implemented to build it?* If building a data warehouse means the design, development, and load of the database, this is potentially achievable in 3 months. If building a data warehouse includes the full life-cycle implementation—from the source systems through your users doing successful decision support processing at their desktop—then 3 months is probably not possible, even under the most aggressive schedule.

I cannot emphasize enough how important it is to take the time to understand your architecture and infrastructures before building your data warehouse. If your architecture is set up to seamlessly handle decision support processing, then it is true that the development of these systems can go very fast. However, as a project manager who is responsible for the project plan, time lines, and budget for development of the data warehouse, wouldn't you prefer to know if you are responsible for setting up the full architecture and infrastructures for implementing the data warehouse or just the design and development of the database itself? Obviously this will have considerable effect on all aspects of the development project, including resources, time lines, tasks, deliverables, and training needs.

SUMMARY

In this chapter, you should have learned the following:

- An architecture is a set of rules or structures providing a framework for the overall design of a system or product.
- A data architecture provides a framework by identifying how data will move throughout the system and be utilized within the corporation.
- The data architecture for a data warehouse has the following distinguishing characteristics:
  - Data is extracted from source systems, databases, and files.
  - The data from the source systems is integrated before being loaded into the data warehouse.
  - The data warehouse is a separate, read-only database designed specifically for decision support processing of large volumes of data.
  - Users access the data warehouse via some front-end tool or application.

- Source fields for a data warehouse may come from different databases, different platforms, and in a variety of data types and formats.
- One database design cannot efficiently provide both operational and decision support functionality.
- The generic data warehouse architecture, as well as many variations, are currently being implemented within companies.
- There is no right way to implement a data warehouse; however, the basic constructs of the data warehouse architecture must be in place.
- Technical infrastructures are the technologies, platforms, databases, gateways, and other components necessary to support the chosen data warehouse architecture.
- Part of building a data warehouse is finding the correct technical solutions to your decision support needs and creating a solid data warehouse architecture within the parameters you have to work with.
- One data warehouse architecture can be implemented in several ways by using different infrastructures.
- Technical training is an important technical infrastructure.
- Identifying data warehouse architecture and infrastructures should be a separate project from the actual development of your data warehouse.

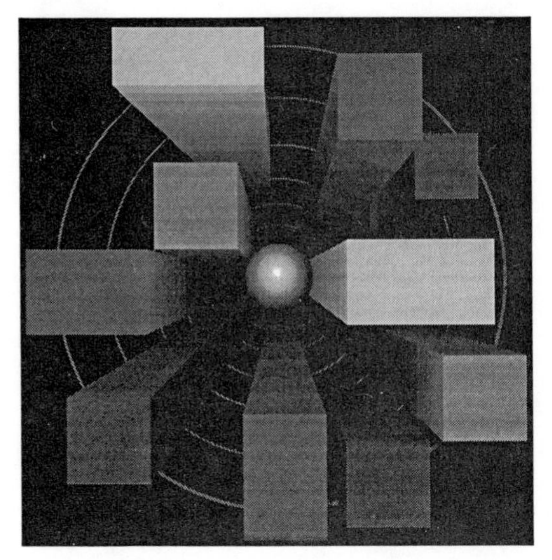

Chapter 4

Critical Success Factors

A FOCUS ON SUCCESS

Many discussions of data warehousing quickly become comparisons of technologies. Our experience, however, is that the particular brand of hardware or software you select is much less important than vendors would have you believe. The true critical success factors in data warehouse deployment converge around aligning technical solutions to business goals.

Data warehouses, unlike other large business systems, exist to facilitate strategic decision making, not day-to-day operations. To develop and deploy a data warehouse project successfully, you need to understand the nuances and ramifications of this distinction.

This chapter presents a framework for understanding how to develop and deploy a successful data warehouse. The remainder of the book expands upon the concepts and solutions presented here.

HOW IS A DATA WAREHOUSE DIFFERENT?

Data warehouses differ dramatically from operational systems in everything—from what they contain to how and when they are used. The following sections explain the most important differences between decision support and operational systems.

A Data Warehouse Incorporates Operational and Historical Data

Data warehouses need years of historical data so users can analyze business trends such as changing demographics or sales. Operational systems need only enough historical information to support day-to-day delivery of products or services.

For example, last year's account balances and transactions are irrelevant in an operational system. In fact, in order to manage costs and performance characteristics, operational systems keep historical information to a minimum. Almost all operational systems purge old transactions, closed accounts, and other information unnecessary for running day-to-day business at least once a year.

In contrast, a decision support system must maintain customers' last year's account balances and transactions as well as today's (or a recent snapshot). Decision support users want to understand the activities that led to an account being closed. They want demographics related to closed accounts. Closed accounts are often as revealing to decision support users as open accounts. Closed accounts are irrelevant to operational systems, because only open accounts are active.

As a result of the need for several years of historical data, a decision support database is often two to three times larger than an operational systems database. It is not at all uncommon to store two or three or even seven years of historical information (often summarized for older data) in a data warehouse. As the cost of disk space continues to plummet relative to the value of information, the trend is clearly headed toward even longer retention periods for historical data in corporate decision support systems.

Periodic Updates Rather than Real-Time

A key point to remember from our definition in Chapter 1 is that analytical databases hold information as of a specific point in time. As such, the strategy for updating a data warehouse is almost always a batch-driven process using a planned, well-defined schedule for refreshing and integrating new data. This is important because end users in a decision support environment dislike having data change in the middle of their analysis activities. A planned schedule allows users to structure decision support activities knowing that

- The warehouse data content will remain stable between refresh cycles.
- Newer data can be expected for integration into the database on a predefined time line.

Occasionally, a concern is voiced about the lack of real-time updates of the data warehouse contents. To address this concern, we must understand the intent of the decision support system.

The idea behind a data warehouse is to facilitate strategic decision making. Such decision making is concerned with understanding trends and patterns in a business that can be proactively addressed with new business models, product strategies, customer relationship development, and so on. If an organization needs the last two hours of sales transactions to make a strategic decision, then there is something seriously wrong with its decision-making process!

Strategic decisions rely—or should rely—on a long-term understanding of trends in the business. Having discussed the relationship between strategic decision making and a long-term view of information in the warehouse, it is also important to understand the need for more frequent data loading when supporting tactical decision making. The goal of tactical decision making is to respond immediately to specific business situations such as

- customer contacts driven by quantitatively derived interaction models
- real-time investment or pricing decisions based on market conditions
- short-term inventory adjustments due to unexpected demand (or lack of demand) for products
- dynamic scheduling or rerouting of equipment based on point-in-time assessment of available options for deployment.

Tactical decision support systems typically require depth of history and richness of information that is characteristic of a data warehouse but have performance and systems availability requirements quite similar to the operational systems environment. The combination of this tactical decision support capability with operational systems requirements are often referred to as an Operational Data Store (ODS). The algorithms deployed in tactical decision support systems are often derived from analysis of information that takes place using the data warehouse.

In both strategic and tactically oriented decision making, the decision support systems use periodic (rather than real-time) update methods. The frequency of these updates ranges anywhere from hourly (or less) for tactically oriented decision support to monthly (or more) for purely strategic decision support. Most data warehouse implementations are positioned somewhere in between these extremes. The specifics of the business problems to be solved and the timeliness of the data required for effective decision making determine the update cycles.

Service Levels for High Availability

The service levels for the data warehouse database are usually not as stringent as those in an operational environment. In today's business environment, most operational systems must be available seven days a week, 24 hours a day. In fact, most mission-critical systems have a disaster recovery plan that provides automatic takeover of essential operations at an off-site location in the case of failure at the organization's primary data center. After all, customers get pretty upset if an ATM won't deliver cash even at midnight on a Friday night (especially at midnight on a Friday night!) or if the computers at passport control can't process an incoming customs clearance. Our society has become dependent on automation to perform tasks round the clock. Both planned and unplanned outages in operational systems are becoming less and less acceptable in today's business environment.

Most data warehouse implementations don't require the investments in high availability typically found with operational systems—initially. Rarely does a decision support user log into the data warehouse environment to look at the latest customer segmentation results at midnight on Friday night. *Initial* deployment of decision support capability is usually quite successful if the system is available for perhaps 12 hours a day for 6 days a week (12 x 6 availability).

This does not mean planning for 12 hours of outage each day, but rather planning to take the data off-line for maintenance. While data is off-line, database loading, index builds, reorganizations of the data files, backups, and other maintenance can be orchestrated without impacting users. Of course, you can perform these tasks while end users have access, but that's much more costly and complicated.

Our recommendation is to initially deploy the data warehouse with a rather modest service level for availability (e.g., 12 x 6) in order to minimize cost and time for the first delivery, but to have a clear plan for increasing availability. As end users become more dependent on the data warehouse and become more sophisticated in the workloads that they construct against the database, the initial modest service level becomes unacceptable because users will demand more. They begin issuing batch-oriented overnight workloads for more complex analyses and scoring models; these require opening up the nightly window for end-user batch query activity. Moreover, in a decentralized corporate decision-making environment, a pilot successfully implemented at a single site must often expand its available hours to end users in different time zones. Eventually, the service level desired for planned availability against the data warehouse edges its way up to 24 x 7.

Still, the consequences of unplanned downtime in a data warehouse are rarely as damaging as in an operational system. Decision support systems, unlike operational systems, are not usually needed for the short-term aspects of running the business. The cost of system downtime in a data warehouse is the opportunity cost of not being able to run queries while the system is down. This is clearly not in the same category as the cost of losing business while an operational system is down. The business impact of waiting a day for the answer to a strategically oriented decision support question is probably pretty small as long as the end user can still ask all the questions necessary for analysis within the throughput constraints of the data warehouse machine. Of course, tactically oriented decision support environments put a much higher premium on the cost of unplanned outages due to the importance of timely decisions.

In strategic decision support, the real disadvantage of system outages is the loss of end-user confidence in the availability of information. If unplanned outages become disruptive to the decision-making process, then users will abandon the data warehouse for other more reliable sources of information. Since decision making is ad hoc by its very nature, it is essential that the warehouse strive to avoid unplanned outages so as not to interfere with the creative processes involved in strategic analysis and decision making.

On the other hand, there is always a cost to maintaining high availability. These costs must be carefully weighed against the value of a 24 x 7 decision support environment. Given advances in technology and the increased robustness of data warehousing tools in the marketplace today, it is reasonable for end users to eventually expect 24 x 7 service at an economical price. Three to four years ago, this would not have been the case. Even so, most strategically oriented decision support environments do not go so far as to provide for an off-site disaster recovery infrastructure. Its cost is usually not justified by the potential lost opportunities, given that disasters are rare.

Interactive Exploration of Information by Business End Users

The question of how data warehouses differ from traditional MIS (Management Information System) reporting environments comes up often in discussions of investing in a data warehouse. The key difference between the two is the interactive and ad hoc nature of data exploration in a warehouse versus the static reporting capabilities of an MIS. A typical MIS reporting system can run batch-oriented reports that are delivered to end users as hard copy or made available on-line to management decision makers. More sophisticated MIS reporting systems can generate parameterized reports to be produced on demand. The limitation of most MIS reporting environments is that information and its organization on reports are limited to a relatively small set of templates. Parameterized reporting environments allow users some flexibility in determining the content of delivered reports but still confine analyses to predefined templates.

A successful data warehouse environment almost always lets users slice and dice information themselves. Although predefined ("canned") queries may be provided for ease of use to casual users (and are recommended to ease the learning curve associated with a decision support system); more sophisticated users should be able to formulate queries that have not been predefined in any way by the warehouse environment. The on-the-fly specification of these ad hoc requests means that users can get answers to questions that were unforeseen by the system designers. The combined flexibility of relational database technology and advanced query tools encourages interactive data exploration in ways that are not possible with predefined reports.

The impact of direct access to information by end users should not be underestimated. In a traditional MIS reporting environment, drilling down to the details behind the numbers requires programming. Writing code to extract and match from multiple source systems in order to generate a detailed custom report takes time. The delay in delivering information to the decision maker diminishes the value of the delivered report and significantly hinders iterative decision making.

When end users have direct access to information, they can ask a series of questions, refining them and drilling down to details until they understand the business issue under scrutiny. Even in a data warehouse, though, programmers are often required to provide the expertise for sophisticated analytic models, but they are much more highly leveraged when trained and certified end users have direct access to data to fulfill their most immediate information requirements.

Database Structures

Designing database structures for a data warehouse entails making quite different trade-offs than in designing them for a traditional operational system. Even if both systems contained exactly the same information (which they wouldn't, because of the need for historical and external information in a data warehouse), their database designs would be significantly different because of the huge difference in access patterns.

In an operational environment, information retrieval typically focuses on very well-defined and highly tuned transactions that use indexed access to find a relatively small number of records (usually less than a few hundred). These transactions usually specify an individual customer, account, or other very selective retrieval criteria that makes primary or foreign key indexing very effective. Highly normalized database designs are common in on-line transaction processing systems. They are effective because they minimize data redundancy and allow for a high degree of data integrity while supporting very efficient data access with highly selective indices.

The access path and unstructured query environment in a Decision Support System (DSS) mandate a different approach to database designs. Users rarely make decisions after retrieving information about a single customer or account. Rather, decisions are driven by examining large customer segments and historical trends in aggregations across hundreds of thousands or even millions of records. Instead of primary key access to database records, aggregations are invoked in which many records are examined with potential filtering or categorization based on customer attributes, account attributes, transaction attributes, and other facts or dimensions relevant to the analysis to be performed.

Dimensional attributes are characteristics that categorize the facts of interest in an analysis. For example, a user interested in the number of dollars invested at a financial services company may want to categorize these dollars by month, product, geographic location of the customer, and so on. The invested dollars are the fact of interest, whereas the dates (month), investment instrument (product), and geography (geographic location of the customer) are the characteristics of interest or dimensional attributes.

Database designs for a warehouse must anticipate the unexpected. This is difficult because, unlike an operational system where transaction behavior is very predictable, decision support queries are constantly evolving. An appropriate database design for a warehouse delivers flexibility, ease of use, and performance to accommodate the unpredictability of query patterns in a DSS.

Some amount of data summarization and other denormalization techniques are usually applicable in a data warehouse design with these goals in mind. Star schema designs, which are discussed in Chapter 9, are derived from a quite popular methodology for denormalizing relational tables in a data warehouse for high performance and ease of use in accessing information. Techniques such as sampling, bit indexing, column partitioning, and other approaches for database design that are quite relevant to data warehouse implementations are virtually unseen in traditional operational database deployments; yet the trade-offs in these approaches must be carefully considered in the context of the business requirements.

WHY WOULD I WANT A DATA WAREHOUSE?

Once you understand how a data warehouse differs from a traditional operational system, the question becomes: Why embark on the investment of time, effort, and cost involved in constructing such a beast? What is the value to the organization? These are the questions to answer before you get involved in obtaining funding and beginning implementation. Knowing why the data warehouse is needed provides a framework for its design and the organization's buy-in.

At a high level, the primary benefits of a data warehouse can be described by four specific capabilities:

1. Allows an integrated and complete view of the organization
2. Provides access to historical information about the organization
3. Institutes an unambiguous source of informational truth within the organization
4. Facilitates DSS without hindering the operational systems

Each of these points is described in more detail below. Applications that make use of these capabilities are discussed later in the chapter.

Total View of the Organization

Most operational systems in large organizations have been built around specific functional areas of deployment. From an operational point of view, this strategy is usually quite appropriate because these specialized systems are efficient and cost-effective. But the result is a collection of "silo" or "smokestack" systems organized around separate products or functions. Interaction between systems is minimal. This works well for operational efficiency but makes decision support in a customer-oriented business environment difficult.

For example, understanding the details of a customer's credit card account is irrelevant when processing a transaction against the customer's checking account. However, business analysts trying to formulate strategies for customer reationship management need access to both credit card and checking account activities—they can't get both kinds of information from smokestack systems.

The data warehouse integrates the information from disparate operational systems into a total view of the organization. Common key structures, an integrated data design, and a unified set of data definitions provide decision support capability that cannot be had in any other way. The resultant total view of the organization gives analysts the information necessary to make sound decisions about strategic issues that have a significant, long-term impact on the business. This is quite different from narrow decisions based on information extracted from a single functional area.

The Past Is the Best Predictor of the Future

By understanding past trends and behaviors and then injecting insights about how the current business environment has evolved from the past, companies can develop a quantitative analysis framework for decision making. Rather than being limited to qualitative decision models, the data warehouse provides end users an analytic foundation for decision making.

For example, consider a company trying to increase its market share by lowering the price of its product. Without historical data on price and product demand, decision makers must make projections based only on intuition and experience to assess the impact a price drop will have on market share. On the other hand, when historical pricing and product movement data are in the warehouse, analysts can predict this impact. The real power of the warehouse in this simple example comes with the ability to pose "what-if" questions to assess the outcome of various pricing strategies. Rather than trying out these strategies in the marketplace, and then waiting to see what happens (with potentially disastrous results), the marketing analyst can test the proposed price cuts in the decision support environment and keep asking questions until the optimal price, market share, and profitability mesh. Of course, access to historical data as the basis for the decision support is essential.

Single Version of Organizational Truth

A data warehouse using integrated data and definitions provides an unambiguous source of informational truth, which gives decision makers a common understanding of the business. Far too often, when an organization uses many unintegrated reporting systems, different decision makers have different versions of the "numbers" which describe the business. Without a common set of quantitative figures, decision makers waste their valuable time attempting to reconcile differences between the figures rather than solving the business problem at hand. The issue isn't really whose numbers are right or wrong. In fact, it is likely that more than one set of distinct numbers is correct. The numbers may be different because data was populated into the reporting databases at different times, or because the reporting systems interpreted numbers differently. A single data warehouse as the source of information for all decision making ensures a common set of data for all decision makers with (hopefully) standards for reporting and interpretation within the organization. This establishes a common foundation of understanding among decision makers and makes the process of reaching agreement on important business issues much more effective.

Support for DSS without Impacting Operational Systems

Contention for resources in the operational systems of a large organization is always a significant issue. Decision support systems are notorious for consuming enormous amounts of resources. The execution of a sophisticated DSS query which will typically scan, join, and aggregate many millions of rows of relational data is nearly insatiable in its desire for memory, CPU, and I/O resources.

When a decision support system coexists in the same environment as the operational systems, disaster will likely result. The first time that a complex DSS query is launched against the data warehouse during a high-volume operational load, the conflict in resource consumption is immediately apparent. The response times in the operational systems, normally under two seconds for interactive workloads, creep to three, then five, and on up in delivered performance. Data center operators responsible for performance monitoring will soon realize that the cause of the change is the DSS query workload consuming a large percent of the resources in the operational environment. It will not be long before an operator puts an end to the resource contention by killing the offending DSS query workload.

The fact is that a DSS workload almost always takes a back seat to operational transactions. Despite the recognized importance of strategic decision making, servicing customers inevitably gets priority. In a successful and growing business there are rarely enough spare cycles in the operational environment to service both systems. As a result, the decision support workload is rarely allowed to compete for resources while the operational systems are running at their peak. Operational peak time is usually during prime business hours, which is also when decision support users are most likely to need information.

The solution is to separate the data warehouse database from the operational database, in a hardware environment distinct from the operational systems, so end users can make decisions when they want to without impacting business operations. This makes sense technically, too, because the hardware and software technology choices for implementation of a robust data warehouse environment are typically quite different from those found in operational systems.

TYPICAL APPLICATION DEPLOYMENTS

A successful data warehouse implementation entails much more than merely placing row upon row of data into a relational database system. There must be a clear business benefit. Applications that maximize core business profitability in ways that can be measured and related directly to the bottom line have the most obvious business benefits. Data warehouses that do this provide information that is actionable and relevant to the business—oftentimes, business models and strategies developed in the data warehouse become part of the production systems. The following concrete examples show how and where a number of data warehouse applications have been successful in different industries.

The Return On Investment (ROI) for any one of these applications usually pays for the company's investment in hardware, software, and people many times over when the application is deployed under appropriate circumstances. Of course, a well-designed data warehouse enables more than just one application, so returns on investment aren't limited to one area.

Fraud Detection

Fraud detection is a popular application of data warehousing because it impacts the bottom line directly in many types of businesses. The idea is to use the decision support capabilities of the data warehouse to develop a fraud detection algorithm and then use it in the operational systems. The ad hoc query and decision support capabilities of the data warehouse facilitate exploration of the data to identify the most appropriate areas in which to concentrate the fraud detection efforts. Using the historical data in the warehouse, models are built to predict likely patterns of fraud so that it can be detected before major losses occur. The models are often implemented in the operational systems with potential feeds from the warehouse to include key historical variables.

The credit card business is, perhaps, one of the best examples of an effective opportunity for deployment of fraud detection algorithms. Patterns of purchasing behavior for individuals show remarkable regularity. Credit card holders demonstrate repeatable patterns in what they buy, where they shop, when they shop (weekends versus specific weekdays as well as time of day), and how much they charge. It is quite feasible to detect fraudulent use of a credit card by looking for irregularities in these established patterns. When a customer normally uses his charge card to buy clothes in downtown Boston twice a month on weekends, and suddenly ten charges appear for stereo equipment and CDs in a single day in New York City (a high-risk zone for fraudulent use of stolen credit cards), fraud is probably occurring.

Of course, actual scenarios where the fraud detection algorithms would need to work are often much more subtle than this example. The key is to use historical information in the data warehouse to characterize patterns of fraud and patterns of legitimate card use by customers and then to provide these algorithms and perhaps key historical variables to the operational systems so that fraud can be prevented in real-time or semi real-time.

Credit cards are certainly not the only targets for fraud detection algorithms. Users of telephone calling cards, like credit card holders, are also amazingly predictable. Their calls to home, work, business associates, and friends follow extremely regular patterns. By characterizing legitimate versus fraudulent calling patterns, effective fraud detection algorithms can be implemented. The same techniques hold true for fraud detection in the use of cellular telephones. Other areas where fraud and abuse are effective include insurance claims payments, welfare payments, retail merchandise returns, airline ticketing, and financial transactions.

Target Marketing

It used to be that organizations improved direct marketing via the acquisition of more list names and making more contacts. Whether in direct-mail marketing or telemarketing, this strategy is no longer effective because the marketplace is saturated. Today, it is the quality, not the quantity, of names contacted that makes the difference. This is where target marketing comes into play. By understanding individual customer demographics, behaviors, and product needs it is possible to use target marketing as a rifle shot to get to the right customers rather than applying a shot gun approach where most of the ammunition ends up as a total miss. Using the historical data warehouse information to develop response models, analysts can predict the probabilities of a contact responding positively to a telemarketing call or direct mail piece before initiating it. Then analysts can use these probabilities and the expected value of the transaction (which can also be modeled from the warehouse) to choose just the right customers for a direct marketing campaign.

Extremely targeted direct marketing can be somewhat of a culture shock to marketing organizations whose direct marketing approaches were developed for mass marketing. A data warehouse allows for a "demassification" of the market. By doing sophisticated analysis with information stored in the data warehouse, marketers can sell to segmented and even individualized targets. Customer segmentation groups customers who have similar characteristics and behaviors in the marketplace together, and customizes communications to them. Individualized targeting customizes marketing communications to each customer.

Ultimately, the goal is to evolve toward "customer segments of size one" in which the marketing message is specific to each individual customer. The depth of customer information in a well-populated data warehouse will allow this sort of customization. Practically speaking, the movement toward individualized customer segments will be incremental in its evolution. As more information becomes available in the warehouse and understanding develops of how to use it effectively, the degree of targeting will increase over time. More precise targeting increases response rates from the intended audience. When the marketing message is customized to the individual, the probability of a positive response to the communication increases substantially. The economic implications of better targeting can be significant because fewer telemarketing calls or direct mail pieces can generate more customer acquisitions or cross sells. For organizations with millions of marketing contacts per year, the impact to the bottom line can be staggering.

Profitability Analysis

It is amazing how little most companies know about their own profitability. Theoretically, average customer profitability can be calculated by dividing total profits by the number of active customers (assuming it is possible to get an accurate count of customers). However, this figure is of little practical use in most industries. The truth is that average profitability is very deceiving because profits are rarely distributed evenly across the customer base. More often, over 80 percent of a company's profits come from less than 20 percent of its customers.

The 80/20 rule applies very strongly when analyzing company profits. Almost every retail bank in North America, for example, falls into this paradigm. In fact, more than half the customers in most retail banks are unprofitable or marginally profitable. Most retail banks are making very healthy overall profits—but they cannot identify their profitable and unprofitable customers. This lack of information is likely to lead to trouble in the future because it is impossible to manage what is not measured and identified.

Consequently, a very important application area in many data warehouse implementations is profitability scoring. Using activity-based costing models and detailed revenue reconciliation, a profit score can be individually assigned to each customer. Activity-based costing charges costs back to individual customers. For example, rather than amortize the cost of a service call center back across all customers as an average cost (those deceiving averages again!), the call center makes charges based on who makes the calls. This means doing much more detailed data collection and integration with customer databases. Of course, not all costs can be charged back to specific customers, but the idea is to use activity-based costing models rather than average cost models to understand the business.

The insights obtained from detailed profitability models can be astounding. It becomes possible to understand profitability according to specific customer segments and to associate profitability results directly with customer behaviors. The decision support capability provided by a data warehouse provides insights into how to best influence customer behaviors to increase overall company profitability. For example, understanding the profitability characteristics of specific customer segments in the retail banking industry may make a group of marginally profitable customers much more profitable merely by moving them from teller-based interactions to ATM and on-line transactions. The action item from such an insight might be to develop a channel management program that identifies users of the more traditional banking channels and then shows the advantages of automated banking, perhaps using special promotions or incentives.

The key in the use of profitability models in any industry is to associate accurate profitability scores to individual customers. This information is then used to strengthen and expand the ongoing relationship to profitable customers and to identify characteristics of profitable customers so that more of them can be acquired, as well as to target unprofitable customers and develop programs to move them into the profitable category. These programs may involve:

- Repricing or restructuring certain products (e.g., service fees for below minimum balance accounts)
- Using educational programs for influencing behavior (e.g., the channel management program described above)
- Introducing new products and services to better target the unprofitable customer segment
- Migrating away from unprofitable customer segments so as to allow better servicing of the profitable customers.

Customer Retention

In today's business environment, competition between companies for the best customers is intense. Retention of existing customers is much more cost-effective than acquiring new customers or trying to win back customers who have been stolen by the competition. This means that while a company is aggressively pursuing the expansion of its customer base through the development of a new customer base or by acquiring customers from its competitors, it must also keep existing customers happy and safe from the competition. An aggressive customer retention program can do this. Using the data warehouse, analysts can develop at-risk scoring models that identify customers in danger of attrition before it occurs.

Customers provide signals about their intentions long before they act upon them—often before they have even become conscious of them. These signals come in the form of interactions or lack of interactions with their service or product provider. The question for the provider is whether or not the data is collected and can be interpreted as information relevant to a retention program. At-risk scoring models can predict what is likely to happen far enough in the future to prevent it from happening.

For example, when the expiration date for a credit card is looming three or four months away, it is very important to have already captured the patron's behavior and instigated an at-risk score to understand whether or not the patron will likely renew the card. In fact, it is usually effective to score at-risk for the patron regularly, rather than just before renewal time, because the patron can stop using the credit card at any time. The key is to use decision support systems to capture and interpret interactions from the customer and use them as the basis for the retention program.

The rates of success in a retention program certainly vary by industry and by each individual program within an industry. However, it is certainly no stretch in most situations to assume that, if identified early enough, at least 10 percent of the customers who leave their provider could be "saved" with an appropriate retention program. The program may involve the use of special promotions aimed at retention, a simple letter or phone call of appreciation, or perhaps some marketing communication to educate and refresh the value proposition of the business relationship in the customer's mind. Of course, such programs aren't free and thus, efforts must be well targeted.

The accuracy of targeting relies directly on the quality of the at-risk scoring models. The quality of these models depends on the quality and accessibility of detailed customer information. The customer information must have enough behavioral content and history to provide predictable models. The customer is talking to you with every interaction. The question is: "Are you listening and what are you going to do about it?" The data warehouse gives companies the information they need to listen to and to take the appropriate actions to successfully target and deploy a customer retention program.

Inventory Management

In the retail industry, where a large part of the business revolves around effective inventory management and merchandising, information is an organization's most lethal competitive weapon. Successful retailing is all about having the right products in the right place at the right time. As WalMart has demonstrated for years, appropriate leverage of information can change an organization's entire profit structure.

In retail, successful business is all about having the right product in the right place at the right time for the right price. It used to be that when a product was out-of-stock, retailers issued "rain checks," ordered the item, and called the customer for a pick-up when it arrived. Today, we live in a consumer-driven society. If an item is unavailable, the customer goes to the competition to buy it elsewhere. If items are out of stock frequently enough, the customer begins going to the competition first.

Although a lack of the right inventory in a retail outlet can be deadly, having too much inventory can be equally disastrous. In a business where profit is counted in pennies on the dollar, managing inventory carrying costs effectively is critical. Having too much inventory means that the capital carrying costs of doing business quickly eat up extremely competitive retail profits. Managing carrying costs is equally critical in manufacturing, especially where the cost-of-goods-sold is very high.

In retail, the problem is particularly difficult because the most profitable items are typically the most unpredictable. Demand for items such as clothing, toys, and music depends on what is "hot" and what is "not." While an item is "hot" profits are high, and having the item on the shelf is very important. On the other hand, when an item is no longer "hot," demand plummets dramatically without much warning. Having a large inventory for an item which is no longer in demand is very undesirable because the carrying costs are so high. The deep price cuts which make selling a "not" item possible diminish profits in an industry where margins are already slim.

For items with high volatility in demand over time, retailers use a technique called trend merchandising. This involves moving product from stores where demand is weak to stores where it is strong. Merchandise managers have long recognized that most trends start in large cities either on the East or West Coast, and then branch out to less urban areas and into the Midwest. Variations in demand depend on customer demographics, climatic differences (for clothing, in particular), and so on. By using information from their data warehouse and trend merchandising techniques, retail merchants can maximize profits for an item while it is in high demand and offload inventory from one store to another to adjust for shifts in demand by geography.

Another aspect of inventory management includes category management, which means optimizing product mix based on consumer demand, product profitability, and limited available shelf space. Supplier management in negotiating pricing, delivery service levels, damaged goods allowances, and so on is yet another important aspect of inventory management.

The key to effective inventory management, of course, is access to information about patterns in demand and performance of suppliers in providing these items, as well as basic information regarding profit margins and shelf space requirements. A data warehouse used for inventory management needs at least 15 to 27 months of historical data to understand year over year trends by item and store. Understanding seasonal effects and the ability to benchmark new items with comparable items in past history generally lead to quite accurate demand forecasts. If the retailer can capture customer demographics, either through individual customer identification or through block group demographics, then applications such as trend merchandising or category management become even more accurate in predicting demand. A successful retailer uses all these analyses on a store-by-store basis, and customizes product mix and inventory levels to each local market.

When inventory is fixed—as it is in rental cars, airline seats, hotel rooms, or rental videos—merchandisers practice yield management. Once an airline seat is sold for a particular leg or a car is rented for two days, the inventory is no longer available for selling to other customers. In these cases, where inventory is "recycled" to meet customer demand, yield management optimization is crucial. The idea is to sell as close to 100 percent of the inventory as possible at the best possible price.

In many industries, it is possible to do this by varying price based on current demand. For example, sophisticated rental car agencies reprice cars every 15 minutes for each location based on demand versus available inventory. Retrospective analysis in a data warehouse using past demand and inventory patterns allows construction of sophisticated pricing algorithms which are then implemented in the operational systems. Tiered pricing structures, such as those common in the airline industry, are another way to optimize yield management in a fixed inventory business. Tiered pricing structures are developed using extensive analysis of historical sales with particular attention to price elasticities.*

Notice that an increase in inventory in this type of business is very different than in a sell-through business. In a fixed inventory business, acquisition of new inventory is a long-term commitment and is typically much more costly than in a traditional retail business. New inventory acquisition adds to the fixed costs of operation. Thus, analysis of long-term business trends becomes even more important in fixed inventory businesses than it is in traditional inventory management analyses.

Credit Risk Analysis

The area of credit risk analysis has become more and more sophisticated as saturation of the marketplace continues to escalate. It is no longer easy to obtain customers when an analysis of credit risk is obvious or simple. Persons with stellar credit histories typically have more credit than they could ever use. Thus, increase in market penetration means accepting and evaluating new credit applications for credit lines, home loans, car loans, and so on from individuals when the decision to extend credit is not always straightforward.

When examining individuals for credit risk scoring, the population is typically divided into three categories—affectionately referred to as "the good, the bad, and the ugly." Individuals categorized as "the good"

*Price elasticity is a measurement of the sensitivity of demand for a product to its pricing. It is formally defined as the difference in units demanded for a product divided by the difference in price for that product. For example, a high price elasticity indicates that a small reduction in price will result in a large increase in demand for the product. Conversely, a small price elasticity indicates that a large price increase or decrease will have little impact on demand for the product.

have immaculate credit histories, stable job histories, high incomes, and an overall assessment of low risk. It would be quite desirable to issue a new credit card to them, but unfortunately they already have more than enough credit, so issuing credit that would actually be used is very difficult. Individuals categorized as "the bad" have bankruptcies, frequent and recent derogatory events in their credit history, and job instability. They are poor credit risks and are avoided in the credit business (although secured credit lines may be quite viable). The individuals in the "ugly" category are the most interesting. These individuals have mixed credit histories. The presence of derogatory entries in an individual's credit history may coexist with a number of positive signals such as high income and job stability. Scoring enables companies to manage bad debt by identifying the best risks among the untapped market of those in the "ugly" category.

In order to accurately assess credit risk, quantitative models for predicting credit payment behavior of individuals based on past history have been developed by every major player in the credit marketplace. Precision in credit risk scoring is the differentiator between competitive organizations. Players with more accurate models have a decided competitive advantage. More accurate models rely on better analytics and better access to information related to credit candidates. Credit risk assessment can be particularly effective when standard credit bureau data is augmented with information regarding customer behaviors taken from an internal data warehouse. By applying proprietary knowledge obtained from internal sources about customer behavior, it is possible to develop models with accuracy that go beyond the standard credit scoring from externally acquired data. The existing customer relationship provides access to information about the individual which substantially lowers the risk of an inaccurate credit assessment. Collecting and maintaining information from multiple source systems into the data warehouse is a prerequisite in successfully deploying this strategy.

Long-Term Value Assessment

Understanding the value of a customer relationship is much more than merely assessing last year's profitability from the customer. What is important is the long-term value of the customer. A marginally profitable customer can easily evolve into a very profitable customer. Of course, that same marginally profitable customer could also evolve into a very unprofitable customer. The trick is to determine which scenario is more likely to occur.

The predictive models for this assessment rely very heavily on access to extensive information in the data warehouse regarding customer behaviors as they relate to the psychographic, synchographic, and demographic composition of the individual. Customer behaviors are captured in the warehouse via activities such as purchases, inquiries, and other interactions with an organization. Psychographics, which describe the makeup of the individual in terms of buying propensities, risk profiles, self-image, and so forth are typically captured using survey devices or feeds from external sources which acquire this information. Synchographics involve obtaining the details regarding the dates of major life events, such as marriage, birth of children, home purchase, departure of children to college, retirement, and so on. Finally, demographic information describes the individual's ethnicity, income level, occupation, and other characteristics which are specific to the person and predictive of long-term behavior.

By analyzing all this information, or whatever portion of it that can be acquired consistently with high-quality results, models can be constructed for predicting long-term profitability for a customer that go beyond a simple retrospective look at last year's results. For example, a student may represent only meager profits while still in college but can evolve into a very profitable customer once graduation takes place and a large salary allows for a substantial disposable income. Identifying potential long-term customers and retaining them through marketing communication and customer care programs is essential. The data warehouse provides both the predictive scoring and the feeds into marketing communication programs and operational systems that enable businesses to keep potential long-term customers.

Pricing

Competitive pricing entails understanding product demand, competitive positioning in the marketplace, and profit margins. All these ought to be captured in a data warehouse. Past history, with adjustments for the marketplace and seasonal factors, shows demand for a product. As discussed earlier, understanding price elasticities provides the basis for making appropriate decisions regarding price versus volume trade-offs in the marketplace. Competitive pricing also entails understanding the price of substitute products and consumer alternatives.

Pricing decisions must also consider the profit margin. Sophisticated models are often constructed from information in the data warehouse to develop pricing structures to maximize profitability. The tiered pricing schedules described earlier in the context of yield management for fixed inventory businesses are a good example. Credit risk, too, ought to be a direct input for a well-thought pricing strategy; any credit institution that uses a single APR (Annual Percentage Rate) and fee structure for all customers is suboptimizing. Risk-adjusted pricing models allow credit accounts with a higher probability of bad debt to be profitable via appropriate pricing strategies that compensate for higher risks with higher APR and fee structures.

Similarly, pricing in the insurance business relies on actuarial analysis of claims experience in well-defined rating groups to establish pricing according to historical claims and premium behavior of large groups of individuals. This type of sophisticated pricing analysis requires extensive access to years of historical data to establish trends in claims and premium experience. The data warehouse enables analysts to pose "what-if" questions regarding profitability outcomes by slicing and dicing information along numerous dimensions and drilling down into detailed data in ways that are nearly impossible to predict. Only the access to information in a data warehouse enables decision makers to do this and thus develop fundamentally new pricing models.

KEY CRITICAL SUCCESS FACTORS

Throughout this book you will find tips on the many factors that determine the success or failure of a data warehouse implementation. In this section, we concentrate on three critical factors that were prerequisites for success in every successful warehouse implementation with which we have been involved. These three critical success factors are:

1. Focus on the business, not the technology
2. Rapid turnaround on deliverables
3. End users on the implementation team

Take it from the experience of many others: You may have the best data warehouse vision in the industry, but without careful adherence to the three critical success factors described in this section the likelihood of a successful implementation of the vision will be in serious jeopardy.

Focus on the Business, Not the Technology

Focusing on the business means addressing strategic directives and the bottom line of the corporation. Don't build a data warehouse as a technical undertaking, or simply by gathering all the data in the corporation into one big database. There must be a clear business imperative for constructing the warehouse. It is not enough to merely state that "information is strategic" and therefore the business needs a data warehouse. To ensure success, there must be a well-defined deliverable with a clear Return On Investment (ROI).

Establishing a return on investment model for the data warehouse is important because all too often the focus in comparing DSS environments is on the size of the database rather than the size of the ROI. This "my database is bigger than your database" mentality may lead to an interesting set of technical issues but rarely leads to a business benefit. In fact, a larger database size incurs higher costs and therefore must yield better returns in order to produce an acceptable ROI for the project.

However, although project success must be evaluated in terms of ROI, true understanding or competitive advantage is rarely obtained in a decision support environment that lacks detailed data. Storing and providing historical access to detailed data almost inevitably results in large databases. The important point is to populate the data warehouse with information that is relevant to real business decisions. The order in which subject areas are populated into the warehouse, as well as the depth of history, must be driven by the business applications. Do not make the data warehouse a dumping ground for all the data in the corporation.

Business considerations, rather than technology considerations, should dictate the data sourcing and implementation approach. We have seen many technology-driven implementations in which a clean, modern relational database system is used to source the data warehouse because the data available from it is high in quality and easily accessible in a normalized form. However, if this isn't the data required for decision making, then it will not be useful to the organization. Our experience is that those 20 year-old VSAM and IMS files with a multitude of "redefines" and other data quality issues do not exist because management is attached to them in any way, but rather because they are critical to the operational systems which run the business. Carefully consider the business implications of the source systems selection for the warehouse. Use technology considerations to provide a risk adjustment factor for assisting in the decisions regarding data sourcing, but make the business requirements the dominant influence.

Lastly, don't get caught up in the technology hype that surrounds data warehousing. Be very aware of the fact that as soon as an organization expresses interest in a data warehouse, the vendor wolves begin circling in anticipation of a sale. Since what the vendors have to sell is technology, it's easy to get dragged into the depths of endless technology evaluations and product demonstrations. This is all fine and good, but stay focused on the business problem and don't get deflected into technology considerations before you have a full understanding of the business requirementss. Technology evaluations without well-defined business requirements quickly become black holes of effort.

Unless business requirements are in place to provide the basis for evaluation, discussions of hardware, database, and tools degenerate into religious debates that merely distract the data warehouse team. Before allowing any vendors to speak to you about SMP (Symmetric Multiprocessing) versus MPP (Massively Parallel Processing) or ROLAP (Relational On-Line Analytic Processing) versus MOLAP (Multi-Dimensional On-Line Analytic Processing) or whatever the current raging religious debates are at the moment, make sure that you have a carefully constructed framework for specifying your business requirements. Otherwise the technology is likely to begin driving the business requirements, rather than the other way around. Making good technology decisions means choosing the tools and platforms that provide the lowest-risk solution for delivering business value to the organization. At all costs, avoid getting pulled into "gee-whiz" technology discussions.

Rapid Turnaround on Deliverables

Any attempt to implement a data warehouse using traditional development methodologies will fail. Traditional forms of project execution, such as the Systems Development Life Cycle (SDLC) approach, involve a long process with many steps: functional analysis, systems design, implementation, User Acceptance Testing (UAT), and (finally) deployment. In this "waterfall" development methodology, each step must be delivered before the next can begin. There are two main problems with this approach in a decision support environment. First, it takes far too long for successful deployment in most business environments. The SDLC types of development methodologies take months to deliver end results because they attempt to be overly thorough in each phase of the project undertaking. Second, this approach is fundamentally contractual in nature and leads to an antagonistic relationship between end users and the development team. The relationship between end users and the development team is discussed in the next section.

Functional specifications describe all of the system's screens, reports, and other capabilities. The functional specification is reviewed by end users and becomes a contract between the developers and the end-user community. Typically, developers blame end users for the inevitable failure of an SDLC project, saying they did not communicate their requirements effectively to the implementation team. The signed-

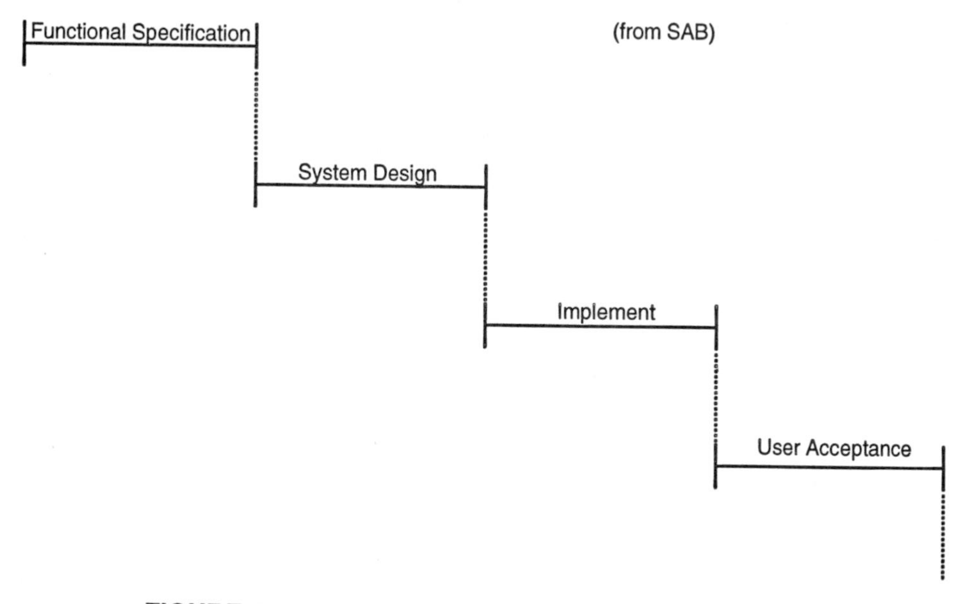

FIGURE 4–1 Traditional waterfall development methodology.

off functional specification becomes contractual proof that the implementation is correct and that review and communication from the end users were inadequate.

Our experience is that the flaw is in the methodology rather than the input provided by the end users. In a decision support environment, a complete specification is simply not possible—the delivered system is guaranteed to lack some desired functionality. The fact is that end users can't predict all the questions they'll ask. Decision support systems do not have well defined and structured screens, reports, and rules as accounting systems or operational environments do. End users of a decision support environment can tell you the first question that they'll ask, but don't know the second question until the first has been answered. Decision making is iterative; a successful development methodology takes this fact into consideration.

The key to success for a data warehouse implementation is rapid turnaround on deliverables using an iterative development methodology. Note that iterative development does not mean that one should bypass the specification, design, implementation, and so forth, steps of the SDLC methodology. Instead, these steps should be undertaken multiple times in a series of iterative refinements to the decision support environment. The point is to allow the specifications and implementation to evolve as end users continue to develop their business requirements through active use of the decision support environment. Adjustments and enhancements to previous iterations can then be made based on user input after hands-on use of the system. It is acceptable to be incomplete or even slightly off-base in the delivery of an iterative cycle for the decision support environment because subsequent refinements will find and address the inadequacies.

Notice in Figure 4-2 that as the iterations converge they become tighter and tighter. This happens because each iteration builds upon its predecessor. Time frames for specification, implementation and delivery of the iterations decrease with each cycle because of the leverage obtained from previous cycles. Only in extreme cases should the cycles exceed 90 to 120 days in duration.

Instituting 90 day cycles in the iterative methodology requires discipline in scoping deliverables. A clear business focus should prioritize requirements to manage scope. Time boxing the deliverables to approximately 90 day ensures rapid delivery of business value and quick feedback from the end users to the implementation team to drive refinement in subsequent iterations. Prioritization should be based on a risk-adjusted ROI to ensure meaningful business deliverables. Subse-

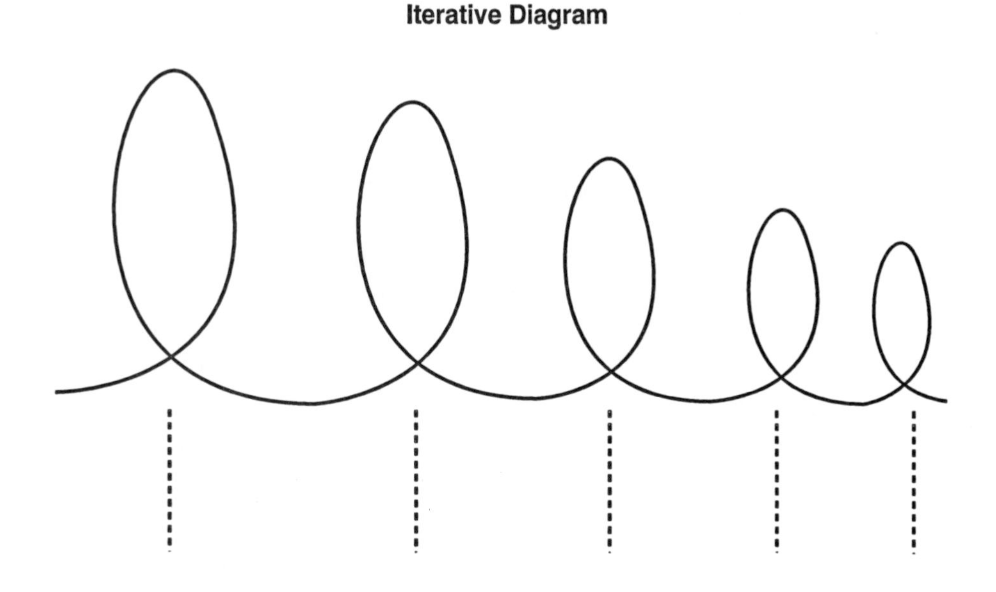

FIGURE 4–2 Iterative development methodology.

quent iterations should be scoped to incrementally address business requirements that were not prioritized within the first 90 day to 120 day time box. Avoid "big bang" delivery models in which enormous amounts of functionality are scoped into a single iteration. If scope begins to exceed three or four months of implementation duration, reexamine and reprioritize the business deliverables within the time box. Manageable scope for deliverables in short time frames goes a long way toward ensuring success and continued commitment by the business to the data warehouse implementation.

The iterative refinements should be undertaken in the context of an overall vision of the architecture and data model for the warehouse. Think of each iteration as filling in puzzle pieces of the complete implementation picture. The picture is not static; the DSS will tend to transform itself and increase in size as the business evolves in its competitive use of information. This means that a certain amount of business and information discovery must take place in the early stages of the project in order to provide a framework for proceeding. However, it is very important not to fall into the trap of the traditional development methodologies by delivering massive amounts of paper specifications and three-ring-binder reports full of entity-relationship diagrams. Development of the framework should be fast and it can be if you focus on what is important to the big picture and fill in the details later, as you refine the iterations.

End Users on the Implementation Team

Direct involvement of end users on the implementation team is probably the single most important critical success factor for a data warehouse implementation. Iterative delivery works well only when end users are active participants on the delivery team for the decision support environment. This participation must go well beyond status reports or monthly steering group meetings. Decision making on design trade-offs should be made with heavy end-user involvement, not with technologists acting alone without business input. The key revelation here is that in a successful data warehouse implementation, there are no technical decisions. There are only business decisions.

The most important role of the technologists in a data warehouse implementation is to demystify the technology issues and translate them into business decisions. Take the issue of storage protection, for example. A discussion with end users about RAID 0 (unprotected disk) versus RAID 1 (mirrored disk) versus RAID 5 (parity protected disks) will be met with blank stares. The technologist's job is to translate the RAID (Redundant Array of Independent Disks) jargon into trade-offs between cost, performance, and availability. Then the end user can make a business decision regarding the data warehouse implementation. When end users participate in design decisions, trade-offs are business driven rather than technology driven. Of course, the technologists should also be influencing the decision with insights about technology futures (e.g., are disk prices likely to go up or down and at what rate?) so that short-sighted decisions are not made.

To extend this example, when technologists translate technical issues into business decisions, end users don't decide between RAID 0 versus RAID 5. The end user can focus on business trade-offs between availability requirements (with RAID 1 providing full disk protection and RAID 0 likely to lead to systems outages at least once per month in a large implementation due to disk spindle failures) versus having twice as much data for a fixed budget (with RAID 0 providing access to twice the data of a RAID 1 implementation because a redundant copy of the data is required in a mirrored protection scheme). When technologists demystify the technology, end users can make the right trade-offs and decisions for the business.

The success of any data warehouse is ultimately measured by the users. If they don't accept the system, or don't use it for everyday decision support, the warehouse is a failure, no matter how well it may perform technically. When end users are part of the design process, they accept the system because they designed it—there are no surprises at delivery time. The right trade-offs are made, and the system meets the requirements end users designed into it. Then and only then will the data warehouse be a success.

SUMMARY

In this chapter, you should have learned the following:

- Data warehouses exist to facilitate strategic and tactical decision making.
- Data warehouses are different from operational systems in these ways:
  - Data warehouses store historical data so users can make sound business decisions. Operational systems store only enough data to support day-to-day business processing.
  - A data warehouse is updated periodically, on a predefined basis; an operational system is updated in real-time.
  - The service levels for a data warehouse are usually not as stringent as those for operational systems. Initially, a data warehouse may be available for 12 hours a day, 6 days a week, though this requirement will increase as users become dependent upon the system.
  - Traditional MIS reporting systems deliver standardized reports that are limited to a small number of templates. The data warehouse must accommodate users performing iterative, ad hoc analysis.
  - The access paths and unstructured query environment require different database structures in a data warehouse than in an operational system where transaction behavior is predictable and much more selective in the number of records required for processing.

  - The data warehouse integrates and consolidates information from multiple operational and external systems into a total view of the whole organization.
- The data warehouse gives users an analytical foundation for making decisions. The historical information in a data warehouse is used to develop applications, algorithms, and models for business decisions.
- An integrated data warehouse gives an organization consistent quantitative figures, so that decision makers can all use the same numbers.
- The data warehouse database has a much higher likelihood of success if it is separate from the operational database, in a hardware environment distinct from the operational systems. That way, end users can use the warehouse without affecting day-to-day operations.
- In the successful warehouses, historical data is used to develop applications with clear business benefits that directly impact the bottom line. Applications that maximize core business benefits in a number of industries include the following.
  - Fraud detection systems detect and prevent fraud before losses are incurred.
  - Target marketing systems give the business an understanding of customer behaviors and product needs so marketing campaigns can be directed to those who will respond positively.
  - Profitability analysis shows companies which individual customers are profitable and which are not, enabling them to develop appropriate customer management programs.
  - Customer retention applications help companies identify and keep their profitable customers, which is much more cost-effective than acquiring new customers.
  - Inventory management allows retailers and manufacturers to have the right products in the right place at the right time, rather than incurring heavy losses from out-of-stock or an over supply of goods.
  - Credit risk analysis enables companies to avoid bad debt by identifying the best risks among prospects with mixed credit histories.
  - Long-term value assessment enables companies to predict which customers will be profitable in the future and which will not.

- Competitive pricing enables companies to develop fundamental new pricing structures by understanding product demand, competitive positioning in the marketplace, and profit margins.

The critical success factors for a data warehouse include

- Design the data warehouse with a focus on the business, not the technology. In successful data warehouse implementations there are no technical decisions—only business decisions.
- Use an iterative development methodology with short cycles and frequent deliveries.
- Include end users on the implementation team. Their participation is necessary for design decisions that will enable the data warehouse to meet the business goals.

Case Study 2

EPA Intranet Helps Policy Makers Protect the Environment

by Chapman Gleason, Systems Manager, Center for Environmental Statistics, U.S. Environmental Protection Agency, and Chip Kelly, SAS Institute Program Manager for Web Enablement

The U.S. Environmental Protection Agency is able to do a faster, more thorough job of analyzing and reporting hazardous waste and pollutants in the air—thanks to Web-enabled software. The EPA's intranet replaces a complex internal network that had users jumping through one technical hoop after another to access several different environmental databases. Now, users click on a ZIP code or the relevant state or county on a map. This accesses summary information from the EPA's Toxic Release Inventory System and several other large database management systems, providing the requested information as graphs.

This Web-based intranet application simplifies public policy professionals' access to critical, national environmental databases—through a single software—to analyze the risks of environmental pollutants and the level of control they require. Employees use it to assess strategic environmental goals. They're able to get quick answers to questions as broad as, "Are releases of toxic chemicals increasing or decreasing?" or as specific as, "How many pounds of chemical *X* was released in *Y* state between 1988 and 1995?"

MORE ON HOW THE EPA INTRANET WORKS

Twenty-one different SAS software products on five desktop UNIX operating systems, Microsoft Windows 3.1, Windows 95, and Windows NT are the linchpin of the EPA's intranet, which logs almost 10,000 hits per day. The EPA's national databases of pollutants, policies, air-quality measurements, toxic-release inventories, and permits reside on products from Software AG, IBM, Lotus, and Oracle.

The network infrastructure supports multiprotocol traffic generated by the agency's TCP/IP, IPX, and SNA networks and links the Washington headquarters with 10 regional sites and a mainframe at the agency's National Computer Center in Research Triangle Park, N.C. T1 circuits link 60 state environmental departments to the mainframe in Research Triangle Park. The

EPA's 20,000 employees at a dozen sites are receiving browser software that assures simplified but timely access to more than 50 critical environmental databases and to Web-based SAS® software on disparate desktop computing platforms. The Web browser software links to Web-enabled SAS software on diverse servers and retrieves data from the appropriate server and mainframe databases.

In Setting Up Its Intranet, the EPA

- Prepared custom installation instructions for SAS software on the EPA's Novell LANs, which run Networked MS Windows.
- Pkzipped the SAS Windows Installation CD-ROM and set up an FTP Server to distribute SAS software to users on Novell LANs.
- Designed and implemented a Lotus Notes Mail-In Data Base and billing strategy to keep track of user population.
- Implemented an SAS Listserver, called EPASAS-L, to allow users to share SAS technical issues and solutions.
- Designed an internal SAS Web using a Lotus Notes InterNotes server and database, which is replicated and published to the Web each hour. This Lotus Notes database is replicated to each EPA region allowing SAS software users at remote sites to document their implementation of SAS software, SAS applications, and SAS software code and share it with other EPA SAS users.
- Implemented a mail user ID for the SAS Notes database, so that users without Notes clients can mail a document (including graphics) to a user ID called epasas.Web@epamail.epa.gov, and the document will automatically be published to the EPA SAS Web.
- Implemented the SAS and Lotus Notes interface allowing SAS programs to write to the SAS/Web via SAS clients on remote systems.

THE EPA WEB

One of the benefits of client-server computing and the popularization of Internet protocols has been the rapid development of the World Wide Web. However, HTML development has languished because of single file names being required in HTML "home pages." One product that has overcome that barrier and that the EPA has used to implement its Web is a Lotus Notes InterNotes Server. An InterNotes server is a Notes server running under Windows NT Advanced Server and has the HTTP daemon running as an NT service. The InterNotes server takes a Notes database and converts the Notes Documents into HTML documents and publishes the Notes Views as HTML links to the Notes Documents. The EPA has used this capability to save software users and developers the learning curve of learning HTML. InterNotes also allows a "macro" level of integration to keep track of hundreds of HTML file names which are prevalent on UNIX systems. Server replication enables publishing to the Internet each hour to allow critical documents maintained in the EPA SAS Web database to be viewable on the Web.

The Lotus Notes Mail-In Data Base feature allows a name, such as "Suggestion Box," to be associated with a Notes database and mail sent to the user ID "Suggestion Box" to be automatically deposited to the Notes Suggestion Box database. The EPA also set up a user ID called Epasas.Web@epamail.epa.gov to allow anyone on an EPA network to submit a mail message to the EPA SAS Web.

DISTRIBUTION AND MANAGEMENT OF SAS LICENSES

One of the fundamental problems in a large geographically dispersed organization is the timely distribution of software upgrades. The EPA has resolved this by setting up a password-protected ftp server and placed a Pkzipped version of the entire SAS CD-ROM on the FTP server. Passwords are changed monthly on this server and only epa.gov systems can FTP to the site.

To keep accurate counts of PC and UNIX software users, the EPA maintains two systems. One requires users to register with an EPA accounting system called TSSMS before securing an SAS software license. This system is the primary billing system used by the agency. The other is a mail system in a Notes database called Epasas.Users. It captures email traffic on people requesting SAS and SAS TSSMS accounts and is replicated daily between Research Triangle Park, N.C., and Washington D.C. so all SAS managers know who has requested SAS accounts.

SUPPORT FOR SOFTWARE USERS

The EPA has implemented several procedures and technologies to provide support for end users and developers. The EPA has an 800 number and analysts that can answer syntax questions for the base product. The agency has also implemented a Listserver called EPASAS-L to provide end users and developers who subscribe to the EPA documentation on how to obtain EMITS (Electronic Mail Interface to Technical Support) and SAS support.

SUMMARY

As the EPA's intranet illustrates, Web and thin-client technologies can have a huge impact on the way decision support systems are used. Because of economical client costs, thin clients offer an attractive way to deliver information to consumers at the low end of the technology spectrum.

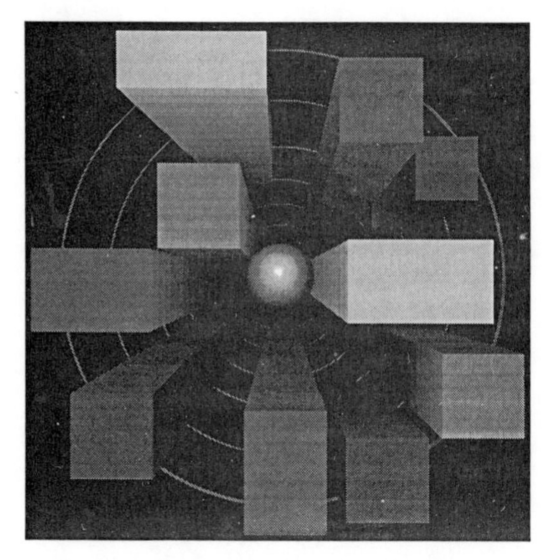

Chapter 5

THE DECISION SUPPORT LIFE CYCLE

LIFE CYCLES FOR SYSTEM DEVELOPMENT

The System Development Life Cycle (SDLC) for on-line transaction processing systems will usually go through several phases: planning, analysis, design, development, testing, and implementation. The development of client-server and distributed systems has modified the traditional SDLC but also moves through a predictable set of tasks and deliverables from the beginning of the life cycle to the implementation of a fully functioning production system.

As would be expected, the development of a data warehouse for decision support also goes through several predictable phases that may simply be called the decision support life cycle. The decision support life cycle, while it may contain many of the same phases, is different from the traditional system development life cycle. The differences in these two approaches to development emerge because the goals and the data structures of on-line transaction-based systems and decision support systems are different.

If you have an in-house methodology being used for project development within your company, do not expect the processes for building a data warehouse to directly map to it. If you do not have the data warehouse knowledge base within your company to modify the methodology, hire someone with this expertise to revise it for you.

ISSUES AFFECTING THE DECISION SUPPORT LIFE CYCLE

The focus of a data warehouse is data, not business processing and their associated functionality. Operational business process functionality is not a major component of the decision support life cycle. This lack of business functionality equates to a much faster development life cycle, as process modeling and other tasks associated with developing business functionality are generally not needed.

A data warehouse for decision support is often loaded with source data from various platforms, databases, and files. The data analysis necessary for data integration so your data warehouse has value across business units or subject areas is not always necessary (and seldom done) in developing operational systems. And to do a good job analyzing data so it has integrated meaning and structures takes some time. The integration of data generally requires the design of processes for data integration as part of your loading. You may also need data cleansing and validation. Additionally, there may be calculations and summarizations being done on the data before it is loaded into the data warehouse database.

Database sizes for decision support systems can be extremely large (terabytes) with single tables potentially holding gigabytes of data. Extremely large database size has a substantial effect on the focus of the development and when in the life cycle certain tasks are done. For instance, capacity planning estimates are done as early as possible in the decision support life cycle, and database and system administration are brought into the life cycle earlier than would be customary in an on-line transaction system.

Additionally the use of advanced tools and specialized technologies may be necessary in the development of decision support systems, which affects tasks, deliverables, training, and project time lines.

THE DECISION SUPPORT LIFE CYCLE IN AN ARCHITECTED ENVIRONMENT

This book focuses primarily on building a data warehouse in an architected environment. It has made a case for establishing the technical infrastructures—which are defined as the training, tools, and technologies needed for the successful development of a data warehouse and identifying the data warehouse data architecture before beginning the development of the data warehouse.

Data processing environments in which data warehouses are created vary widely. It is entirely possible to build a data warehouse without the use of data conversion technologies, with minimalistic technical infrastructures, and in an extremely fast time frame. An environment where source data is homogeneous and easy to locate and extract, where only simple data integration is needed, and where front-end data access is available and usable may be a good candidate for a much faster, less architected development approach.

However, many corporations have extremely sophisticated data processing environments and must be able to technically integrate a variety of information sources, platforms, technologies, data structures, and databases to provide decision support information to users having a wide range of data access requirements and capabilities. These companies will find an architected approach required for the successful development of a data warehouse. Unfortunately, many companies have tried building a data warehouse without establishing the correct architectures and infrastructures and hence have not been successful with their efforts.

The decision support life cycle described in this chapter covers the full life cycle development of a data warehouse in an architected environment. The decision support life cycle is targeted to heterogeneous, sophisticated environments requiring practical and realistic guidelines for data warehouse development.

THE PHASES OF THE DECISION SUPPORT LIFE CYCLE (DECISION SUPPORT LIFE CYCLE)

The phases of the decision support life cycle are

1. Planning
2. Gathering data requirements and modeling
3. Physical database design and development
4. Data sourcing, integration, and mapping
5. Populating the data warehouse
6. Automating the data management process
7. Creating the starter set of reports
8. Data validation and testing
9. Training
10. Rollout

The phases of the decision support life cycle and the central points of focus for each phase will now be explained.

Phase 1: Planning

Planning for a data warehouse encompasses many of the same tasks as any other type of system development project. Creating a project plan and defining realistic time estimates may be difficult for the novice (or even the experienced!) project manager, in part because there are altogether new tasks within the decision support life cycle. It may be helpful to review the remainder of this chapter in detail before creating the project plan.

It is imperative that the data warehouse data architecture and technical infrastructures be thought through *before* the project development begins. If the data architecture and technical infrastructures have not been established, all of the architecture and infrastructure analysis will need to be added to your project plan as tasks with the appropriate deliverables, adding substantial time and complexity to your overall project plan.

Planning for a data warehouse, as shown in Figure 5–1, is concerned with

- Defining and/or clarifying the project scope
- Creating the project plan
- Defining the necessary technical resources, both internal and external
- Defining the business participants and responsibilities
- Defining the tasks and deliverables
- Defining time lines
- Defining the final project deliverables

In addition, there are technical considerations for full life cycle development of a data warehouse that may not have been part of the technical infrastructures but will be part of the development life cycle.

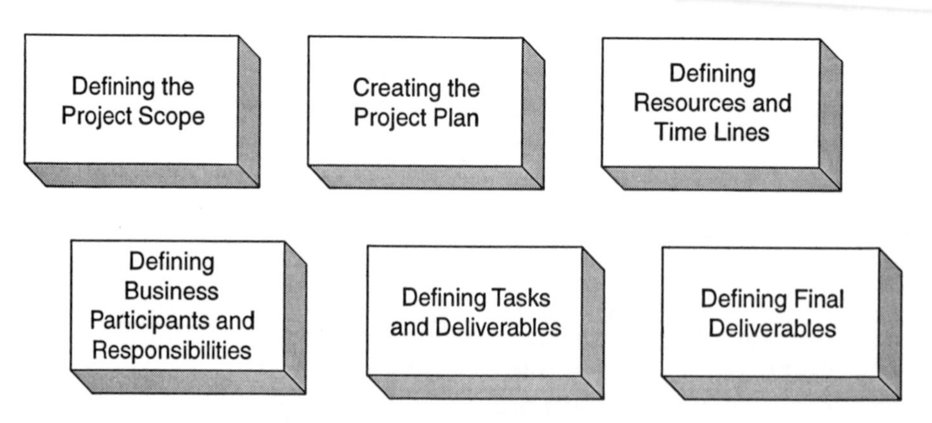

FIGURE 5–1 Phase 1 of the decision support life cycle: project planning.

These technical considerations will need to be included in the planning process and project plan, with appropriate tasks and deliverables, as they require technical resources and time. These may include

- Capacity planning
- Data integration strategies
- Archiving strategies (if appropriate)
- Procedures for end-user access to archived data (if appropriate)
- Data refresh/update strategies
- Operations and job scheduling strategies
- Metadata management strategies

If the following technical infrastructures are not in place, their implementation will also need to be part of your project plan:

- LAN/WAN technology
- Platform selection
- Database connectivity
- Database gateways
- Database Management System (DBMS) load utilities
- Configured workstations
- Front-end data access tools

Phase 2: Gathering Data Requirements and Modeling

This phase of the life cycle is concerned with understanding the business needs and data requirements of the users of the system. It also includes modeling these requirements. The entire requirements phase can be accomplished in as little as 4 weeks but should not take more than 6 weeks or so. If the process takes longer, you probably have too broad a scope to accomplish in a single pass. Take another look at your scope and see if it needs some realistic revision. You may need to scale back or divide up the project into multiple projects.

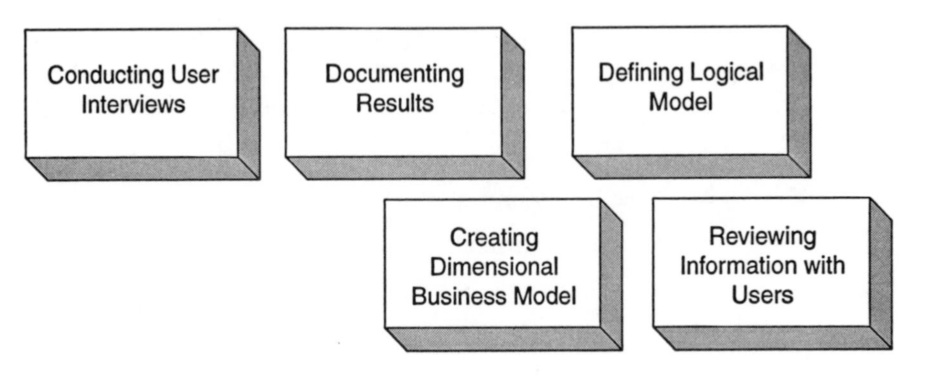

FIGURE 5–2 Phase 2 of the decision support life cycle: Gathering data requirements and modeling the data.

Gathering Data Requirements. Gathering data requirements includes understanding

- How the user does business
- What the business drivers are
- What attributes the user needs
- Which attributes are absolutely required and which attributes are a "wish list"
- What the business hierarchies are
- What data users use now and what would they like to have
- What levels of detail or summary the users need
- What type of front-end data access tool will be used
- How the user expects to see the results of their queries

Gathering requirements may be difficult for the following reasons:

- The business objective of the data warehouse has not been specifically defined, so it is impossible to gather the requirements to fulfill the objective.
- The scope of the data warehouse is too broad, so analysts need to gather requirements from too many areas and people.

- There is often a misunderstanding of decision support versus operational processing, which causes the analyst to fluctuate back and forth between them while gathering requirements. Additionally, the difference between data requirements for the two types of systems is also often difficult to communicate well to end users during requirements gathering.

To minimize these dilemmas, tasks, deliverables, and schedules should be defined that will assist analysts in moving through this phase quickly. See Chapter 7 for detailed information on interviewing users, the use of facilitated sessions, and gathering requirements.

The process of building a data warehouse is iterative in nature. Once the first round of data is loaded into the data warehouse and users have a chance to see what data is available to them, there will be changes and additions requested. This is to be expected and is a normal part of the decision support life cycle. This phase of the life cycle should be kept short because the iterative process is an effective means of fine-tuning data needs and a fairly large amount of time must be spent on sourcing data analysis.

Information collected during this requirements gathering will directly feed the data modeling.

Data Modeling. The central focus of this task in the life cycle is to provide

- A logical data model covering the scope of the development project including relationships, cardinality, attributes, definitions, and candidate keys.

or

- A dimensional business model that diagrams the facts, dimensions, hierarchies, relationships, and candidate keys for the scope of the development project.

The following issues can affect the timing of the data warehouse development and should be addressed before development begins if they were not resolved as technical infrastructures.

- How will derived data be reflected in your model?
- Are there clear procedures within the corporation with respect to logical models? Do you have a choice to build a logical data model or Dimensional Business Model, or must you create an ERD (Entity Relationship Diagram)?
- If you are using a CASE tool, will the tool allow the transformation of a denormalized logical model to the physical mode for Data Definition Language (DDL) generation?
- Are there procedures in place within the data modeling group so that data types and other modeling objects are shared among data warehouse projects?
- Do your modelers understand differences in the general design of data warehouses and are they familiar with star schemas?

Phase 3: Physical Database Design and Development

This phase of the decision support life cycle covers database design and denormalization. It also has tasks critical to decision support processing and development. For the database design phase of the life cycle, as detailed in Figure 5-3, the focus will be on

- Designing the database, including fact tables, relationship tables, and description (lookup) tables
- Denormalizing the data
- Identifying keys
- Creating indexing strategies
- Creating appropriate database objects

For this phase, it is imperative that you get training and have an understanding of

- Decision support concepts
- The concepts of hierarchies, dimensions, and facts
- Star schema database design concepts

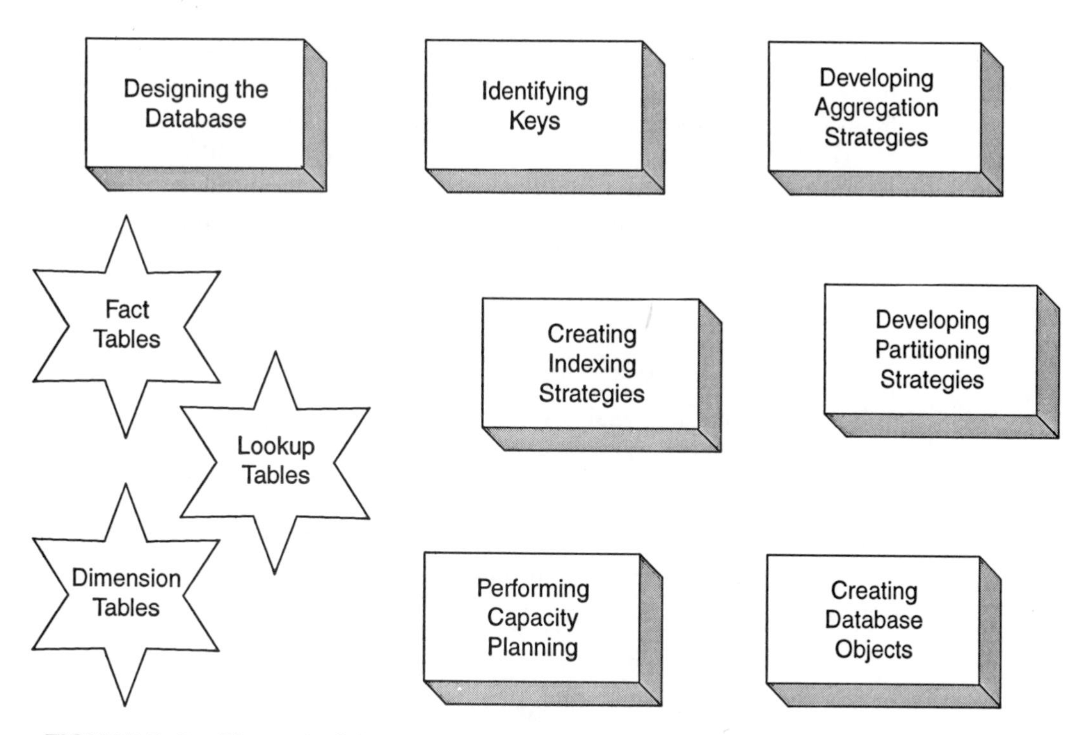

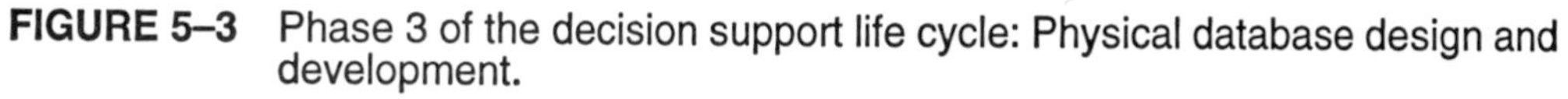

FIGURE 5–3 Phase 3 of the decision support life cycle: Physical database design and development.

Obviously, you will also need the expertise of a good Database Administrator (DBA) on the implementation database. Chapter 9, "Designing the Database for a Data Warehouse," has detailed information that will assist you with this process.

At this stage you should also

- Develop aggregation strategies (in association with the two preceding phases)
- Develop partitioning strategies
- Refine capacity planning estimates

Phase 4: Data Sourcing, Integration, and Mapping

This is a phase that is done in conjunction with the database design phase, because you will need your target data warehouse database design for the source to target mapping. This phase, shown in Figure 5-4, is generally the most time-consuming and encompasses locating the source of the data in the operational systems, doing analysis to understand what types of data integration may be needed, writing integration specifications, and mapping the source data to target data warehouse database design. This investigation is crucial to determine what data can actually be captured. During this phase you will be

- Defining the possible source systems
- Determining file layouts
- Performing data analysis to determine the best (and cleanest if possible) source of data
- Performing data analysis to integrate the data
- Developing written data conversion specifications for each field and refining your integration strategy
- Mapping source to target data

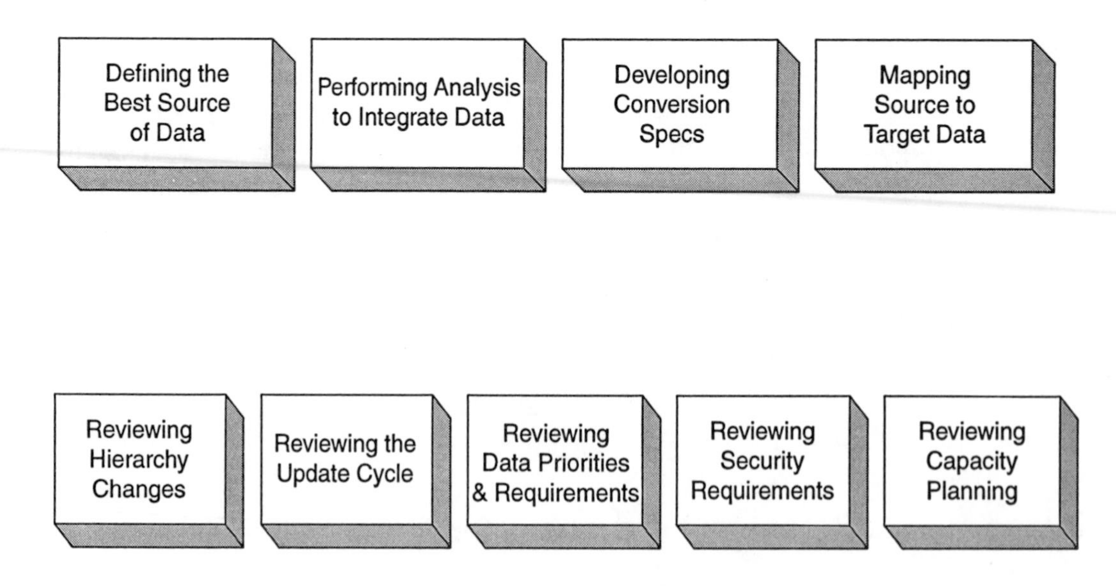

FIGURE 5-4 Phase 4 of the decision support life cycle: Data sourcing, Integration, and Mapping.

The data that is actually possible to source, which is often quite different from the data requested by the end users, may modify your requirements, dimensional business model, and database design. For information on the specifics that need to be gathered for each source field, please see Chapter 8, "Data Integration."

Phase 5: Populating the Data Warehouse

The full process of extracting, converting, and loading data into the target database will often be done with the assistance of data conversion technology. Using a data conversion tool will affect the timing of the life-cycle phases and may consolidate tasks and deliverables. The focus of this phase, illustrated in Figure 5-5, is

- Developing programs or using tools to extract and move the data
- Developing load strategies
- Developing the procedures to load the data into the warehouse
- Developing programs or using data conversion tools to integrate data
- Developing update/refresh strategies
- Testing extract, integration, and load programs and procedures

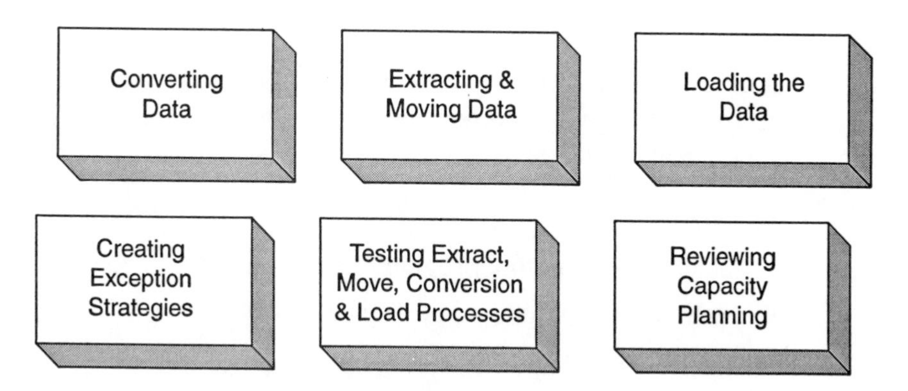

FIGURE 5–5 Phase 5 of the decision support life cycle: Populating the data warehouse.

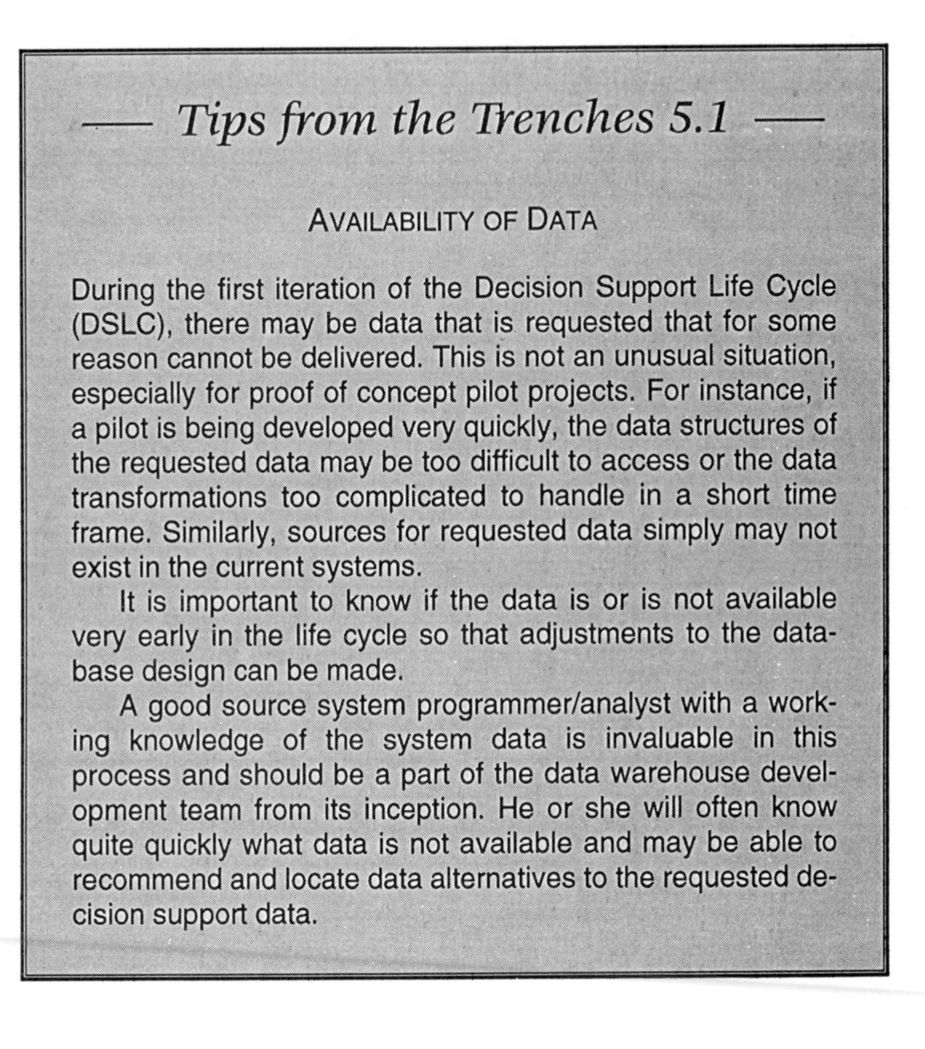

— *Tips from the Trenches 5.1* —

AVAILABILITY OF DATA

During the first iteration of the Decision Support Life Cycle (DSLC), there may be data that is requested that for some reason cannot be delivered. This is not an unusual situation, especially for proof of concept pilot projects. For instance, if a pilot is being developed very quickly, the data structures of the requested data may be too difficult to access or the data transformations too complicated to handle in a short time frame. Similarly, sources for requested data simply may not exist in the current systems.

It is important to know if the data is or is not available very early in the life cycle so that adjustments to the database design can be made.

A good source system programmer/analyst with a working knowledge of the system data is invaluable in this process and should be a part of the data warehouse development team from its inception. He or she will often know quite quickly what data is not available and may be able to recommend and locate data alternatives to the requested decision support data.

Technical infrastructures should be in place to assist with the crucial steps of data mapping, conversion, extraction, and loading. These infrastructures may include

- DBA expertise
- Data conversion tool programming expertise
- Source programming expertise
- Quality assurance procedures
- Capacity planning expertise
- System/platform expertise

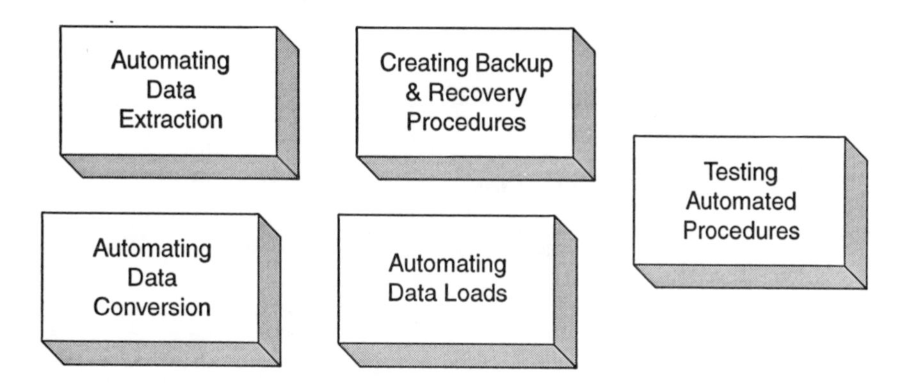

FIGURE 5–6 Phase 6 of the decision support life cycle: Automating data load procedures.

Phase 6: Automating the Data Load Process

This phase is concerned with automating the extraction, integration, and load of the data warehouse. This phase, as shown in Figure 5-6, will include

- Automating and scheduling the data extraction process
- Automating and scheduling the data conversion process
- Automating and scheduling the data load process
- Creating backup and recovery procedures
- Conducting a full test of all the automated procedures

Phase 7: Creating the Starter Set of Reports

Development of a starter set of reports can begin as soon as you have loaded a test subset of data. DSS application development is generally done through the use of data access tools to prebuild several reports. Figure 5-7 shows the major tasks in this phase. DSS application development and data access tools are discussed at length in Chapter 10.

Structured navigation paths to access predefined reports or data directly must also be developed. This may be as complex as writing Visual Basic code or as simple as configuring the interface of a tool. This phase will also drive data validation and performance tuning. Actual de-

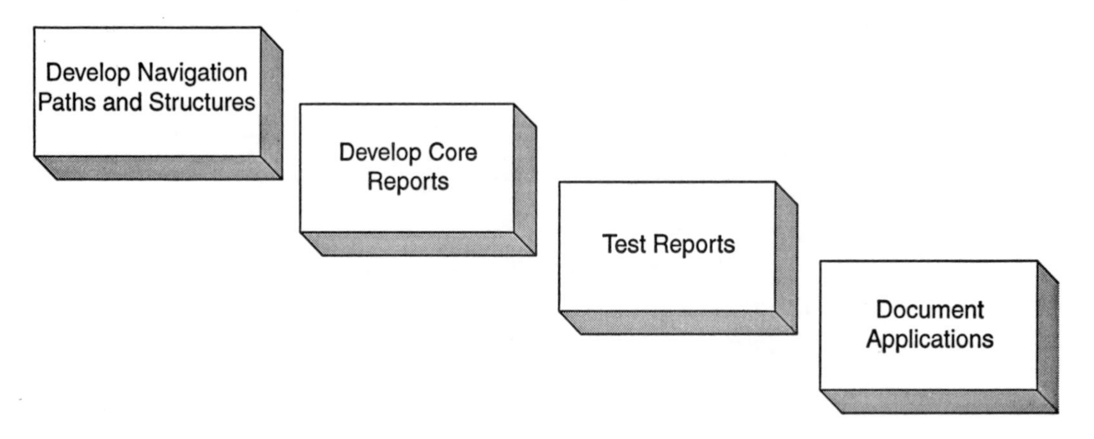

FIGURE 5–7 Phase 7 of the decision support life cycle: Application development—creating the starter set of reports.

velopment of a starter set of reports may only require several weeks of effort; however, you should plan for a larger number of elapsed weeks in your project schedule to account for the time required to correct data-related issues.

This phase is concerned with

- Creating the starter set of predefined reports
- Testing reports
- Documenting applications
- Developing navigation paths

Phase 8: Data Validation and Testing

You should include standard data validation processes throughout the data extract, integration, and load development phases. Basic checks on record counts—and other traditional development concepts—apply for the data warehouse also. In addition, once the data access front end has been put in place, additional data validation can occur.

Phases 7 and 8 are the catalysts for iterative changes within the decision support life cycle as users work with the front-end tools to interact with the data. Development will move back up the decision support life cycle to the analysis phase, working itself back down as the data-

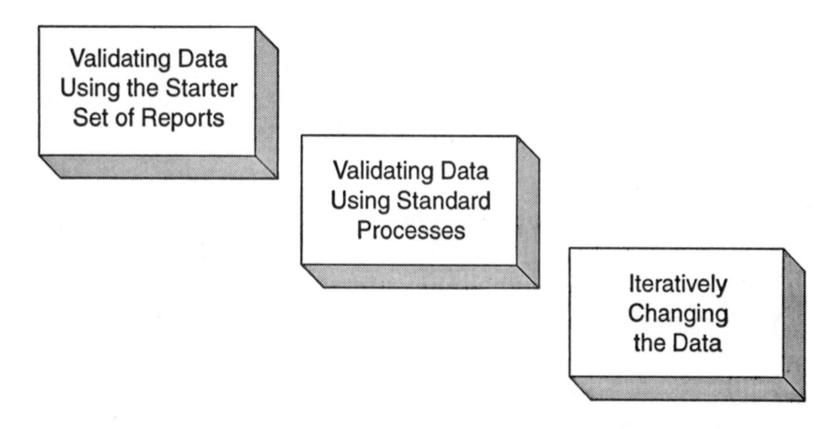

FIGURE 5–8 Phase 8 of the decision support life cycle: Data validation and testing.

base modifications are made. These new data modifications will be located, extracted, mapped, integrated, and loaded into the data warehouse. Figure 5-8 illustrates the primary elements of this phase.

Phase 9: Training

The training phase of the decision support life cycle, as shown in Figure 5-9, is focused on creating training programs for the user community. A one-day training course on the front-end tool is *not* enough. To gain real business value from your warehouse development, users of all levels will need to be trained in

- The scope of the data in the warehouse
- The front-end access tool and how it works
- How to access and navigate metadata to get information on the data in the warehouse
- The DSS application or starter set of reports—the capabilities and navigation paths
- Ongoing training/user assistance as the system evolves

See Chapter 11 for a discussion of training and support for your data warehouse.

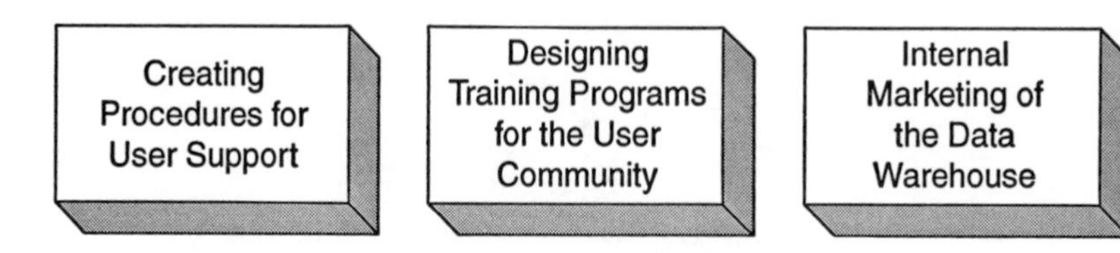

FIGURE 5–9 Phase 9 of the decision support life cycle: Training and user support.

Phase 10: Rollout

The rollout phase of the life cycle, Figure 5-10 includes the necessary tasks for the deployment of your data warehouse to the user community. These may include

- Installing the physical infrastructures for all users. The components that must be in place for the end user are the LAN/WAN, database connectivity, configured workstations, data access software, and managed metadata.
- Deploying the DSS application.
- Creating end-user support structures.
- Creating procedures for adding new reports and expanding the DSS application.
- Setting up procedures to back up the DSS application, not just the data warehouse.
- Creating procedures for investigating and resolving data integrity related issues.

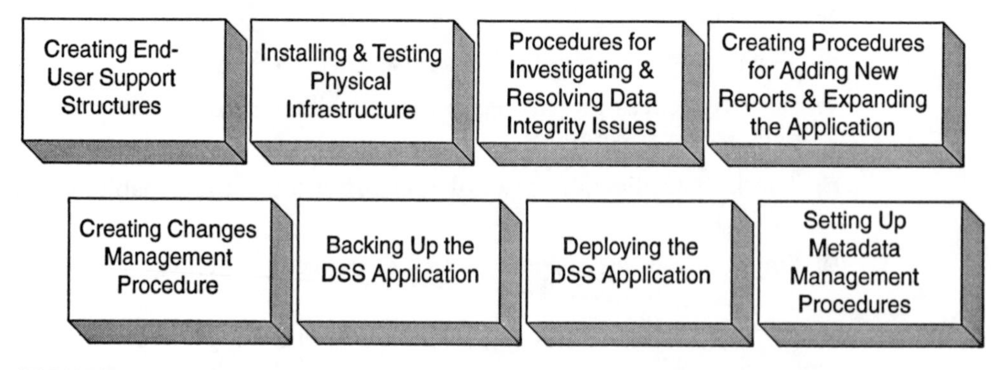

FIGURE 5–10 Phase 10 of the decision support life cycle: Data warehouse rollout.

- Setting up procedures for metadata management.
- Creating change management procedures.

SUMMARY

In this chapter, you should have learned the following:

- The lack of traditional business functionality inherent in decision support systems equates to a much faster development life cycle, as process modeling and other tasks associated with developing business functionality are not generally needed.
- The evaluation, acquisition, and use of advanced tools and specialized technologies may be necessary in the development of decision support systems, which affects tasks, deliverables, training, and time lines within the decision support life cycle.
- The different phases of the decision support life cycle are
  - Planning
  - Gathering data requirements and modeling
  - Physical database design and development
  - Data sourcing, integration, and mapping
  - Populating the data warehouse
  - Automating the data management process
  - Creating the starter set of reports
  - Data validation and testing
  - Rollout and end-user support

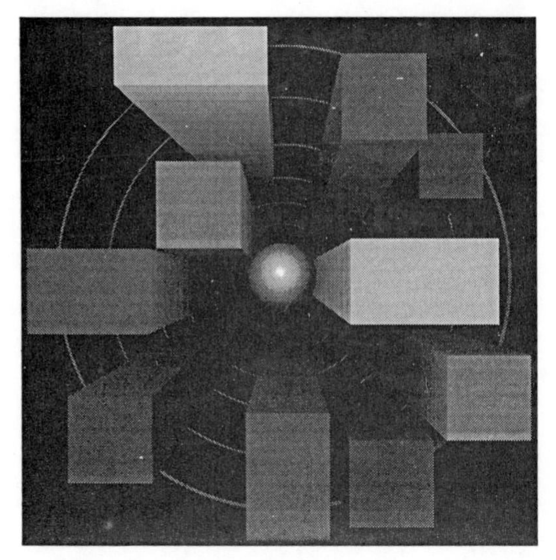

Chapter 6

Getting Started with Data Warehouse Development

THE PROOF IS IN THE PILOT

Before creating a full-blown data warehouse, many companies first do a pilot project to get their feet wet, gain experience, show users the value of decision support information, or perhaps do a proof of concept for higher management or for a steering committee. It is amazing how many of these pilot projects are not successful or take altogether too long before deliverables are in front of the users.

If you want a successful data warehouse pilot project, a few basics should be handled from the very beginning. These are

- Clarify the purpose of the pilot project. What is the goal?
- Treat the pilot as a development project—allocate appropriate resources and a project manager.

Clarify the Purpose and Goal of the Pilot Project

Why are you doing a pilot project? If the answer is to see if a decision support system will provide a competitive edge for the corporation, an automatic bell should go off in your head. This is not a good reason to do a pilot project—it is much too broad and will be difficult to achieve.

What is the goal of the data warehouse pilot project? The answer to this question will determine how to proceed successfully with the development of your pilot. If you are doing a "proof of concept" pilot, the goal may be to show users how a system can provide useful, decision support information. In other words, you are proving that the concept of a data warehouse for decision support is viable and valuable to the end user and can assist them in their decision making.

One way to prove that a data warehouse for decision support will assist users in decision making is to get the data in front of the users in a way that is easily accessible, within a relatively short time frame. The primary focus, then, would be to develop a good, accessible database design and put time and attention into assisting users in understanding the navigation and capabilities of the decision support data. This may include providing short decision support training classes, finding front-end data access software that users are comfortable with and work well with, and working with them to create predefined queries.

The focus of the proof of concept pilot will be on the data and the users' interaction with the decision support information. Understanding how this information will assist them in decision making will prove that the concept of a data warehouse is viable and valuable to the corporation. This can often be accomplished with a small subset of data.

The proof of concept pilot is completely different from an architecture and infrastructure pilot. An architecture and infrastructure pilot is developed to figure out how all the components of a data warehouse work together and to understand and gain experience with the phases of the decision support life cycle. Such a pilot would develop a very small decision support database but have data flowing through the entire data warehouse architecture. The communications, gateways, data conversion tools, refresh/update strategies, and front-end software—all of the technologies required to bring data from the source systems into a decision support data warehouse for easy access by a user—would be used and tested.

The main goals of this type of pilot are

- Understanding the complexities involved in developing a data warehouse for decision support
- Gaining experience with new tools and technologies
- Getting a sense of realistic time lines and learning curves for tasks
- A data warehouse providing decision support information to users

A proof of concept data warehouse pilot project can usually be done in a much shorter time frame than an architecture and infrastructure pilot, because all the technical components may not need to be in place. Technologies that are familiar to the developers, programmers, and Database Administrators (DBAs) may be used in a proof of concept pilot. However, the architecture and infrastructure pilot, while taking longer, will provide a stronger knowledge base so that future projects will go more smoothly and quickly.

Doing a pilot project of either type has many advantages and will produce for you

- A first cut of a Dimensional Business Model
- Ideas on how to design your physical database
- An understanding of the cleanliness of your data
- A working prototype of a data warehouse
- Concrete analytical examples to serve as thought starters for your end users
- An understanding of how your data access tool works

Treat the Pilot like a Development Project

Building a data warehouse for decision support is very often thought of as "no big deal"—simply a matter of dropping some data into a database and using a query tool on them. You might hear how finance or purchasing, for instance, is "throwing together" a decision support system because they are tired of waiting for reports.

The idea of finding a way to access information more easily is not new. Programmers have been providing reports by creating extract files off different systems and applications for years. Doing a database dump or using one of the multiple extract files within the company and putting a front-end query tool on it is not the type of data warehouse pilot being recommended here. In fact, this type of approach creates more problems than it solves and wreaks havoc on your data warehouse data architecture. Both types of pilots, either a proof of concept pilot or architecture and infrastructure pilot (and probably any other kind), require an understanding of decision support concepts and a sound database design.

Approach a data warehouse pilot project for what it is—a development project. It should be funded, have a project manager who understands the steps within the decision support life cycle, and have the associated tasks and deliverables that will keep the pilot moving well. A successful data warehouse pilot project requires this.

Building on the Pilot

The data warehouse pilot project is rarely a throwaway. You can refine the pilot and then move on to the next subject area. Usually the next subject area of the warehouse is built upon the first, or the iterative process builds upon the existing database. Since pilot projects are quite often used as the basis of ongoing data warehouse development projects, designing the database with an eye toward the future is a very good idea.

The base data should be designed well so that moving from a proof of concept pilot to a more fully developed data warehouse, for instance, may not require a full redesign of the database. The development cycle in such a situation would then be centered more on considering requirements and modification for full volumes, finding technical solutions, and creating strategies for making all the architectural components work together.

Since the database for the pilot project has an extremely high chance of being built upon, you must take the time to design the data well. The database design of a data warehouse for decision support will be discussed in detail in Chapter 9.

With respect to pilot projects you should also be aware that several vendors in the marketplace are providing an abbreviated proof of concept. These projects, which typically last between two and four weeks, provide a visual idea of the possibilities and the benefits of a data warehouse in your environment. A subset of your data is generally loaded into a database and sample applications may be developed. You will gain the most from this type of project if you assign one or more of your data warehouse project team members to work with the vendor.

Keep in mind that vendor-supplied abbreviated pilots also bear several risks, including

- A misconception that you can really build a data warehouse in two to four weeks.
- Not understanding the complete infrastructure required to support a production data warehouse.
- Large data volumes are significantly different than small prototype volumes, both in database design and data administration.
- The full life cycle is not considered, many shortcuts are made due to time constraints.
- You may end up with only a partial understanding of full life cycle data warehouse development—just enough to be dangerous, but not enough to be effective.

CHOOSING A BUSINESS AREA FOR DATA WAREHOUSE DEVELOPMENT

If you are committed to building a data warehouse for decision support and have not yet made a decision on the business area to pilot, consider first what drives the revenues for your company. This will usually be a primary consideration in developing a data warehouse. Then consider

- Sales analysis
- Marketing

- Market segmentation
- Customer profiles

Although many areas within the company can benefit from decision support information, these areas lend themselves well to decision support processing. Sales analysis, marketing, customer profiling, and market segmentation are especially beneficial areas for development as companies seek to become more competitive.

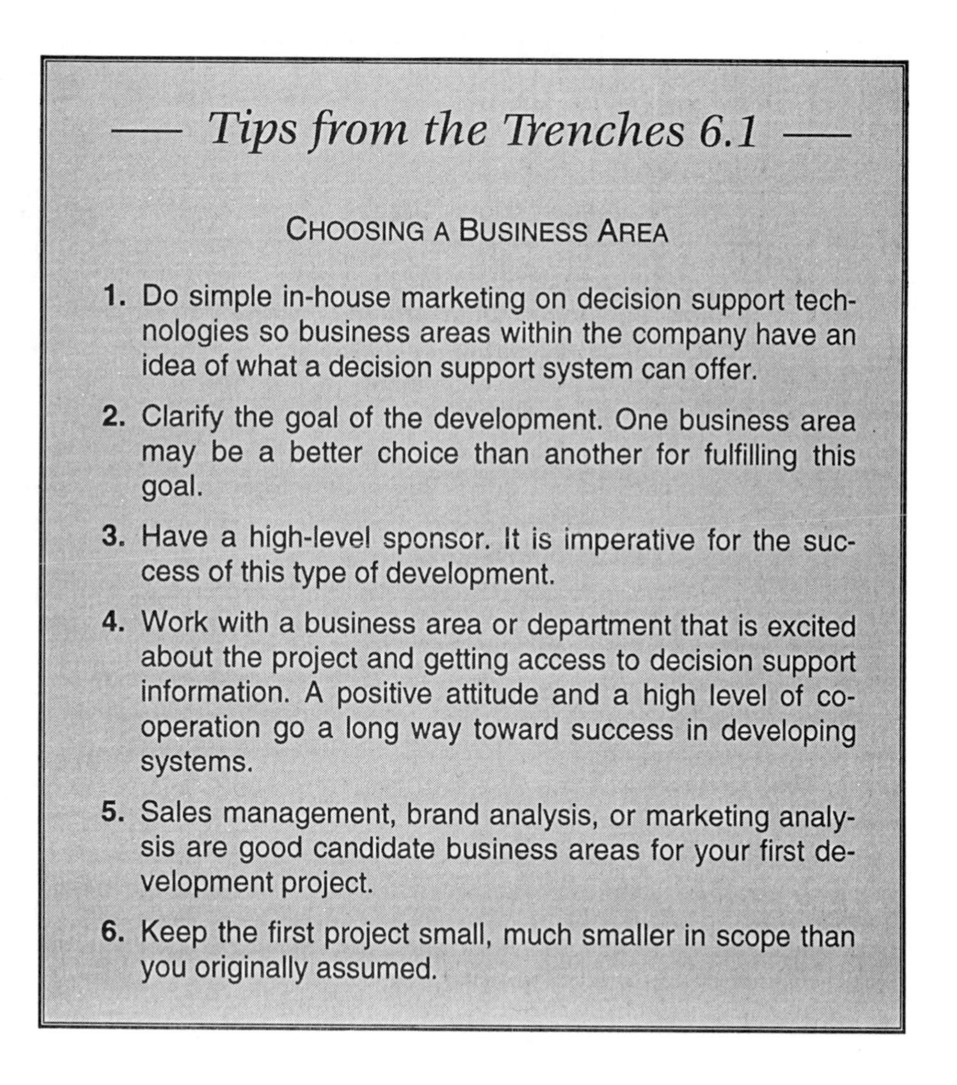

— *Tips from the Trenches 6.1* —

CHOOSING A BUSINESS AREA

1. Do simple in-house marketing on decision support technologies so business areas within the company have an idea of what a decision support system can offer.
2. Clarify the goal of the development. One business area may be a better choice than another for fulfilling this goal.
3. Have a high-level sponsor. It is imperative for the success of this type of development.
4. Work with a business area or department that is excited about the project and getting access to decision support information. A positive attitude and a high level of cooperation go a long way toward success in developing systems.
5. Sales management, brand analysis, or marketing analysis are good candidate business areas for your first development project.
6. Keep the first project small, much smaller in scope than you originally assumed.

Sales and marketing analysis are good candidates for your first warehouse. These areas are quite data reliant—analysts are looking at the numbers to make business decisions on a daily basis already. Providing good quality, multidimensional data that can be manipulated across many dimensions would be using data as a corporate resource. These areas drive the revenue for the organization and are keys to business success.

Market segmentation and customer profiling—understanding what products are being sold, where they are selling, what is affecting their sales, and who they are being sold to—are fundamental to business profitability and success.

This type of fundamental information, within most corporations, is incomplete or nonsense, and getting to it is difficult. It is also of incredible value to decision makers.

Using historical data to build strong customer profiles and creating targeted marketing strategies from these profiles is one key to keeping a corporation competitive. For this reason, marketing and its associated specialties are good candidates for data warehouse development.

Customer profiling, while a great candidate for decision support processing and desperately needed within a corporation, may be challenging to implement on your first project. This is because many companies do not have wholehouse definitions of customers across divisions or business units; hence, consolidating information on a customer can be quite difficult. Also, depending on the type of business, many companies do not gather information from their production systems on a customer level but on an account level, which makes data integration for a customer extremely difficult.

Market segmentation is also difficult if your company has not defined its segments across business units or from a warehouse perspective.

ENSURING A SUCCESSFUL DATA WAREHOUSE

Now that you have chosen a subject area for your pilot project, you are ready to get started! In our experience, we have found the following eight points, "the big eight," are critical to ensure a successful data warehouse development project.

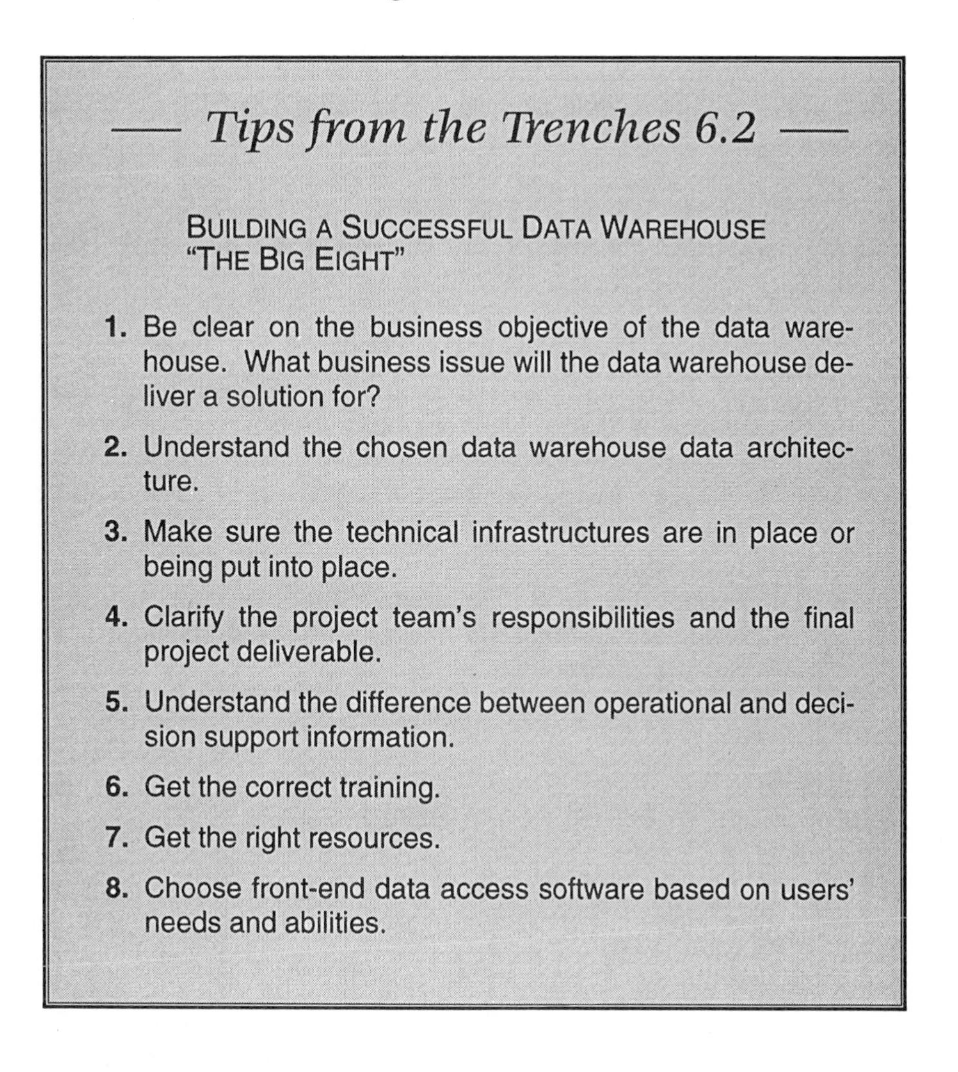

— Tips from the Trenches 6.2 —

BUILDING A SUCCESSFUL DATA WAREHOUSE
"THE BIG EIGHT"

1. Be clear on the business objective of the data warehouse. What business issue will the data warehouse deliver a solution for?
2. Understand the chosen data warehouse data architecture.
3. Make sure the technical infrastructures are in place or being put into place.
4. Clarify the project team's responsibilities and the final project deliverable.
5. Understand the difference between operational and decision support information.
6. Get the correct training.
7. Get the right resources.
8. Choose front-end data access software based on users' needs and abilities.

Be Clear on the Business Objective of Your Data Warehouse

One of the first questions to clarify in any type of data warehouse development is simple: What is the business objective of your data warehouse? Your business objective for developing a data warehouse will have a broad-range effect on what gets developed, what data goes into the data warehouse, and your parameters for success. A data warehouse business objective should be specific, written, and measurable. The business objective will be the driving force in determining the scope of the project and will provide boundaries so that the scope isn't continually changing and expanding.

Understand the Chosen Data Warehouse Architecture

A diagram of your data warehouse architecture should be on the desk of every member of the development team. This is the high-level blueprint that will be used to develop the decision support system. The choice of data architecture and infrastructures will determine many aspects of how the system is developed, such as types of database design and granularity levels (which will affect the overall size of your warehouse), options for update/refresh technologies (perhaps you will need replication technologies), training needs, and timing within the development life cycle. The architecture and infrastructure also provide a solid basis for explaining decision support system development within the corporation.

Make Sure the Technical Infrastructures Are in Place or Being Put in Place

The technical infrastructures—the tools, platforms, databases, communications, training, and so on—usually require substantial time to put into place. New hardware and software may need to be purchased and installed; data integration tools must be reviewed and chosen; and networks, gateways, and communications must be set up. These technologies take time to purchase, install, learn, and fine-tune. Technical infrastructures should be determined and in the process of installation before the warehouse development begins.

Clarify the Project Team's Responsibility and Final Deliverable

Building a data warehouse for decision support in an architected environment brings together many departments, technologies, and skills within the information technology group. Decision support systems also require substantial input from the business users if they are to be successful. It is common for the information technology group to team up with a business area to cosponsor and cofund a data warehouse project.

Depending on the organizational structure of your company, development of a warehouse extending horizontally across many business units may inherently have political difficulties that need navigation. Especially in situations where development is crossing departmental boundaries, it is a good idea to clarify the responsibilities of everyone, both business and information technology, involved in the development. For instance, clarify responsibility for

- The owner of the project and his/her responsibility
- Defining the scope of the project
- Bringing the end users to the table for requirements gathering
- Physical versus logical database design
- Choosing, learning, and using the data integration tool
- Data access software selection, purchase, and training
- Finding the best source of data
- Setting up and testing networks, gateways, and databases
- Choosing platforms and buying and installing hardware and software
- Establishing security
- Creating the starter set of reports
- User support and training

All companies set up their development teams differently. Some companies create a team that encompasses all the necessary skills. Other companies have their own corporate infrastructures well developed, making it immediately evident what department or person would be responsible for specific tasks. Other companies are quite disorganized in their development and would benefit greatly by clarifying what group, department, or person is responsible for the different tasks that make up the full life-cycle development of a data warehouse for decision support. Clarifying responsibilities and what the final deliverable will be is an especially important aspect of a successful project.

Make Sure the Members of the Project Team and the Users Understand the Difference between Operational and Decision Support Data

Operational data is used to run the day-to-day operations of the business, while decision support data supports analytical processing used for decision making and strategic planning. Decision support data is usually historical in nature, since monitoring trends, gauging profitability, or understanding what products are being bought are analytical processing that requires an understanding of how the data is changing over time. The definition of decision support data and how you will be using such data in your company should be used as the basis of gathering data requirements and doing database design. Whenever there is confusion about data content, especially required levels of detail, always go back to the definitions of decision support data and analytical processing.

Get the Correct Training

It is extremely important that the project team members have a good understanding of decision support technologies. They should understand the difference between transaction processing and analytical processing systems and understand the phases in the decision support life cycle. Team members should also understand why the database design for decision support systems is different from on-line transaction systems, and how that design is different. Get the training needed to provide a solid base of decision support knowledge to all the team members before the project starts. Find a class in building a data warehouse and actively seek out decision support articles, books, and knowledgeable people. Get vendor training in the data conversion tool of choice and set aside some time in the project plan for practicing with the tool. Choices in front-end data access software are extremely varied in sophistication and functionality. Certain members of the team should be well trained in whatever software is chosen. It is quite difficult to expound on the wonders of all the fantastic decision support data if the front end is more sophisticated than you are!

Get the Right Resources

Many companies may not have development teams with expertise in decision support processing and development. As with any other new development, finding someone who has done it before and whose knowledge you can leverage will speed up your development. A very experienced project manager who has never implemented a data warehouse will not know all that is neccessary for a project, so don't expect him or her to. Provide someone to guide and coach that person—he or she will quickly learn the ropes. If you do not have decision support development expertise within your corporation, be encouraged to find a consultant with this expertise. Developers who have had experience working through the development cycle and in finding technical solutions to the thornier issues in data warehouse development are extremely valuable. The amount of time the company will save with a consultant who is experienced in data warehouse development, data warehouse data architecture, and/or data conversion technologies is substantial.

Additionally, find other companies that have successfully implemented and are using their warehouses. These companies can provide valuable information on what worked for them, where they hit development snags, how they incorporated database change procedures, how they marketed and rolled out the data warehouse, information on products and vendors that work, as well as a multitude of other information that only experience can provide.

For your data warehouse development project, resources or skills that you will need include

- Someone with experience building data warehouses to assist you in creating the project plan and to keep the project moving through all of the obstacles
- Architecture and infrastructure planning experience
- A data architect who has experience with data warehouse development and fine-tuned data analysis skills for the data integration
- Good source system personnel who have access to the actual data
- A well-versed DBA and star schema database design expertise

- A hands-on project manager, preferably one with decision support experience and a technical background
- Team members (end users) with a good understanding of the business, the data, and how they are used are imperative to a successful data warehouse project

In addition you will need access to the personnel who handle networking, communications, workstation and software installation, capacity planning, operations, and training.

Choose Front-End Data Access Software Based on User Needs and Abilities

Many of the query tools on the market are extremely sophisticated and are directed toward application development. They require a good knowledge of relational databases in addition to the underlying data structures and are not readily learned by business users. The choice of query tools can significantly affect how well the data warehouse is received in the user community, how eager or reluctant (due to perceived or real learning curve) users will be in using the warehouse, and how positively the corporate grapevine will influence the acceptance and use of the warehouse.

Making data truly accessible is a significant aspect of warehouse development. It is often misunderstood or overlooked. A realistic appraisal of users' needs, abilities, and comfort level with front-end technology and then use of the appropriate front-end software are absolute requirements for a successful data warehouse for decision support. An entire chapter, Chapter 10, is devoted to making timely data accessible and should provide you with substantive assistance in this critical area of data warehouse development.

SUMMARY

In this chapter, you should have learned the following:

- The data warehouse pilot should be approached like any other development project, with the appropriate funding, resources, and a project manager who understands the decision support life cycle.

- The primary focus of a proof of concept pilot will be on the front end and the user's interaction with the decision support information. This type of pilot can often be accomplished with a small subset of data.
- An architecture and infrastructure pilot is developed to gain experience in the technicalities of how all the components of the data warehouse architecture work together. Additionally, you will gain experience with the full decision support life cycle.
- The database for the pilot project has a high chance of being built upon, so the database, even for a small project, must be designed well.
- Abbreviated proof of concept pilots, taking only a few weeks, are being offered by vendors to provide a visual idea of the possibilities and benefits of the data warehouse. Be clear on the benefits and risks of such pilots, so you can use them to your best advantage.
- Clarify the goal of your pilot project development; one business area may be a better choice than another for fulfilling this goal and increasing your likelihood of success.
- Always have a high-level sponsor for the development of a data warehouse.
- Sales management, brand analysis, and marketing are good candidates for choosing a business area for your initial development. Customer profiling and market segmentation are greatly needed within companies but may be more challenging.
- "The big eight" are fundamental aspects of building a successful data warehouse that should not be ignored. See Tips from the Trenches 6.2 on "the big eight."
- The resources or skills that you will need to build a data warehouse include
  - Someone with experience building data warehouses to assist you in creating the project plan and to keep the project moving through all of the obstacles.
  - A cross section of users who know the business well and have a specific business problem to address.

- Architecture and infrastructure planning experience.
- A data architect who has experience with data warehouse development and fine-tuned data analysis skills for the data integration.
- Good source system personnel who have access to the actual data.
- A well-versed DBA and star schema database design expertise.
- A hands-on project manager, preferably one with decision support experience and a technical background.
- Team members (end users) with a good understanding of the business, the data, and how they are used are imperative to a successful data warehouse project.
- Access to personnel who handle networking, communications, workstation and software installation, capacity planning, operations, and training.
- A realistic appraisal of the users' analysis needs, abilities, and comfort level with front-end technology, and the purchase of the appropriate front-end software to respond to these different levels of users, is an absolute requirement for a successfully used data warehouse.

Case Study 3

Moving through the Obstacles to Implementation

by Mark Thompson, Manager of Market Planning, Hoffman Engineering, Mark Johnson, President, InER-G Solutions, Ltd., and Vidette Poe

Hoffman Engineering Company, an ISO 9001 certified company, is the leading North American supplier of electrical and electronic enclosures used for a wide range of industrial applications. They have five manufacturing locations throughout North America and over 6,000 SKUs.

Hoffman sells their products through industrial distributors throughout North America and markets their products globally via parent company affiliates with direct and distribution sales organizations. This business paradigm, in addition to their stability in the market for over 50 years, resulted in Hoffman becoming primarily a product-driven organization.

Historically, Hoffman's strong distribution channel enabled it to be distributor versus end-user customer focused. Never really needing to be a strong marketing organization, Hoffman had no real customer focused information or processes from the end-consumer perspective. As their market became more competitive, Hoffman acknowledged that understanding their customer base and becoming more customer-centric would improve their supply chain management that would ultimately translate into an improved bottom line. Understanding their customers' product needs would also give them more control over their manufacturing process.

In 1994, Hoffman recognized that their sales analysis and reporting system was unable to support the business decision-making process required to achieve their long-term growth objectives. Like many other organizations, Hoffman Information Technology (IT) had developed a reporting backlog causing requests for new reports to take several weeks or months of development time before being put into the hands of the end user. Since the delivery of sales and analysis reports required considerable time between request and fulfillment, by the time the user received the requested report, they already had several more reports that were needed or had a different way they wanted to see the data displayed.

Realistically looking at their sales measurement and reporting capabilities, Hoffman observed the following:

- The Sales Analysis and Reporting system had inflexible output that was not user friendly
- Extensive data validation was necessary to determine the nature and extent of a problem or opportunity
- Inconsistent numbers were being generated from different reports
- Accurate sales measurement and analysis were difficult, if not impossible, because of these inconsistent numbers
- Meetings were spent debating the validity of data as opposed to making business decisions

Due to the limitations of the reporting systems and the inconsistency of their data, Hoffman could not answer fundamental business questions about their sales, products, and customers, such as

- What products are our largest distributors stocking?
- To whom are our products being sold?
- How much of our annual price increase was accepted versus discounted?
- How can we better optimize our inventory?

Hoffman was making business decisions with respect to sales measurement, analysis, and forecasting with inconsistent or conflicting data.

In the fourth quarter of 1994, with an intent of becoming more customer-centric and to remedy the inefficiencies in their reporting systems, Hoffman decided to develop a data warehouse. The original objectives of their data warehouse were to

- Implement a market-based forecasting process
- Facilitate the sales and marketing measurement process
- Understand the customers' present and future product requirements so they could satisfy these requirements more profitably

At that time, Hoffman hired a consulting company, InER-G Solutions, Ltd., to assist them in the planning and prototyping of a data warehouse. Hoffman described the following phases in building their data warehouse:

- Developing a prototype
- Implementing
- Migrating data from mainframe to the data warehouse server
- Connecting the data warehouse server to user's PC
- Rolling out the warehouse to users to begin using it

DEVELOPING A PROTOTYPE

Developing the prototype encompassed the process of project planning through prototyping. Using a tool called InER-G*Cycle* as a repository for the data and analysis gathered throughout the data warehouse life cycle this phase consisted of the following steps:

- Facilitating discussions and having interviews with 10 to 12 business users from forecasting, product planning, manufacturing, marketing, sales, and finance to determine their requirements for the data warehouse
- Documenting and analyzing business drivers
- Modeling the requirements and attributing the model
- Designing the prototype database based on the user requirements and business drivers
- Prototyping these requirements to ascertain if the database design would meet business requirements
- Using the prototype to make appropriate modifications to the data structures and overall database design

The full process of prototyping, from planning through the physical prototype, took approximately 12 weeks. During this time, Hoffman found inconsistencies in their data and began making process and reporting changes.

IMPLEMENTING

After a successful prototyping phase, Hoffman moved forward with the data warehouse implementation. This implementation phase consisted of the following:

- Doing source-to-target field mapping
- Creating specifications for data integration for the fields
- Acquiring a server
- Refining the database design from the prototype using a star schema-oriented relational model
- Creating the extract and load programs for the AS400
- Populating the database
- Building the first front-end applications with Cognos' Impromptu tool

MIGRATING DATA FROM MAINFRAME TO THE DATA WAREHOUSE SERVER

At the time of the data warehouse implementation, Hoffman was in the process of converting their production systems from a Cullinet mainframe to a JD Edwards/AS400 platform. The data warehouse source data was migrated from the mainframe to an AS/400 data warehouse server running DB2/400.

CONNECTING THE DATA WAREHOUSE SERVER TO USERS' PCS

Hoffman used Windows on the desktop with a Novell LAN Server and Client Access for mainframe connectivity. End users, familiar with the Windows environment, did not want to move to the Win/OS2 client for performance and functionality reasons. This created a substantial problem since there was no easy way to connect the AS400 to a client workstation for both "Windows only" and "Win/OS2." The IBM TCP/IP interface for the AS400 was the connectivity solution. Evaluating alternatives and implementing a workable solution to the Windows versus Win/OS2 environment took five to six months.

ROLLING OUT THE WAREHOUSE TO USERS TO BEGIN USING IT

Hoffman has analysts within the different functional areas of their business. The first rollout of their data warehouse was to three of these analysts within the sales and marketing group. These three analysts became the first data warehouse power users, supporting five to ten people each. Currently, there are six power users on this decision support system, supporting a number of people in a variety of business functions.

Because users now have access to information that had never been available to them before, requests for information are coming in from other departments and from the highest levels of management. In an effort to accommodate these requests, Hoffman has plans to deploy the data warehouse to both the finance and operations departments.

The initial prototype front-end applications were created using Impromptu and PowerPlay by Cognos. Limitations of the tool's ability to work with the volume of data needed to answer specific business questions led Hoffman to begin looking for a different multidimentional analysis tool.

The following process was used to evaluate and choose a new multidimentional analysis tool for their data warehouse:

- Contacting different multidimensional analysis tool vendors and gathering information
- Requesting that vendors do a proof of concept using Hoffman's data
- Visiting sites and talking with companies where the vendor had implemented their multidimentional analysis tool

The multidimentional analysis application chosen by Hoffman was SalesTracker from Silvon Software, Inc.

OBSTACLES TO BUILDING THE DATA WAREHOUSE

Hoffman had to navigate the following obstacles to successfully implement their data warehouse:

- IT organizational changes.
- Conversion of business systems.
- Senior management changes.
- The data warehouse was never a top priority initiative.

IT Organizational Changes

Immediately after the prototype project was approved, the current Vice-President of IT assumed different responsibilities at Hoffman. The new Vice-President of IT was hired from outside Hoffman and requested an evaluation of the PC and mainframe systems performance and architecture. As a result, the data warehouse project resources and deliverables needed to be rejustified.

Conversion of the Business Systems

Two months after the prototype was completed, it was apparent to Hoffman that their Cullinet/mainframe operating systems needed to be replaced. A project team was assembled and after a long evaluation process, the JD Edwards/AS400 solution was selected and approved. Immediately afterwards, all IT and user resources were refocused to implement the JD Edwards/AS400 system. During this evaluation and implementation process, minimal resources were allocated to the data warehouse project.

Senior Management Changes

At the same time the multidimensional application of the data warehouse was implemented, Hoffman's president received new responsibilities within Hoffman's parent company. This resulted in internal promotions and new assignments of some senior management personnel. Although this did not directly affect the data warehouse project, it impacted Hoffman because a new management team was forming, determining roles and responsibilities, and assessing resource requirements for current initiatives.

The Data Warehouse Was Never a Top Priority Initiative

Although the data warehouse was approved by the President and his staff, the project was not a top priority initiative. Hence, when other projects needed resources and/or staffing, personnel were taken off of the data warehouse project and reassigned. As a result, the time line of the project and the ability to create deliverables were affected.

HOFFMAN'S NEXT STEPS

Hoffman has defined their next steps in creating a more robust decision support environment as follows:

- Implement an executive information system. Hoffman will initially be using the Impromptu tool as in the original prototype. They will then conduct interviews to review information requirements and determine the data needed to satisfy those requirements.
- Load external data which will supplement their existing analysis
- Deploy to other functional departments. As mentioned above, Hoffman is planning to roll out the data warehouse to the Finance and Operations departments
- Deploy to Pilot sales offices. Silvon Software, Inc., makers of SalesTracker, have another tool which enables a subset of data to be downloaded to remote users.
- Add a data mining tool. Hoffman will be evaluating a data mining tool which will enable them to conduct more robust data analysis across a broader spectrum.

WHAT HOFFMAN HAS LEARNED

- Data warehousing is a process and needs to be incorporated into existing business processes.
- Data accuracy is not a one-time event.
- Project leader and IT skill requirements are critical.
- Select consultants and software applications carefully.

50/50 HINDSIGHT

"Having gotten as far with your data warehousing as you are now, what would you do differently?"

- Hold more firmly to delivery dates, whether for in-house resources or outside consultants.
- To have greater success with moving forward in warehouse development, the data warehouse needs to be a business priority for the corporation. Perhaps not the top corporate priority, but definitely closer to the top of the list than to the bottom.

SUGGESTIONS TO OTHERS WHO ARE BEGINNING THE DATA WAREHOUSING PROCESS

"What are a few of the key suggestions you would give to those beginning this process?"

- Most importantly, talk to other businesses and people who have implemented a data warehouse.

These discussions will yield a tremendous amount of useful information and insight on the battles they have gone through and the obstacles that must be overcome, including technology issues, tools and software experiences, services and consulting referrals, providing you with a realistic view of data warehouse development.

- Determine your organizational readiness. Companies need to realistically ascertain the resource needs and skill sets that are required to successfully implement a data warehouse. You need to do a careful readiness assessment of your current resource skills sets and those that need to be acquired/added, corporate commitment to the development process, funding, resource allocation between different projects within the company, the need for outside expertise, and the overall budget required.
- Pick your data warehouse partners carefully. Whether consultants, associates, new hires, or vendor partnerships, pick your data warehouse partners carefully. Get referrals from business associates. Choose partners who have a demonstrated track record. Remember that bigger is not always better when looking for external consulting assistance.
- Pick the internal project manager carefully. The internal sponsors and project manager need to be personally committed beyond a "general agreement" that data warehousing is a good idea.

SUMMARY

Developing a data warehouse at Hoffman was not an easy process. It has taken several years and movement through many obstacles to bring the warehouse to fruition and build it into a system that supports their decision making. Now that Hoffman has gotten this far in the process, they are actively witnessing the rewards of having access to information that is vital to their decision-making process. Use of the data warehouse has improved Hoffman's sales force performance and measurements, including their distribution channel. They can now analyze operations and manufacturing resources more efficiently. The data warehouse has also enhanced Hoffman's analysis of marketing programs and their strategic planning.

Additionally, the availability of information is changing how Hoffman works. With information available to them that was not available before, the management team is now being challenged to work differently and to increase the level of sophistication in how they handle the business. New business models and marketing programs are being created to target customers more effectively and improve market share.

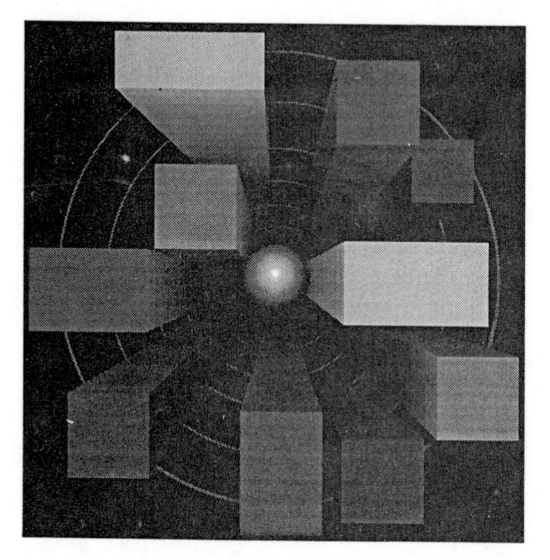

Chapter 7

GATHERING DATA REQUIREMENTS

A PROPER MINDSET

It is important to understand that building a data warehouse is somewhat different from developing transaction systems. This is especially true when you are trying to gather requirements from the users. Typically, system development revolves around well-defined specifications. The paradox in building a data warehouse is that you may need to develop a system to support undefined requests.

Your job as a data warehouse developer is to recognize that your main focus in developing this system is to provide information to users. One ramification of this is that you have to be much more open-minded when you gather data requirements; without prior decision support experience, your users may not always know what their next question could be. Another part of your challenge is that many users have not had training in analytical processing and have not had experience using the advanced decision support front-end tools that are currently on the market. This lack of experience means that they cannot imagine or visualize the broad range of capabilities that may be available to them.

USER INTERVIEWS

The Purpose of Interviews

The primary purpose of collecting end-user requirements for a data warehouse is to understand how users conduct their business, what data they currently use, and what they would like to do in the future. This gives you, the data warehouse developer, the business perspective that must be delivered to the user population. A key point to keep in mind throughout the project is that users will always ask questions of the decision support system from their frame of reference. If you do not understand that frame of reference, you could deliver a system that may theoretically be fabulous, but end users will have trouble using it, or the performance will be incredibly poor since you have designed for a completely different set of parameters.

The main things that you need to come away with from the interview process are

- A broad understanding of the end-user's business
- Specific details about the data and key elements to be included in the initial implementation of the data warehouse

- An understanding of the core use of the initial data
- An understanding of the common information that may be used for another business unit or when additions are made
- An understanding of other users who need to access or could leverage the initial data

To ensure success, it is important to have systems analysts or data modelers participate in the interviewing process. If your staff has not been exposed to data warehouse and decision support development, it will be well worth the investment to have an experienced DSS consultant in your project team during this phase.

Setting Up Successful Interviews

The most successful projects have input from key people within the end-user community. These people tend to be very much in demand. You need to make sure that they understand the importance of their participation and give them plenty of advance notice to ensure their availability.

Who to Interview

To gain the complete understanding of the business, whom you choose to interview is important. You will need a cross section of the following groups:

- Analysts and users from the target business functions
- Managers from the target business functions
- Analysts and users from related business functions
- Managers from related business functions
- Executives

Within the cross section of the above groups, it is important that you interview the highly technical power users. Additionally, you will need to talk to key influencers, whether or not they are technically savvy. A brief description about the structure of the interview and goal for talking with each of the above groups follow.

Key End Users and Analysts from the Target Business Functions. Spend time with the people who will be the primary audience for the system. The focus for this interview is to understand the day-to-day analysis—what is performed manually, what reports are created, and what types of ad hoc questions are being handled.

You should try to limit the number of people interviewed at one time to a maximum of four.

These interviews will take a minimum of two hours. They could take as long as four if the users have a great deal of information they wish to share.

The first interviews you conduct tend to take longer than subsequent interviews as terms and practices are learned. Try to be sensitive to the interpersonal dynamics of a group. Try to keep any single interview with peers, rather than with managers and employees. Some people are reluctant to speak freely in an interview with their boss or their boss's boss.

Managers from the Target Business Functions. Again, these interviews should take two hours, with a maximum of four people. The primary goal here is to understand the business objectives. In the best world, how would your staff spend their time? What analyses do you wish you could get more frequently? What analyses do you perform yourself? What do you do with reports that are provided to you?

Analysts and Users from Related Business Functions. Again, a two-hour interview with no more than four people should provide the information you need. The most useful people to talk to are those who interact directly with the data and/or business function that is the primary target. Keep this group focused on how they could use the same data and what related data is integrated to perform additional analysis. The focus of this interview is to understand the dependencies and shared data between the business groups.

Managers from Related Business Functions. It may prove useful to conduct individual interviews with this group since they will have diverse responsibilities. These interviews could be reduced to one hour.

Executives. The executive sponsor and related executives should be interviewed individually. The interviews should be 30 minutes long, at most one hour. Even getting this much time may be a challenge for this level in the organization. Executive interviews should be done last. The executive vision will pull together all the pieces of the puzzle that you have been collecting from the other interviews. This level of interview is critical to understanding the overall goals for the company. Executives tend to have a great deal of vision of where they want their department/division to be in the immediate future and for the next three to five years.

This is also a visible sign of support to the rest of the organization of the importance of this project. Other people on the interview schedule will take the sessions more seriously when they see high-level involvement.

What to Ask End Users

First of all, you will ask different questions of the executives than of the managers and analysts. So let's start with the managers and analysts.

Job Responsibilities

- Describe your position.
- How is your performance measured?
- What are the key business issues you face today?

Current Analysis. It is important to understand the flow of information into and out of the department. In many cases the effort to simply handle incoming information, perform cursory analysis, and then create outgoing reports takes up all of many analysts' time. The ability to expedite and automate these processes will be very well received by the analysts.

What You Receive

- What reports do you currently get?
- Which ones do you use?

- How often do you receive this report?
- What do you look for? (Look for what is highlighted.)
- What else do you do with this?

More often than not, users start with a hard copy report and add several calculations by hand or rekey the data into a spreadsheet for further analysis. Do not feel badly if you find people doing this in your company. You will begin to appreciate the need for the data warehouse and your efforts!

What You Create

- What reports do you create?
- How often do you perform this analysis?
- Who gets this information?
- Do other groups create this same report? If so, who?
- How is it used?
- How long does it take you to create it?
- Where do you get the information?
- If you had the time, what are the next steps you would take to analyze this information?

Ad Hoc Analysis. Most end users will not be able to define what their ad hoc requirements are. From their perspective, if they have all the data they might ever need for the last 10 years at the transaction level of detail, they will be able to perform their analyses. Since this is rather unrealistic, you must ask probing questions to understand the nature of the ad hoc questions. This will allow you to predict the type of analyses that may be required in the future.

- What kinds of ad hoc analyses do you do?
- Who asks the original question? Customer, manager, high-level executive . . . ?
- How do you fulfill these requests today?
- Do you have any examples of what you have done in the past?

Business Analysis. If you are familiar with the business, you may pose a series of specific questions that are topical. For instance,

- How do you develop promotional programs?
- How do you evaluate promotional effectiveness?
- How often do you perform vendor reviews?
- What analysis is performed to support the decision to buy?
- How do you manage your inventory levels?

Data Specific Information. Make sure that you understand, *down to a field level,* what data the user thinks they need. Also understand which fields are classified as mandatory for their analysis.

- Where do they think the data comes from?
- How often is it updated?
- What level of detail is needed?

Wish List Information. What would you want to be able to do if there were no financial, time, or technical constraints in your way? (Golfing four days a week is not a valid answer.) In many cases, their wildest imagination barely begins to touch on what you may already be planning to include as part of your data warehouse and decision support solution. Just make sure to bring them back to reality. Remember, good project management and interviewing skills include managing end-users' expectations.

Other Data Sourcing Information. Then explore other data sources. Make sure that you ask the same questions as above.

Business Hierarchies. Understand the business hierarchies within the data sources. Get up and draw on the board what you think the structures look like, or better yet, have the end users draw them for you. Almost every organization sells products, has an internal sales structure, and tracks performance over time. For each of these dimensions, make sure you understand the following:

- At what level do you currently perform most of your analysis? Why? Sometimes it is where it makes sense; other times it is because that is all end users have access to.
- What is the lowest level of detail that exists in the organization?
- Are there multiple hierarchies? For example, often there will be a rollup of stores into marketing areas and a different rollup into the internal sales structure for the company.
- When does your fiscal year end?
- What are the other characteristics of time? For instance, shipment information is monthly, but syndicated POS data comes in 13 4-week periods, and you set up your business calendar on a 4-4-5 week structure per quarter.

If you do not know where to start, look at the reports. Where are there subtotals? Grand totals? What are the primary headings of the reports? This will give you the starting point for the dimensions, as well as the hierarchies within those dimensions.

What have you missed?

- Ask them what else they think you need to know that you have not yet asked.

As you work your way through the process, make sure that you understand the business hierarchical relationships. Almost every data warehouse will have at least a product, a geography, and a time hierarchy.

Do not promise anything in the meetings. After you have completed the entire interviewing process, priorities may change or key data elements may not be available. The goal of the interview process is to share information, not to cut deals.

What to Ask Executives

Be brief and concise with your questions; you will have very little time with this type of person. Also, don't bring in 10 people to ask questions and/or to observe. Include two, or at most, three people. If you have any specific questions about analysis or information this executive uses, ask who can provide you with an in-depth understanding of that analysis rather than getting into the details at the moment.

Here are some questions you may want to ask:

- What are your job responsibilities?
- What are your corporate objectives?
- What are the critical success factors for meeting those objectives?
- What could prevent you from meeting those objectives?
- What are the most pressing business problems you see today?
- What is the financial impact of solving these business problems?
- What is it that you want information about on a daily basis?
- What opportunities exist to improve profits?
- How do you compare to your competitors?

Also be prepared to discuss how the project is going. This person will probably have an interest in the progress and cooperation of his or her staff. If you have any *major* issues, be prepared to bring them up with a suggestion for what you will need to resolve the issue.

Documenting What You Heard

Writing up what you are learning in the interviews should be done as you go rather than waiting until all the interviews have been completed. By the time you have talked to everyone, you may not be able to remember who said what—even if you keep thorough notes. Some people like to record the interviews on tape. If you choose to do this, make sure that you ask before doing so.

The interview summaries serve several key purposes:

- Capture the knowledge and what was said
- Advance your understanding of the business
- Serve as valuable documentation for the future
- Provide documentation to educate new team members

Always summarize what you have learned in writing. This is critical for understanding and integrating data requirements for your data warehouse. Interview documentation also serves as a valuable road map into the future.

Organize the information into the following sections:

- *How the Business Works.* Include a summary of the business function.
- *Job Responsibilities.* Include a brief summary of what was shared.
- *Analysis.* Include a description of the different types of analyses that are currently performed. Examples are sales trend analysis, promotion analysis, price gap analysis, and claims summary. Also include a description of the types of analysis they would like to perform.
- *Data Requirements.* Include a description of each data field that was mentioned, and as much detail as you know about that field, including its possible sources and how it is used.
  - Dimensions. Include a list of the dimensions of the business. Examples are product, time, and geography. See below for a discussion of dimensions.
  - Hierarchies within dimensions. Examples are weekly, monthly, quarterly, and yearly within the time dimension.
- *Miscellaneous.* This section serves to capture other important concepts.

After you have completed writing the summary, share it with everyone who was interviewed. Get their input; you may be surprised at some of the misunderstandings that can occur.

After each group has approved its summary, bring it all together. This can be as simple as publishing all of the final interview summaries to writing a full analysis of the overall research.

As you take the time to document, remember that this will provide the foundation for future data warehouse and decision support development efforts. Also, if you do a good job, when you are wildly successful you can quickly transition a replacement in, so you can tackle your new job when you are promoted.

What You Have to Know for DSS

So now you have more details about the business than you ever wanted to know. How do you wade through all those details to determine how to build your data warehouse? First, let's review what you really need to know:

- Business entities and their attributes
- Relationships between the entities, including all the hierarchical relationships
- What business measures are used for analysis
- The base facts required to create the business measures
- Specific calculations used to create new facts
- If and how the facts can be aggregated

FACILITATION VIA ALIGNMENT

When gathering data requirements for your data warehouse, you may wish to consider using facilitation via alignment. Facilitation via alignment is a process of gathering data requirements and reconciling business issues with a facilitator that is specifically trained to move the group into alignment. For example, we recently used this process in a project tasked with creating a wholehouse definition and the associated attributes for "customer" across 12 business units with very different business goals and processes. Given the inherent problems in working on an enterprise level across business units, facilitation via alignment enabled us to work through the issues exceptionally quickly.

When using this process in the requirements gathering phase, you will be able to gather specific data attributes, reconcile definitions, document the hierarchies and dimensions, and create matrices for sourcing information within two to four sessions of four to eight hours each. This will substantially cut down the time needed to be carved out of the end-users' calendars, which can often be difficult to schedule.

We would also highly recommend using facilitation via alignment for the planning phase of your data warehouse development to move through refining your scope and outlining and defining the associated tasks and deliverables quickly. It is our experience that using a facilitator trained in alignment facilitation cuts the planning time in half.

DEVELOPING THE DATA MODEL

Data modeling is really the process of translating business concepts into a diagrammatic format that can be converted into actual physical data structures. Explanations of both dimensional business models and logical data models and their relevance to data warehouse development follow.

Dimensional Business Model

The users have a business model that drives how they perform their day-to-day business. Although they may not be experts at heuristic processing, end users usually have a fairly good idea of the metrics they care about, the dimensions by which they look at information, the hierarchies within the dimensions, and how these metrics relate to each other.

The data warehouse must reflect this end-user business model. A simple way to organize all of the information you have gathered is to segregate business entities and attributes into facts and dimensions. This is called a dimensional business model as shown in Figure 7-1.

A dimensional business model is a set of diagrams developed in presentation software, requiring no specialized tools. It is a simple model showing metrics, dimensions, and relationships that can easily be presented back to users for verification. When presenting to users,

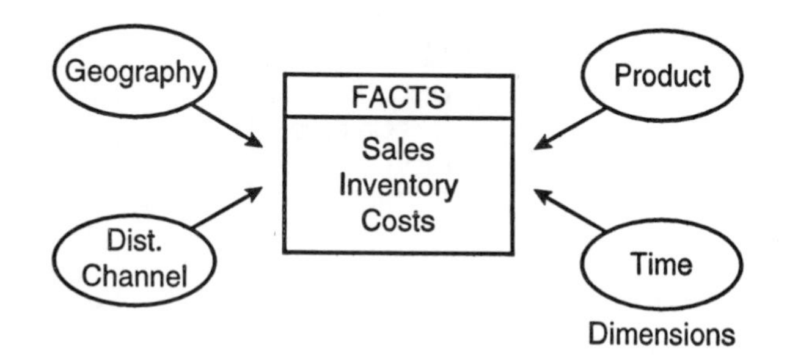

FIGURE 7–1 Example of a high-level dimensional business model.

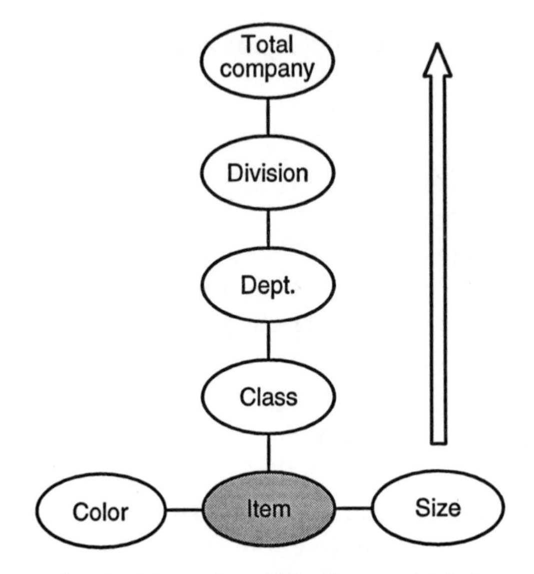

FIGURE 7–2 Example of a hierarchy within the product dimension for a retailer.

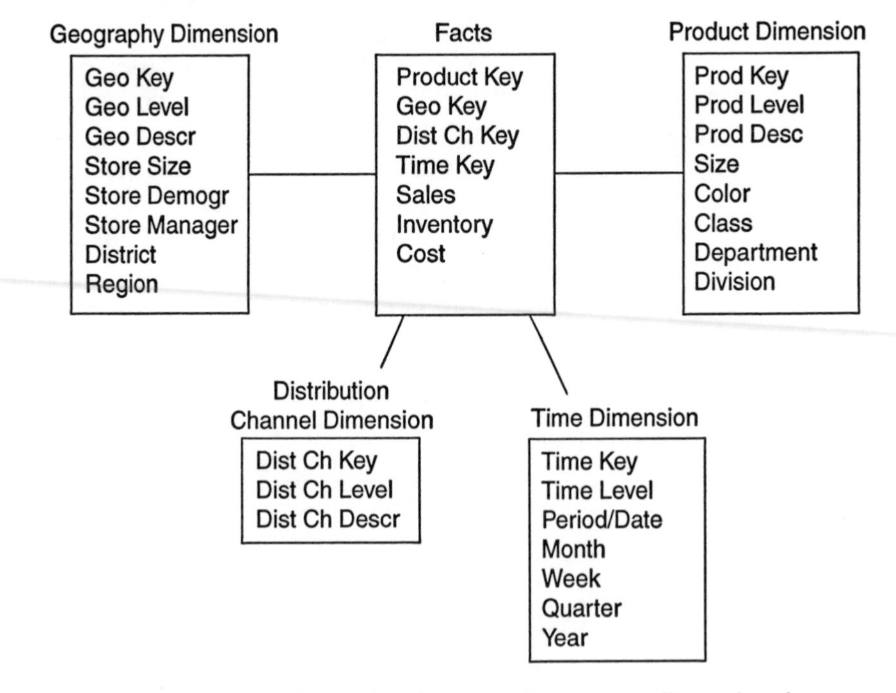

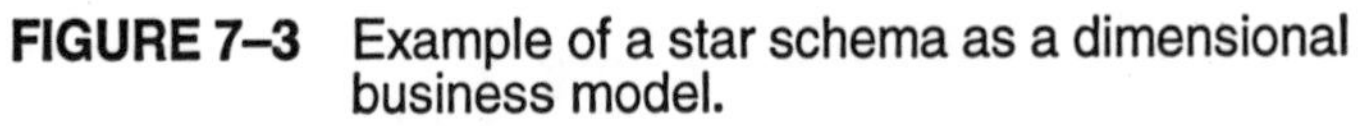
FIGURE 7–3 Example of a star schema as a dimensional business model.

start with the dimensions; then move into details about each individual dimension.

Within each dimension, or group, you will define the hierarchy (Figure 7-2). Then review the facts and associated attributes.

The data model could also be a graphical description of the simple star schema. In that case, the logical model and the physical models will be identical with the exception of physical table partitioning. Figure 7-3 shows an example.

With any of these diagrams, you must use business labels and not internal table or column names. At this time, you can also confirm the proper business terms that will be used during the implementation of the data warehouse front-end access tool.

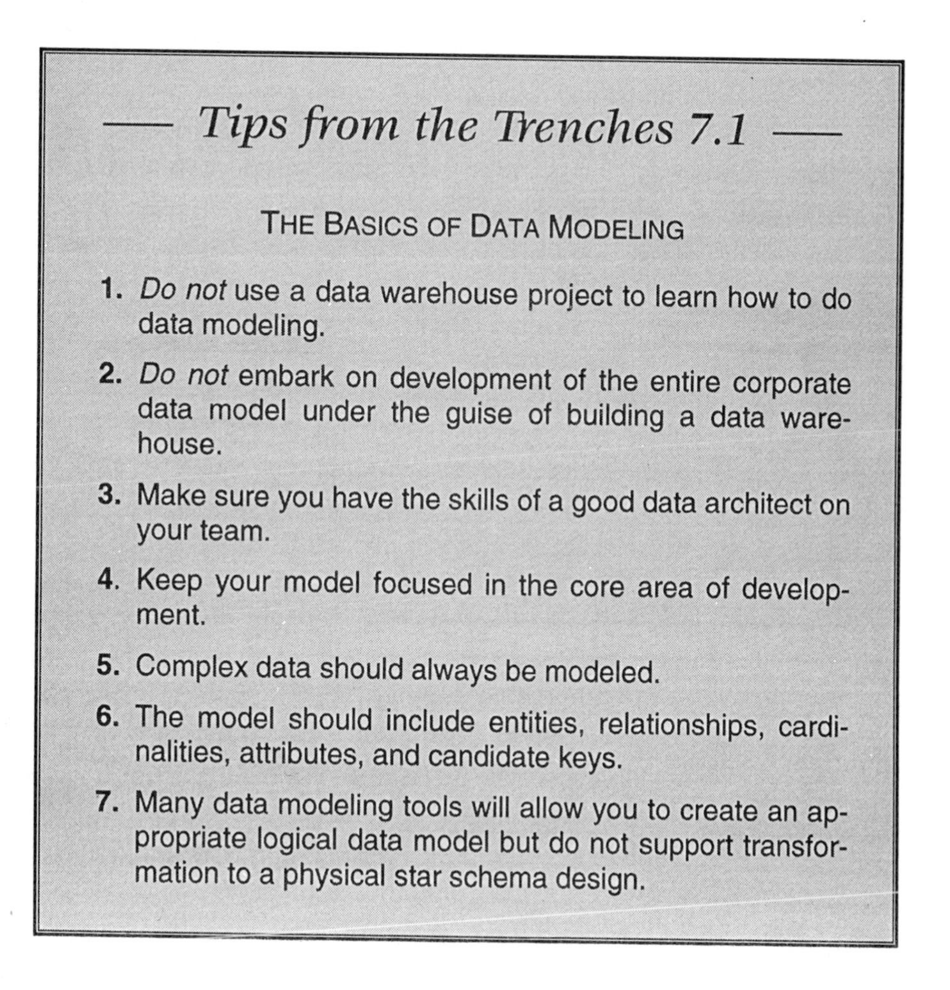

— *Tips from the Trenches 7.1* —

THE BASICS OF DATA MODELING

1. *Do not* use a data warehouse project to learn how to do data modeling.
2. *Do not* embark on development of the entire corporate data model under the guise of building a data warehouse.
3. Make sure you have the skills of a good data architect on your team.
4. Keep your model focused in the core area of development.
5. Complex data should always be modeled.
6. The model should include entities, relationships, cardinalities, attributes, and candidate keys.
7. Many data modeling tools will allow you to create an appropriate logical data model but do not support transformation to a physical star schema design.

Logical Data Model

Traditional logical data modeling, such as the development of entity relationship diagrams, is sometimes applied to data warehouse development. The need to document a detailed logical data model is driven, to a large degree, by your corporate culture. Some organizations do not have a data modeling function and do not have an enterprisewide data model. At the other end of the spectrum, some companies have entire groups that specialize in data modeling. This type of organization may also have in place, or is well on its way to having, a corporate data model. Your organization may require that a logical data model be developed with the standard tool prior to allowing any tables to be created in any corporate database. It is important to note that a successful data warehouse does not require the development of a full and complete logical data model. However, it does require that you have these data modeling, architecture, and analysis skills available to you, whichever model you choose to use. In many cases, the development of a Dimensional Business Model is sufficient to drive the development of a data warehouse.

SUMMARY

In this chapter, you should have learned the following:

- A good method of gathering requirements for a data warehouse is by conducting a series of interviews with a cross section of the user community within the scope of your project
- The fundamentals of interviewing—whom to interview, what to ask, and what the primary goal of the interview will be.
- The structure of the interview is important—limit interviews to a maximum of two per day, with a maximum of four users. Interviews should last only two to four hours.
- Always capture a rough draft of the information gathered at the interview within two hours.
- What you need to know for decision support systems is:
  - Business entities and their attributes
  - Relationships between entities

- Hierarchies
- What facts are used
- What the base facts are
- What calculations are used to create new facts
- If and how the facts can be aggregated

- The dimensional business model is a simple way to segregate and diagram the facts and dimensions gathered throughout the interviewing process, and are easily understood by users. These can often be used to replace an Entity Relationship Diagram (ERD).
- If data structures are simple, a full logical data model may not be required for the development of a data warehouse—a dimensional business model can be used instead. For extremely complex data, you may wish to do an ERD. Do so only for the scope of your project
- Do not use the data warehouse project to learn how to do data modeling.
- Many tools will allow you to create an appropriate logical model but do not support transformation into a physical star schema.

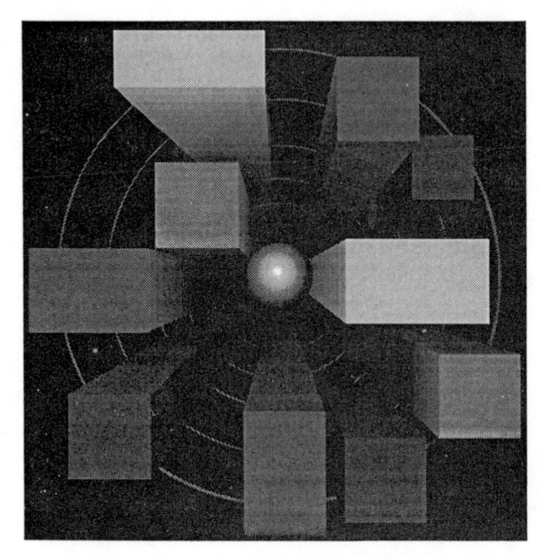

Chapter 8

DATA INTEGRATION

INTRODUCTION

Imagine yourself as the director of the marketing organization of a retail bank. One of the key areas of interest you would like to have a better understanding of is the relationship between the demographics of your customers and the kinds of financial products they tend to use. This will help tremendously in focusing your advertising campaigns to the specific households representing certain age groups and income levels, allowing you to derive higher value per dollar spent in your advertising budget. You think it would help to have a data warehouse to collect account information from systems across the bank that provide support for the various products the bank offers. You also think that additional information from an external vendor who specializes in gathering demographic statistics would help to categorize and sort the account information already available regarding your customers. With this in mind, you explore the idea of building a data warehouse that will provide this information to your de-partment.

THE METAMORPHOSIS OF DATA TO INFORMATION

The business user usually knows what information they want from a data warehouse. However they may not always understand if the data available will actually provide the information they want. For example, the marketing group may want to compile all the data collected by transaction systems that support teller activity, loans, credit cards, ATM, real estate, and investment accounts on a daily basis. The systems that collect this data were primarily, if not solely designed, to conduct a transaction specific to the operation of that particular business function. The information the marketing department is interested in finding out about a customer is likely to be very different from what is necessary to process a transaction and perform the proper accounting to manage a savings or checking account. However, if that data (transaction amount, transaction type, account type, account number, transaction location, etc.) is collected and sorted according to geographical region, age group, or income level—suddenly it is no longer disparate bits of data but a profile of information that allows the marketing director to get a report, graph, or even a three-dimensional landscape representation of account activity of current customers within definable ranges or dimensions. This is an example of the metamorphosis from data to information.

DEFINING DATA VERSUS INFORMATION

Now we are in a position to differentiate between data and information. Often we hear these words used interchangeably, but they are quite distinct in their meaning and this difference is why we build data warehouses. When we refer to the term "data," it implies a collection of discrete elements such as a file. Data is collected and stored in a data structure designed to be used by a computer system supporting a specific process. Operational systems process data to support the daily business activities of the organization.

When data is merged, aggregated, derived, sorted, structured, and displayed, as described in the above scenario, it becomes "information." This is why we build data warehouses: to provide a staging area to collect, integrate, and store data to perform actions with it that enrich and enhance the value of the data to, quite literally, transform the data into information.

DATA INTEGRATION

The data integration process can be thought of as "preprocessing" data to standardize names and values, resolving discrepancies in representation of the data, merging together common values, resolving "equivalent" values of data from disparate sources that approximately represent the same business facts, and establishing various access paths by identifying primary, alternate, and nonunique keys. This is the added value that the integrated data warehouse provides as a staging area for data that is ready to be turned into information. Doing the work up front to be sure the business user will be able to compare "apples to apples" and not be tempted or forced to compare "apples" to "eggplant" or "apples" to "fruit" is the purpose of the data integration process.

The steps required to integrate data will be repeated over and over again regardless of whether it is to perform the initial development of the target data warehouse, add new sources to an existing target data warehouse, or to distribute data from the warehouse to business users who might be using query tools or importing the data into other corporate systems. In fact, the data integration process is the "product" even

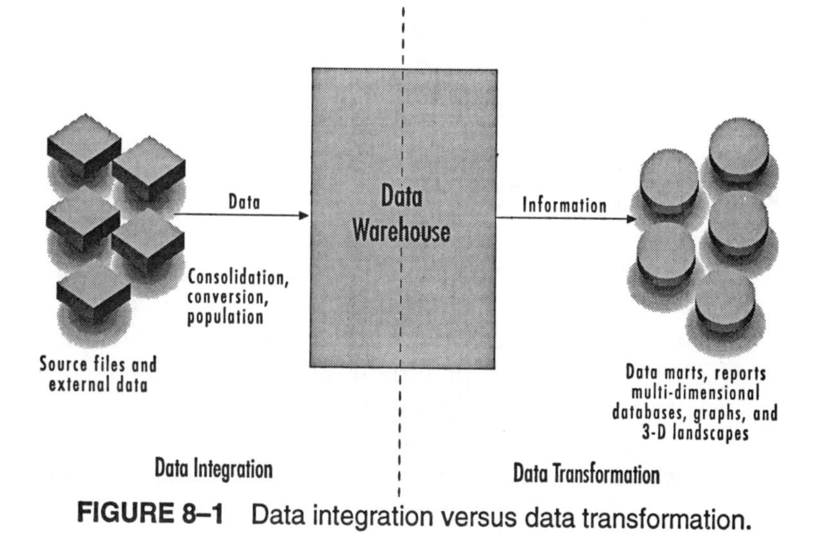

FIGURE 8–1 Data integration versus data transformation.

more so than the data warehouse itself. In other words, the process is the deliverable.

It is impossible to integrate data without having a "point of view." Data is created from the "point of view" of its usage in the source operational system. The data warehouse will have a different "point of view" from the source data because it is being built for a specific business purpose that is not being supported currently by any other systems in the organization. The business objectives for building the data warehouse give it its "point of view." If the purpose of the data warehouse is to support a particular business area within the organization, it simplifies the point of view and the integration process can proceed more quickly. It may be necessary to be concerned with maintaining a neutral point of view if the business purpose of the data warehouse is to provide information for anyone across the organization who wants to collect data to perform analysis for any kind of business reason. In this case we are required to wear many hats and get as many points of view as possible about the source data to provide a flexible data structure that will be powerful enough to serve the requests of a variety of business areas. (This approach is far more difficult and prone to failure due to nonspecific business objectives.) In either case it is important to understand the "point of view" being taken by the data warehouse and realize that a successful data warehouse implementation derives its "point of view" from the benefits the business sponsors expect to realize by building it.

DATA ARCHITECTURE

The data architecture is the underlying framework of the data warehouse. It must be established early in the project based on the business objectives, constraints, and priorities of the organization. The questions answered while determining the data architecture will drive the process for sourcing, integrating, storing, and accessing data from the data warehouse. The data model of the data warehouse will also be derived based on the data architecture and the business user's access requirements. The data architecture and data modeling efforts will drive the physical database design of the data warehouse. Once the data

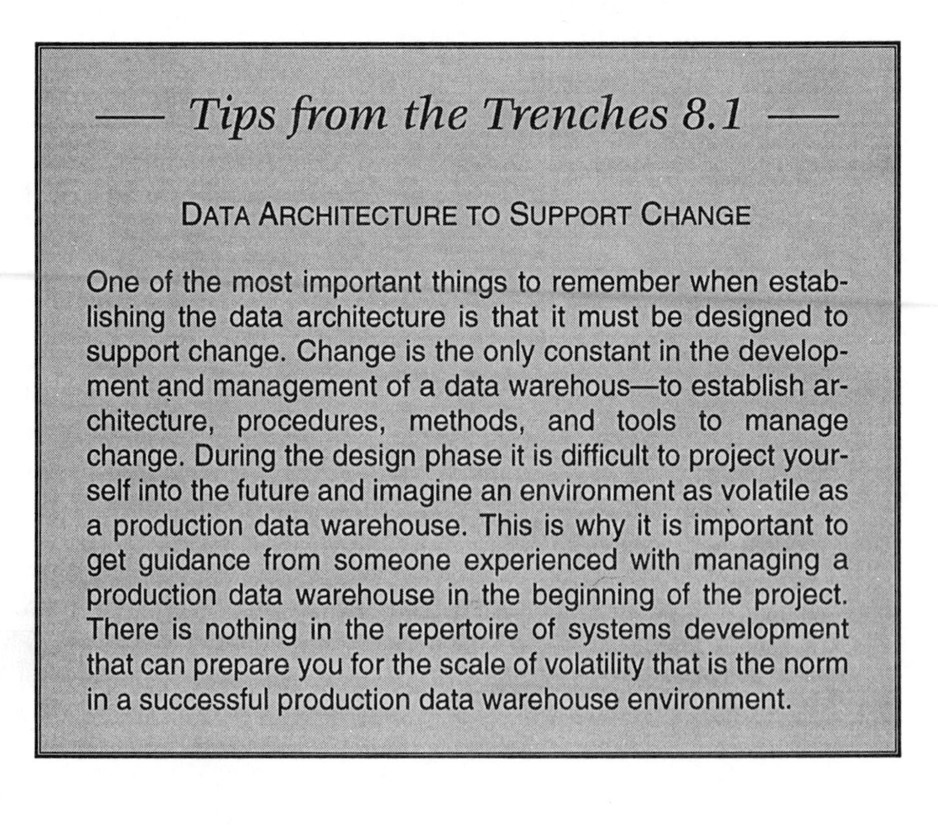

— *Tips from the Trenches 8.1* —

DATA ARCHITECTURE TO SUPPORT CHANGE

One of the most important things to remember when establishing the data architecture is that it must be designed to support change. Change is the only constant in the development and management of a data warehous—to establish architecture, procedures, methods, and tools to manage change. During the design phase it is difficult to project yourself into the future and imagine an environment as volatile as a production data warehouse. This is why it is important to get guidance from someone experienced with managing a production data warehouse in the beginning of the project. There is nothing in the repertoire of systems development that can prepare you for the scale of volatility that is the norm in a successful production data warehouse environment.

warehouse architecture is defined, the data integration process, which consolidates and converts the content of the source data into the target data warehouse, can be performed over and over again as new sources are identified.

METADATA

Metadata is data about data. Metadata is found in documentation describing source systems. For example, metadata describing the data element "transaction type" is

name (tran-type)

definition (The particular kind of transaction recorded such as "deposit," "debit," "transfer," etc.)

data type and length [char(5]

allowable values (01 = debit, 02=credit, 03=transfer)
key identifier (primary key or foreign key)

Metadata is used to analyze the source files selected to populate the target data warehouse. It is also produced at every point along the way as data goes through the data integration process. Therefore, it is an important by-product of the data integration process. The efficient management of a production data warehouse relies heavily on the collection and storage of metadata. Metadata is used for understanding the content of the source, all of the conversion steps it passes through, and how it is finally described in the data warehouse or target system. Metadata, such as definitions and business rules that describe calculations for derived data, is essential to business users who want to understand the content of the data warehouse. Metadata is used by developers who rely on it to help them develop the programs, queries, controls, and procedures to manage and manipulate the warehouse data. Metadata is also used for creating reports and graphs in front-end data access tools, as well as for the management of enterprisewide data and report changes for the end-user. Change management relies on metadata to administer all of the related objects (data model, conversion programs, load jobs, data definition language (ddl), etc.) in the warehouse that are impacted by a change request.

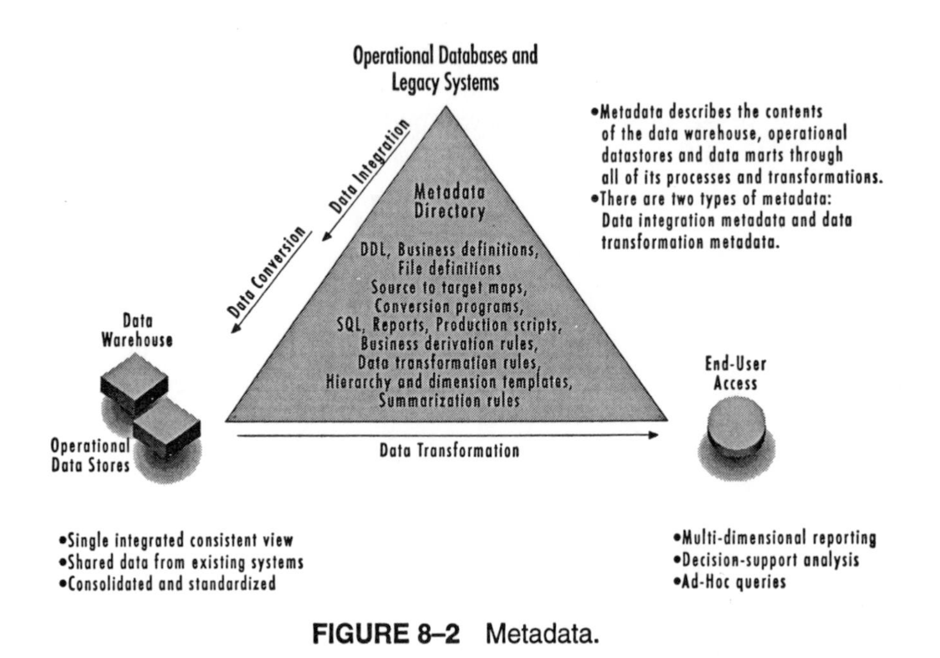

FIGURE 8–2 Metadata.

THE DATA INTEGRATION PROCESS

The data integration process can be used for any migration project where data from source files must be populated into a new integrated database. The data integration process consists of the following phases:

- **Data sourcing** focuses on the meaning of the data by identifying the source files and fields that will support the business objectives and requirements of the target system. *The deliverable is the correct source files and fields that fulfill the business objective of the target system (data warehouse).*
- **Data consolidation** focuses on the structure of the data by consolidating the sources into a single integrated target structure whether it is the initial model or adding new sources into an existing model. *The deliverable is an integrated data model or physical database design.*

- **Data conversion** focuses on the content of the data by specifying how to alter the source data to fit into the integrated target data structure. *The deliverable is the conversion specifications used by programmers to load the source data into the target database.*

- **Data population** focuses on the steps that need to be performed to physically load the source data into the integrated target data structure. *The deliverable is the conversion programs run to load the source data into the target database.*

DATA SOURCING

The first step in data integration is making sure you have the "right" data. Understanding what the business user expects to gain from building the data warehouse is critical to determining if the sources of data selected to populate the warehouse will render the expected benefits. Sourcing data is where the analysis process begins. A good data warehouse data analyst must be part analyst, part modeler, and part sleuth. They must not take for granted that the sources identified will deliver the expected benefit. It is their responsibility to perform some initial analysis (and sleuthing) to get a fundamental understanding of the source data. This will enable them to determine if it is complete enough so that, when integrated, it will provide the expected business value.

Often customers already know the internal systems from which they want to source. They have probably already tried alternative methods to access that data to produce the reports they want and have failed to achieve the desired results. They may not know if there are other sources more appropriate to their objectives or the availability of external data from information services that can augment what is collected by the internal systems to extend the business value of the data they want. It is essential to spend the time up front to find out what data is available internally, what formats and platforms it is already being delivered on, and if it will contribute to the business value of the data warehouse.

Taking a thorough inventory of sources available allows us to prioritize and scope the initial load of the data warehouse and guarantees a better chance for success. Review the user interface being designed to access the data. Understand the way the user wants to use the data. What is the specific business problem they want to resolve? The cost and time it takes to analyze, convert, integrate, and populate a data warehouse may be considerable. Making sure the initial population of the data warehouse renders business value will depend on taking a thorough inventory of the sources available.

DATA CONSOLIDATION

Data consolidation is a data modeling activity. As described in the preceding sections It is the process of analyzing and combining data from disparate sources or systems into a single, integrated data structure. Data consolidation is accomplished by identifying data that is common across the various source files, investigating the business rules that govern the usage of the data, and determining the new integrated data model that represents an accurate consolidation of the source data. Data consolidation is performed during the initial modeling of the data warehouse and every time a new source is added. An example of one type of data integration that often occurs for a data warehouse follows.

In many companies, keys in existing systems have intelligence built into the format. This is a very common practice in the design of operational systems; this intelligence must be broken out, integrated with the other fields that the intelligence represents, and mapped to the appropriate target fields before being loaded into a data warehouse. For example, Product Number has codes built into the format (Figure 8-3).

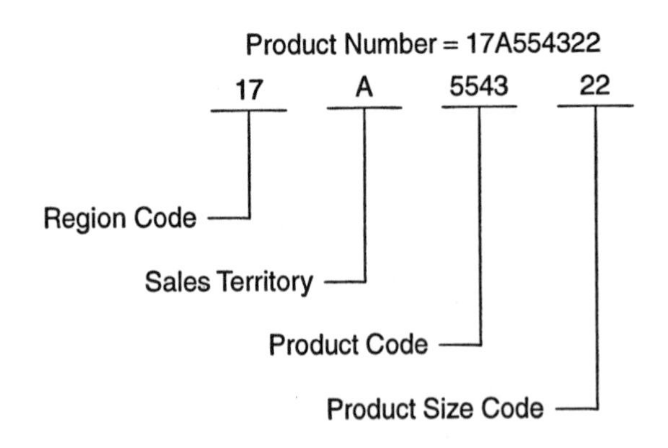

FIGURE 8–3 A field with codes built into the key.

Keys with intelligent codes built in that have not been properly dissected and integrated present decision support report challenges. For instance, using Figure 8–4, with no data dissection and integration being done, how would you compare sales on all of the products for specific sales territories within a region? The majority of the data warehouses will be either relational or multidimensional database technology. They are accessed with SQL or a multidimensional querying language, neither of which easily lend themselves to queries to pull embedded knowledge out of a data structure.

To do reporting on the sales of all products for certain territories within a region, a cross-reference/data integration algorithm would be established to transform the data in the Product Number field from the different source systems. This data integration algorithm would map the source data to several different relational fields in the data warehouse database and make the actual Product Number a consistent data type and format. This is one example of the type of data integration often needed in a data warehouse.

UNDERSTANDING THE PROCESS OF DATA CONSOLIDATION

These are the steps for performing the data consolidation process:

- Analyze source data documentation
- Flatten out data into logical records
- Perform domain analysis
- Determine primary keys
- Determine foreign keys

The deliverable is an integrated data model or physical data warehouse database design.

Analyze Source Data Documentation (Metadata). Source data documentation metadata is necessary to review and refer to throughout the analysis process. It will provide the first blush of knowledge about the source data. The way to assess the quality of the documentation is by examining the contents for completeness, consistency, depth, availability, and currency. The following list can be used to assess the quality of the documentation.

- Completeness—Every field in the files documented.
- Depth—Detailed information available.
- Accessibility—Ease of access to documentation (electronic versus hardcopy).
- Currency—Up-to-date information.
- Consistency—Multiple references of the same fields (synonyms) consistently described.

The following are examples of metadata that, depending on the thoroughness of the documentation, represent the kind of information you should expect to get about the source data:

- System overview description.
- File name and description of its use or purpose.
- Data element (or attribute) name and description, data type, length, range of values, valid values (if it has a finite domain of values such

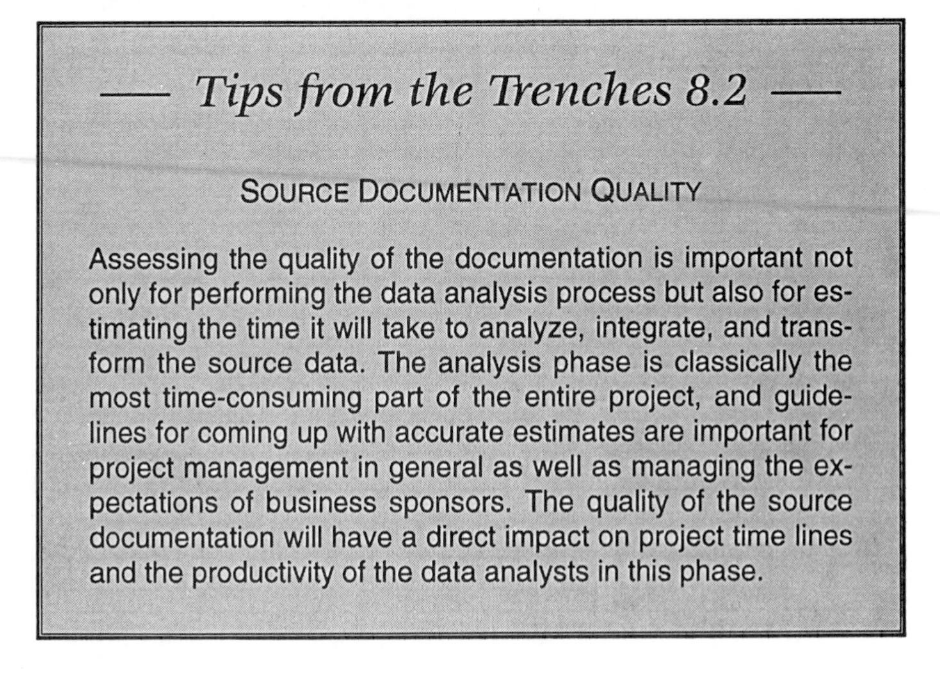

— *Tips from the Trenches 8.2* —

SOURCE DOCUMENTATION QUALITY

Assessing the quality of the documentation is important not only for performing the data analysis process but also for estimating the time it will take to analyze, integrate, and transform the source data. The analysis phase is classically the most time-consuming part of the entire project, and guidelines for coming up with accurate estimates are important for project management in general as well as managing the expectations of business sponsors. The quality of the source documentation will have a direct impact on project time lines and the productivity of the data analysts in this phase.

as "State Code"), value definitions, position in the file (depending on the file format), null rule, default value (the value inserted when there is no specific data to populate the field), whether it is a primary key, alternate key, foreign key, nonunique key, and control information necessary to understand the file formats.

"Flatten Out" the Data into Logical Records. Once we have the documentation, one of the first things to determine is the file format of the data. The analysis process must initially focus on the format of the source data. For instance, the process for doing this if the data is from an IMS database would be to link together "segments." If the data is being converted from an IDMS database, we would need to "walk the set" from parent to child records and link them together into logical record types. Quite often data is formatted into a file called a "flat file" (which we always thought was a misnomer and should have been called a "fat file!"). These are sequential files that are padded with control characters or fields to include multiple logical records of information in one file. This was used as a convenient way to store different logical file types together in the same physical file during a time when space was at a premium.

A logical record is a grouping of related information which has a key or identifier. For example, customer information may have a customer identifier followed by name, address, age, employment history, credit history, rental history, and so forth, grouped together in one file. If we start to examine this, we quickly discover that a person has a name, age, and current address but may have had many jobs which can be identified by dates of employment. In this case the main record would be the customer record followed by a second record type that would have employer name, address, phone number, position, years employed, start date, and so on. This job history information would be stored in a second record type. Because a customer may have had many jobs, there are likely to be multiple job history records for each customer record. To associate the job history with the correct customer information, there is a control field that would indicate which job history records went with which customer records. It is usually structured so that after each customer the different record types of related information follow, then a control field indicating the new customer record, and the next related record types, and so on for all the customer records in the file. Once this is flattened out, the flat file may end up being represented by as many as 20 logical files!

Data provided by external data providers for demographic or financial information or data that has been stored in an internal COBOL table using an "occurs clause" are often formatted in this way. The only way to know how the data is structured is by referring to the documentation that comes with the external vendor data or reading the COBOL copybook and related system documentation to understand the way the file was constructed. A program will need to be written during this phase in the analysis process referencing the control data to separate the source data correctly into separate files so that it can be accurately understood and analyzed. Failure to do this would make analysis impossible because each field in the sequential file would have multiple, unrelated values associated with it. In other words, the data is meaningless if it is just dumped into another file or table without the file processing to separate it out. This flattening out process will convert the data first into normal form (every field represents only one business fact). It should be noted that this step must be performed to convert the data to populate the warehouse whether or not we perform data-driven analysis.

The control information provided by the data provider (such as record type) is used to understand how the data is formatted. This is

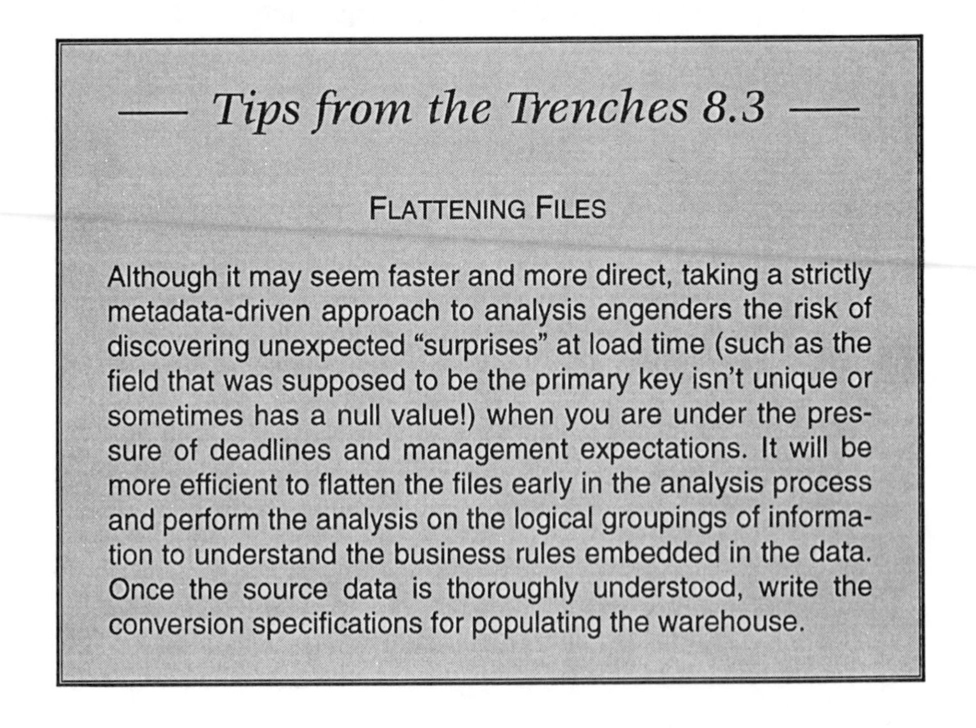

— *Tips from the Trenches 8.3* —

FLATTENING FILES

Although it may seem faster and more direct, taking a strictly metadata-driven approach to analysis engenders the risk of discovering unexpected "surprises" at load time (such as the field that was supposed to be the primary key isn't unique or sometimes has a null value!) when you are under the pressure of deadlines and management expectations. It will be more efficient to flatten the files early in the analysis process and perform the analysis on the logical groupings of information to understand the business rules embedded in the data. Once the source data is thoroughly understood, write the conversion specifications for populating the warehouse.

data that is significant to the conversion process of the data but not significant to the business content that is being populated into the warehouse. It is important that the data analysts responsible for writing the conversion specifications for the data don't inadvertently proliferate this system data into the warehouse.

Perform Domain Analysis. Once the data has been processed into logical records, we are ready to begin analyzing the data itself. The first area of analysis focuses on the content of each attribute in the source file. This is referred to as domain analysis. The reason for this is that, by definition, each attribute contains characteristic information that participates in a specific domain.

The domain of an attribute describes the content of the data and is defined by the data type (character, alphanumeric, integer, etc.); the length of the attribute; the expected range of values associated with the attribute based on a minimum and maximum (if it is defined); the default value of the attribute, which gets populated if there is no specific value supplied to put in the field, such as a "blank," a "0," or a phrase such as "not known." Some attributes have a finite set of allowed values (for example, "gender" would have the two values "male" or "female"). Another characteristic of an attribute that defines its domain is the "null" rule associated with it. This means it may be defined as a mandatory field in the record. In this case the null rule will be "NOT NULL," meaning it must have a value. Otherwise, the rule would be "NULLS ALLOWED."

The analysis of the domain of each attribute compared to the metadata, or documentation, provided about the source data, will reveal how "clean" the data is. As we mentioned earlier, it is likely that errors have crept into the data and it is very difficult to discover without a thorough analysis process. If discrepancies are discovered between the actual data and the metadata, it is the responsibility of the data analyst to inform the business sponsor and the data steward (person responsible for accuracy of the data) of the source data. The discrepancies may be actual errors or "undocumented features or changes" to the source file. Either way this must be identified and documented and taken into consideration during the data integration process to ensure data quality in the data warehouse.

The first step in domain analysis is to understand if the domain information actually matches the documented information about the data. Even if there are no apparent errors, the meaning of the data can start to "drift." The potential areas of concern are if the actual data reveals additional values that are not documented in an allowed value set. The usage may have changed to add values that were never documented and it is critical to find out what they mean so they can be converted correctly into the warehouse. It is also significant, although less critical, to discover if documented values are not present at all in the data set. There could be many reasons for this. For instance, the sample of data may not be sufficient to cover all the cases (for example, regional sales data with a sample from only one region will not have the values representing the other regions represented in the data). Another reason may be that the value documented is infrequently used because it is dependent on a business rule that applies only at specific times of the year or under special processing.

The data type, length, and null value rules are other areas of significance in understanding whether the differences are within the range of the documented information. If the actual data conflicts with the documented information, it must be determined if there was a change that was not documented or if the processing system where the data originated does not enforce these rules, therefore allowing the errors to creep in. Understanding the true nature of the data you are responsible for integrating and converting is essential to writing accurate conversion specifications for populating the data warehouse. For example, if a null rule is not enforced, then there is a risk that a key field may have a null value which would cause it to fail in the load process.

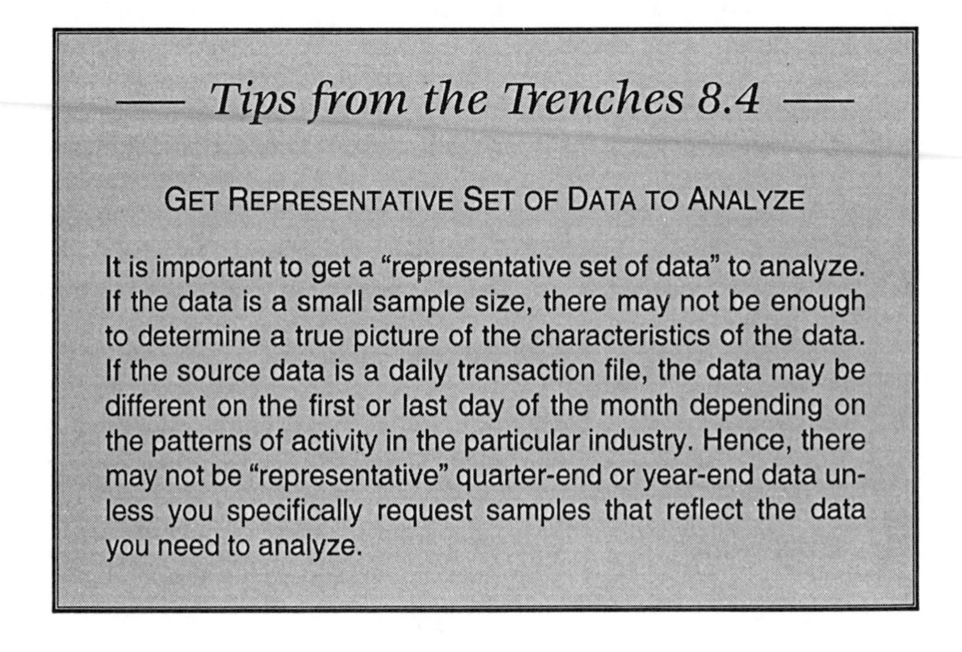

Tips from the Trenches 8.4

GET REPRESENTATIVE SET OF DATA TO ANALYZE

It is important to get a "representative set of data" to analyze. If the data is a small sample size, there may not be enough to determine a true picture of the characteristics of the data. If the source data is a daily transaction file, the data may be different on the first or last day of the month depending on the patterns of activity in the particular industry. Hence, there may not be "representative" quarter-end or year-end data unless you specifically request samples that reflect the data you need to analyze.

Determine the Primary Keys Once domain analysis is performed, each file will have certain unique fields that have distinct values which could be considered candidates for the primary key or identifier of the file information. In the domain analysis process it should be determined whether the documented primary key is, in fact, unique. If it is not, then it must be determined if there is an error in the sample data or if there is an additional field that needs to be concatenated with that primary key to make it unique (often a date field serves this purpose and sometimes a record type or system-generated control field is used to establish uniqueness). This is why the data analyst should carefully analyze the data for business content and logical identifiers instead of proliferating system data into the warehouse because it was used by the source system to enforce uniqueness.

Candidate keys are all of the potential ways to uniquely identify a record. For the purpose of converting data into a data warehouse, most of the time it is preferable to use a field that carries actual business-relevant information into the warehouse instead of system-generated identifiers. System-generated identifiers proliferated in operational systems, especially On Line Analytical Processing (OLTP) systems, to promote speed of processing and data management, especially with a lot of update and insert activity. The architecture of the data warehouse is different from typical OLTP systems because it is designed primarily for bulk loading and unloading data and read-only access which generally precludes the necessity for a system-generated key. Another reason to avoid system-generated keys is that often the access paths required for many data warehouse queries can be supplied by simply hitting the index because the key information is the only business content required. This speeds up rather than slows down a query because the Database Management System (DBMS) doesn't have to go through the second lookup for the actual data as would be needed if the key were system-generated.

An exception to this occurs when the key is representative of a field that is identified as a synonym or analog to other identifiers of source files from different systems. It is likely that it is targeted to be integrated with these files in the warehouse and may need to be treated differently than a typical primary key. Even if these keys are clearly synonyms in a business context, because of the different formats from the different source systems, it may be important to create a single system-generated warehouse key as an identifier to cross-reference all the source file identifiers. This may end up adding an extra join or "lookup" but promotes the integration of data from multiple systems to provide a cross-organizational view of information.

Another significant analysis task when determining the primary keys is discovering whether there are additional logical groupings of data embedded in a logical record. This is known as second normal form. If we go back to our customer example, we could take the address information and recognize that there are several attributes in the logical record devoted to describing address information. A customer can have many addresses associated with their file. We may want to break out address information into a separate record and will then have to identify a primary key that will uniquely identify that address as belonging to a particular customer and perhaps another address type field that describes the usage of that address (such as "home," "mailing," "office"). Understanding additional groupings of data embedded in a logical record is consequential for analyzing the source data to determine

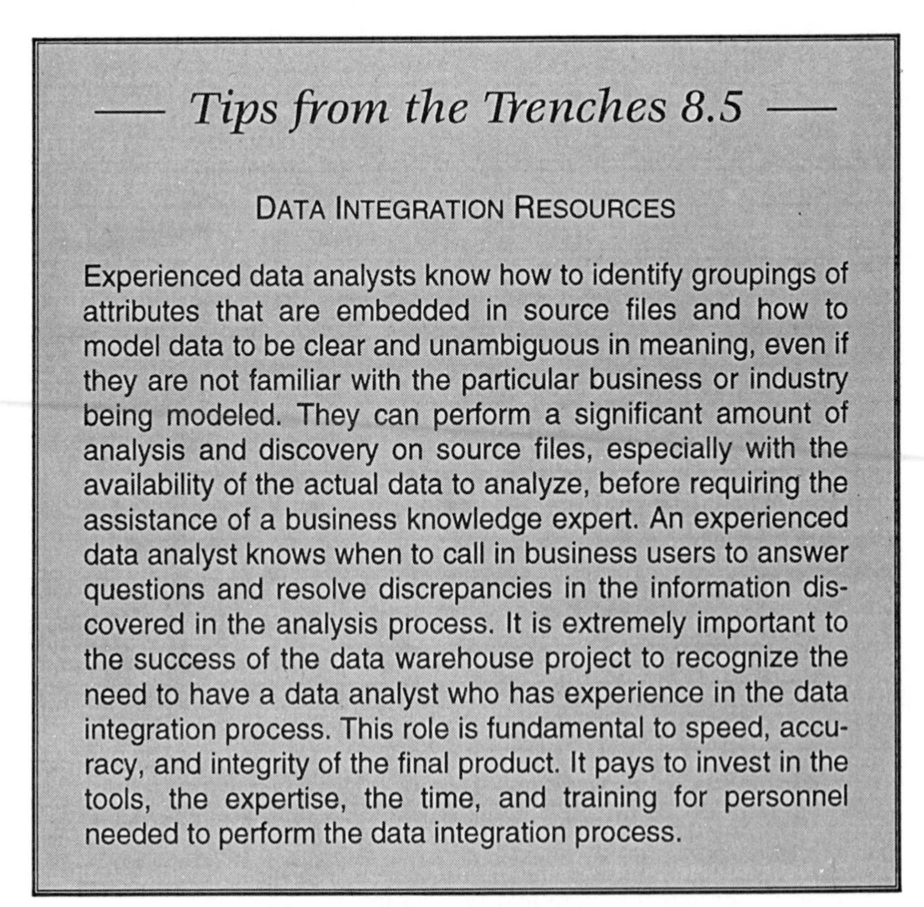

— *Tips from the Trenches 8.5* —

Data Integration Resources

Experienced data analysts know how to identify groupings of attributes that are embedded in source files and how to model data to be clear and unambiguous in meaning, even if they are not familiar with the particular business or industry being modeled. They can perform a significant amount of analysis and discovery on source files, especially with the availability of the actual data to analyze, before requiring the assistance of a business knowledge expert. An experienced data analyst knows when to call in business users to answer questions and resolve discrepancies in the information discovered in the analysis process. It is extremely important to the success of the data warehouse project to recognize the need to have a data analyst who has experience in the data integration process. This role is fundamental to speed, accuracy, and integrity of the final product. It pays to invest in the tools, the expertise, the time, and training for personnel needed to perform the data integration process.

the target data warehouse model or writing the conversion specifications for populating an existing model.

If the target model has address information separate from the customer information then the specifications must be very clear to convert the correct address from the source to the data warehouse data structure. In the example presented in Figure 8-4, the specifications must be written so it is clear that, when loading the data from the source file, the appropriate source address is loaded into the target table with the corresponding address type. The program must be written to read the Home Address and populate the Customer ID associated with it, and then populate the Address Type with the value representing "home" before moving each field into the data warehouse table. The program will have to process the source record for every address type populated, in this case three times to populate home, mailing, and office address information.

Source Customer File	Data Warehouse Customer Address Table
Customer ID	Customer ID
Customer Name	Address Type
Customer Home Street Address	Street Address
Customer Home City	City
Customer Home State	State
Customer Home Country	Country
Customer Home Postal Code	Postal Code
Customer Mailing Street Address	
Customer Mailing City	
Customer Mailing State	
Customer Mailing Country	
Customer Mailing Postal Code	
Customer Office Street Address	
Customer Office City	
Customer Office State	
Customer Office Country	
Customer Office Postal Code	

FIGURE 8–4 Second normal form source mapped to new target data structure.

Determine Foreign Keys Once we have analyzed the individual fields for the domain information and determined the logical records and primary keys, we are ready to identify the interrelationships between logical files. Ideally each attribute within a set of logical records from a single source is represented only once—in the logical record with other attributes of like business meaning. For example, we would not expect "Customer Home State" to be repeated in more than one logical record from a single source system. The exception to this is if the attribute is a "foreign key." As mentioned earlier, one of the tasks in identifying overlapping data is determining if attributes in different records are synonyms. The domain analysis performed on each attribute earlier in the process can greatly assist us in determining if there are synonyms (data elements that have common business meaning even though the names are different) between attributes in different files by presenting a subset of attributes that have overlapping domain values.

The process of discovering synonyms across files is critical to the integration process because it establishes the connections between logical records. In our example at the beginning of this section, we discussed a customer record that may have a separate set of job history following it. The Customer ID in the Customer record and the Customer ID in the Job History record would be synonyms and associating them demonstrates the logical connection between these two records. The Customer ID in the Job History record is called a foreign key because it represents the same field as the Primary Key in the Customer record and it is the way relational databases "point" to the related information. This is called "referencing by value." The value for Customer ID in the Customer record matches the value for Customer ID in the Job History record, so we know the job history attributes describe the customer identified by that Customer ID. The processing that accesses data described in this matter is referred to as a "join." It is critical to identify the synonyms across files to correctly represent the related data so that the data model can be designed accurately and conversion specifications can be written to populate the warehouse to reflect the logical relationships of the source data. Foreign keys are the most common synonyms found in the analysis process.

An important consideration when identifying foreign keys is clearly understanding the business meaning of the overlapping domain information. For example, social security number in the Customer record is likely to refer to the customer's social security number. There may be another logical record from the same source system that has a social security number which we are tempted to identify as a synonym because we think it is an alternative way the source system used to identify the customer. This could be the case, and it is certainly a logical assumption; however, it may also represent a different business fact, such as the social security number of the customer's beneficiary or next of kin. This would be an example of uncovering homonyms, two attributes with the same name that represent different business facts.

This phase of analysis is extremely critical because it is typically the point when overlapping data within a single source system is identified. The business rules implicit in the data relationships are uncovered through a thorough understanding of the true business meaning of the data. Homonyms, data with the same name that mean different things, such as our social security number example, and analogs are usually uncovered at this phase if they haven't been identified earlier. This phase of the analysis process is when the data analyst will need to draw assistance liberally from the business knowledge experts.

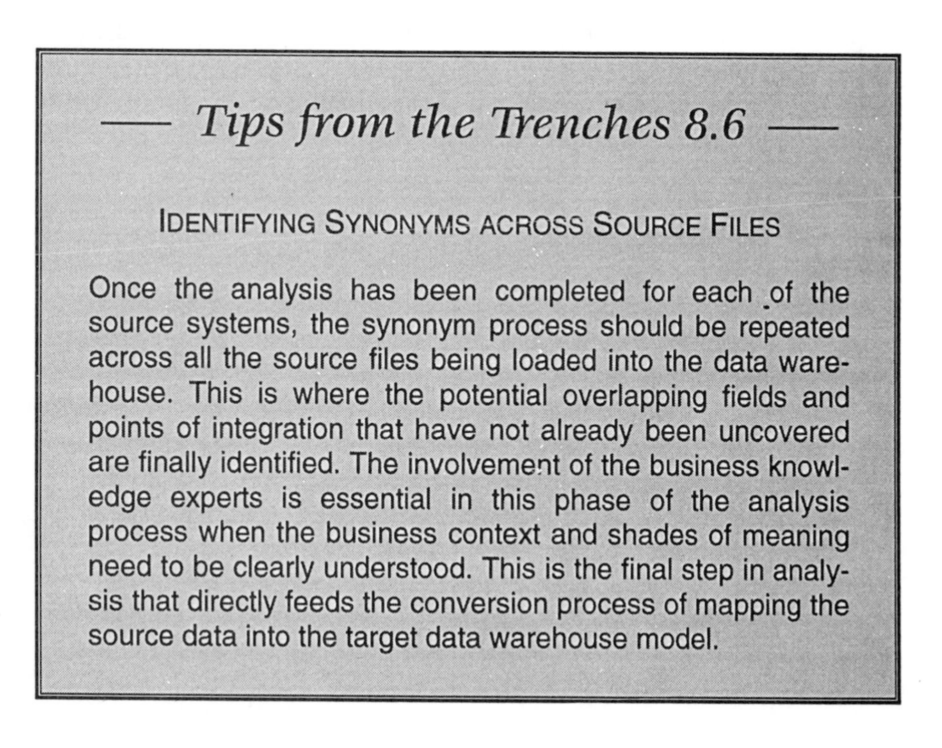

— *Tips from the Trenches 8.6* —

IDENTIFYING SYNONYMS ACROSS SOURCE FILES

Once the analysis has been completed for each of the source systems, the synonym process should be repeated across all the source files being loaded into the data warehouse. This is where the potential overlapping fields and points of integration that have not already been uncovered are finally identified. The involvement of the business knowledge experts is essential in this phase of the analysis process when the business context and shades of meaning need to be clearly understood. This is the final step in analysis that directly feeds the conversion process of mapping the source data into the target data warehouse model.

ADDITIONAL DATA ANALYSIS NEEDED FOR DATA CONSOLIDATION

The following additional data analysis is needed for data consolidation:

- Subject Area Analysis
- Synonyms, Homonyms, and Analogs
- Analyzing Data to Integrate It into an Existing Data Warehouse.
- Understanding Business Rules and Nuances of Meaning
- Data-Driven Analysis

Subject Area Analysis

Subject areas represent collections of data elements and files which are related to each other and, by definition, to a certain topic or area of concern within the organization. The most common subject areas chosen for data integration are customer, account, transaction or event, product, organizational unit, person, and location. These subject areas are typically the underpinnings of a data warehouse and most of the data captured and stored describes or supports these primary areas. Determining the correct subject areas for a data warehouse is the art of identifying the over-

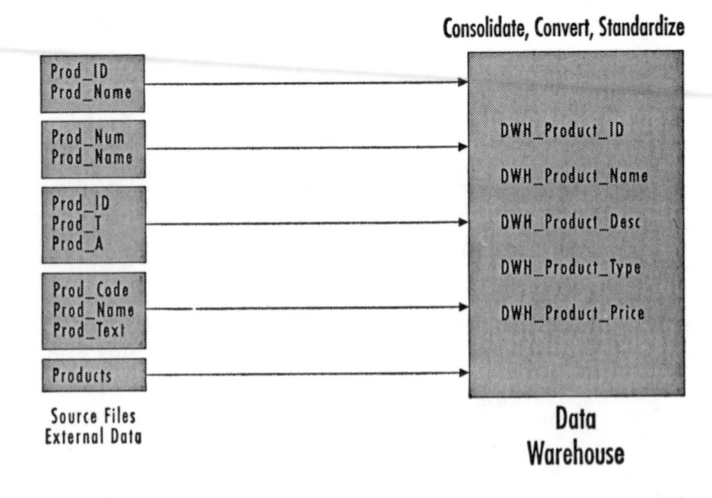

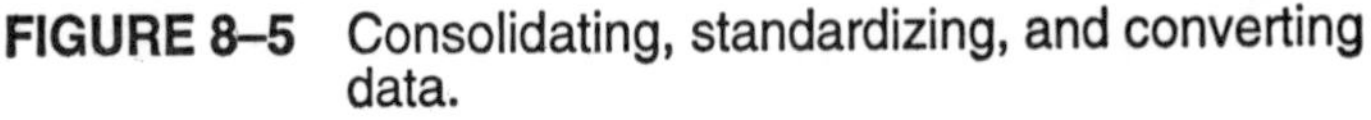

FIGURE 8–5 Consolidating, standardizing, and converting data.

lapping areas of data within the source files selected to populate the data warehouse. Usually there are specific attributes which often point to subject areas such as Customer ID, Account ID, Org Code, Product ID, and so on. During the data consolidation phase it is the job of the data modeler/analyst to discover the set of overlapping data in the source files that constitutes a subject area and determine how to render an integrated yet meaningful data structure of different subject areas of data to support the business objective of the data warehouse.

Synonyms, Homonyms, and Analogs

Data consolidation involves the analysis of the interrelationships between the source files that have been selected to provide the source of data to the warehouse. The data modeler/analyst is challenged to identify the overlapping data from the various source files by determining the data elements that have common business meaning even though the names are different (synonyms). For example, in one file a data element that identifies a product may be called "PROD-NUM"; in another file the data element that identifies a product might be called "Product-ID." As they represent the same business fact in each file they are synoynyms.

Additionally, it is just as important to distinguish the data elements across different sources that may have the same name but represent different business facts (homonyms). For example, in one file there is a data element called "PROD-CODE" and in another file the exact same name "PROD-CODE" occurs. However, upon careful analysis, the meaning of PROD-CODE in the first file represents a unique numeric identifier for a specific product while "PROD-CODE" in the second file represents a value that describes a type of product which would not be unique. These are homonyms.

The real challenge is identifying the data elements in the sources that have "equivalent" values (analogs). Identifying and resolving the "equivalent" meanings between data elements (analogs) for the purpose of integration do not imply that the data elements are incorrect in the context of their original operational systems. It is important to distinguish this critical point from data scrubbing which is performed when there are errors discovered in the source data. Analogous data often appears to be a synonym but has shades of differences in the meanings of the overlapping data elements which are significant to the business understanding of the data. If these differences and similarities are not identified and understood in the modeling and analysis process, the source data will not be integrated correctly. It cannot be emphasized enough that this is where the lion's share of effort is spent in understanding how to design the data warehouse to achieve data integration.

For example, in one file there is a data element called "product-type" which describes the various groupings of products, such as, "checking and savings," "homeowner loans," "retirement fund management." Another file has a similar data element called "PROD-TYPE" that has values such as "business checking," "small business loan," "secured credit card savings," and the like. Upon first inspection these data elements may seem like synonyms. However, upon further analysis it is determined that the first data element "product-type" represents groupings of services while the data element from the other source file, "PROD-TYPE," represents specific product offerings. The information represented by these two data elements has some overlapping values and the business meaning is related, but they do not represent the exact same business fact so cannot be considered synonyms. Finding, understanding, and consolidating these subtle differences in meaning is what makes analyzing analogs both critical and time-consuming.

The failure to understand the importance of correctly identifying synonyms, homonyms, and especially analogs in the source files will result in one or two unfortunate scenarios. If we fail to identify these overlapping data elements, we end up populating a warehouse with disparate data that fail to provide the true integration points across files. This will result in the propagation of the existing vertical view of the data, adding little additional value to the warehouse. If we fail to distinguish the differences between synonyms, homonyms, and analogs, we end up creating even more confusion by integrating data which is actually different, although similar in meaning, without resolving the differences in the conversion process. This second scenario is more detrimental because it results in a falsely cohesive view of the data which delivers the wrong information. Instead of adding value by building a data warehouse, what actually happens is the reverse. The data warehousing effort has succeeded in rendering the source data less meaningful than it was in its original state.

An integrated data warehouse model is designed to support the common data elements of the source files. Those shared data elements are converted into a neutral format to derive "horizontal" business value by making data available to queries that cross organizational and system boundaries. The rest of the data is populated into the model at the level of depth and breadth that is necessary to support the queries that will provide the business users with the information they require to make their business decisions.

ANALYZING DATA TO INTEGRATE IT INTO AN EXISTING DATA WAREHOUSE

Understanding the source system data and the integration points between the source files selected to populate the warehouse is the objective of the analysis process whether we are modeling a warehouse for the first time or populating data to an existing warehouse on an ongoing basis. However, once there is a "fixed target," an existing data warehouse that has already been populated with data, the challenge is inte-

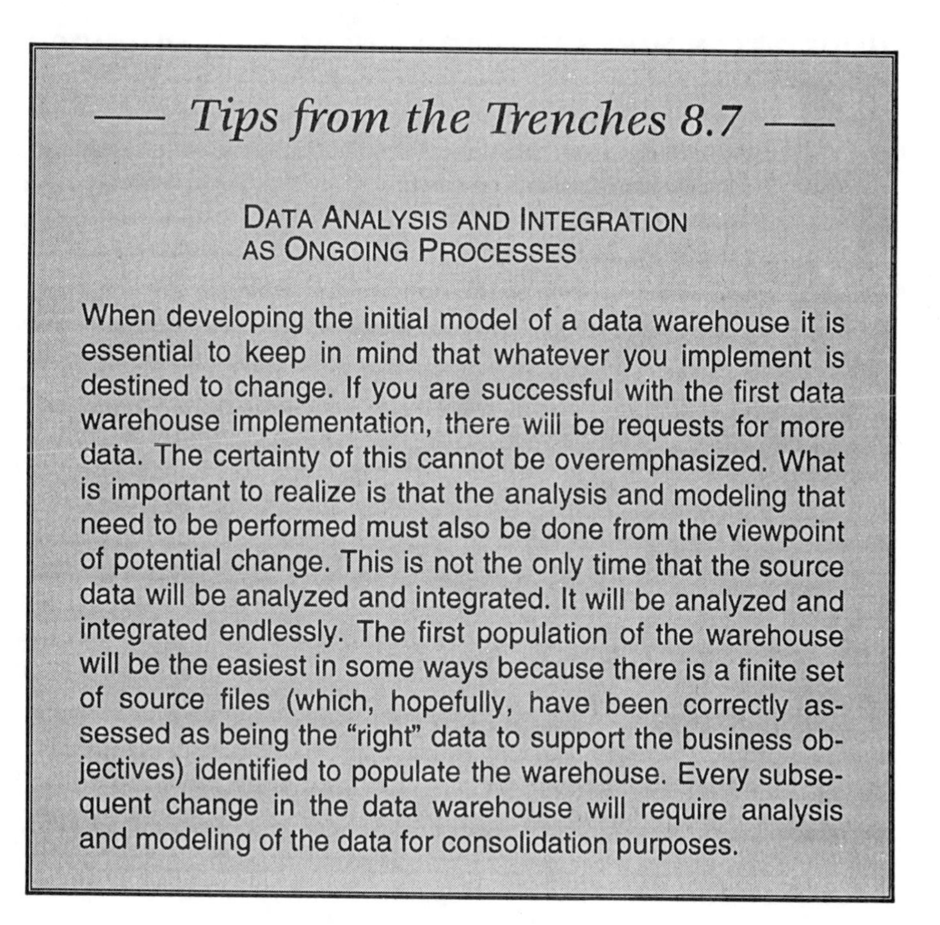

— Tips from the Trenches 8.7 —

DATA ANALYSIS AND INTEGRATION AS ONGOING PROCESSES

When developing the initial model of a data warehouse it is essential to keep in mind that whatever you implement is destined to change. If you are successful with the first data warehouse implementation, there will be requests for more data. The certainty of this cannot be overemphasized. What is important to realize is that the analysis and modeling that need to be performed must also be done from the viewpoint of potential change. This is not the only time that the source data will be analyzed and integrated. It will be analyzed and integrated endlessly. The first population of the warehouse will be the easiest in some ways because there is a finite set of source files (which, hopefully, have been correctly assessed as being the "right" data to support the business objectives) identified to populate the warehouse. Every subsequent change in the data warehouse will require analysis and modeling of the data for consolidation purposes.

grating the new source files with the existing database design. It is the job of data modelers and analysts to make exacting distinctions between the shades of meaning in data elements when analyzing data to be integrated into an existing warehouse. The requirements for adding the new source files may diverge from the original objective of the data warehouse and the expectations to be gained from the addition of the new data may be a "point of view" that is divergent from the initial design of the warehouse. If this is true, it is extremely important to manage the expectations of the business users requesting the new data regarding the usability of the data for their purposes. However, it is to everyone's advantage to pay attention to these distinctions because the quality and veracity of the data and ultimately the usability and success of the data warehouse will depend on it.

UNDERSTANDING BUSINESS RULES AND NUANCES OF MEANING

By uncovering the underlying business rules inherent in the usage of the data in the source systems, we are able to identify overlapping data between the different source files. The usage of the data in the operational system is what gives the data its business meaning. The patterns of data that exist in the operating systems are the footprints of the business rules that govern its usage. Understanding the business rules will help the analyst identify common subject areas, correctly distinguish between synonyms, homonyms, and analogs, as well as identify the primary and alternate keys existing in the data. The way an analyst goes about discovering the meaning of the data is dependent on the structure and culture of the organization and the tools and time frame available to perform the analysis. Another factor that will contribute to the approach of the data analysis is if the data model for the warehouse has been built or not. If the data analysis process is expected to result in a data model to be used for building the data warehouse, the approach is different than if the analysis process is to fit a source file into an existing data warehouse.

To get an understanding of business rules and nuances of meaning, let's look at a familiar example found in the banking industry. The data warehouse may have the original point of view of collecting all the information about account activity or transactions across all departments in the bank to analyze the data for patterns and trends in the usage of products and services. This is a product or sales-driven point of view. (Incidentally, this is probably the most common business objective for building data warehouses across all industries and market segments.) Because this data warehouse successfully fulfilled the need to understand the product and sales activity, the marketing organization now wants to take the next step and populate the warehouse with customer information so they can discover the product penetration specific to customer demographics enabling them to target specific customer segments for new products and services.

This prompts the marketing organization to initiate a request to add new sources to the warehouse with customer information that will integrate with the existing data in the warehouse describing account, product, and transaction history. The marketing organization is actually requesting a new "point of view" of the data in the warehouse. Now it is the job of the data analyst to understand if the source files identified to be integrated into the data warehouse can successfully provide the marketing organization with this new "point of view" that they want.

Unfortunately for the marketing organization, the majority of banks and financial institutions do not have sufficient information available to specifically identify a customer. Financial institutions are account-driven and an account can have many account names associated with it. The usage of the account may vary based on the needs of the person(s) who opened it or are named on it. If, out of frustration in being unable to determine a true customer, the data analyst decides the business rule will be "the first name on the account will be considered to be the primary user of the account and we will identify that person as the customer." However, there is no way to really know who the primary user of the account is even if you are able to collect and analyze all the account activity. This information is not available in the bank's account-driven source systems. We could all probably stop to think of a bank account scenario of our own that would not conform to this business rule if we consider only our checking, savings, credit card, car loan, mortgage, and investment accounts.

If the data is populated into the warehouse using this business rule ("the first name on the account will be considered to be the primary user of the account and we will identify that person as the customer"), the marketing organization would get a false sense of confidence in the information they gathered from the warehouse unless they were clearly informed of the decision to use this business rule and understood the implications. You may be thinking that a different business rule could be adopted to give a more accurate view of customer such as "every name on the account will be considered a customer," but this strategy would also be a false representation of information regarding account activity. Again consider your own accounts as an example. You will realize that there are many cases where someone is named on an account of yours or you are named on someone else's account and have never had any direct activity associated with that account. (Trustees, guarantors, fiduciaries, etc. come to mind instantly.)

If the marketing organization is aware of, or, even better, selects the business rule to be used to populate the warehouse with customer data, it is critical for the data analyst to be sure they are aware of the difference in the shades of meaning between a customer and someone who is named on an account. This is a good example of an analog (data which has equivalent meaning). As another example, imagine a situation where the automobile loan department instituted a business process that associated a customer identifier, separate from an account number, for every person who opens an account for a car loan which clearly identified that customer as the person buying or making the payments on the car loan as opposed to a person named on the account who was a guarantor or a lien holder. When the analyst reviews the data from the automobile loan department system and compares the data with the customer information that comes from credit cards, demand deposit (checking and savings) accounts, and other departments in the banks, they will have to understand how to integrate the customer ID with customer information from the other areas.

Since there is an account ID in every source file that can be clearly identified as synonyms they cannot associate customer ID with account ID—so now what? The analogous or equivalent data elements are customer ID and a combination of account ID and account holder name or account ID and first account holder name. The analogous data elements represent approximately the same business fact, but differences in the shades of meaning between the two are significant. A business decision must be made by the business sponsor who understands the differences in meaning between the analogous data elements and grasps the implications of integrating customer ID with the account ID and account holder name and agrees to populate the data warehouse with these data elements integrated as customer ID.

The thoroughness of the analysis performed to integrate the data and document the decisions made will have a direct effect on the evolution of the data warehouse. The failure to do this will eventually result in "murky" data and the quality and usability of the data warehouse will degrade with every new source file that is added. Conversely, if the analysis and integration of data is scrupulously performed and documented, the data warehouse will evolve into a repository of valuable corporate information. The judicious care in not only integrating data, but also integrating the various "points of view" that will invariably be imposed on the data warehouse will provide a synergistic source of corporate knowledge and an invaluable tool for decision making.

Data-Driven Analysis. Because we haven't been particularly consistent in our proliferation of data structures to support our operational systems over the years, we are required to take particular care in analyzing the business rules embedded in the data which are the footprints of the processing that occurs. This is the delicate art of alchemy that is the hallmark of experienced data analysts. To rely solely on source system documentation (metadata) is folly. Even if documentation was written when a system was first built, it is rarely kept up to date as changes are made.

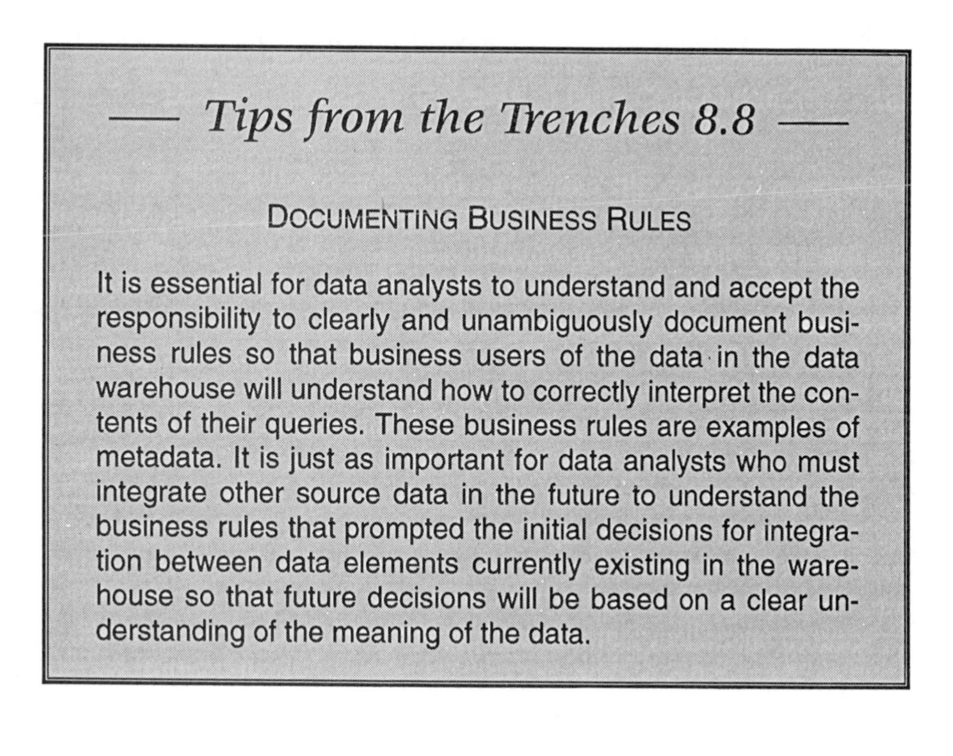

— *Tips from the Trenches 8.8* —

Documenting Business Rules

It is essential for data analysts to understand and accept the responsibility to clearly and unambiguously document business rules so that business users of the data in the data warehouse will understand how to correctly interpret the contents of their queries. These business rules are examples of metadata. It is just as important for data analysts who must integrate other source data in the future to understand the business rules that prompted the initial decisions for integration between data elements currently existing in the warehouse so that future decisions will be based on a clear understanding of the meaning of the data.

Anyone who programs or who has supported production applications knows how often bug fixes get documented. When a system goes down in the middle of the night and the user is screaming because the batch job that records and resolves all account activity for the previous day is halted, any shortcut that can be taken to simply get it up and running again is justified. It is a rare occurrence that the bleary-eyed programmer who received a call in the wee hours requiring her or him to get out of a warm bed will be inspired (or expected and encouraged) to stay and document the exact actions taken and changes made after successfully fixing the system. Even if they were conscientious enough to document thoroughly what occurred and the actions taken, it is likely that it remained in a log somewhere and never found its way into the system documentation handed out upon request. This is why the importance of maintaining metadata in the data warehouse environment is emphasized. It would be impossible to keep up with the requests for changes and additions to the data warehouse without accurate, up-to-date metadata.

Given the reality of operational emergencies that affect most systems, it is prudent to use the actual data in addition to the documentation provided about the data as a basis for analysis. This is called data-driven analysis. The biggest problem with data-driven analysis is that, without tools, it is really difficult to do a thorough job because there is so much data. How can we analyze all of that data to discover if there are anomalies (that surely exist) which contradict the documentation? Once we begin to realize the quantity of metadata we generate by performing a thorough, systematic analysis of actual data, we will probably use our analysis skills to take a different approach. This is when we will start to figure out how to bribe the source systems' developers to find time to provide detailed explanations. Otherwise, we end up burying our heads in the system documentation and using the "cross your fingers" technique when it comes time to load the data warehouse.

Expect the analysis phase of the data integration process to be the longest. It always is. The reason is that there are very few tools available to assist data analysts in the formidable task of pawing through data and uncovering the undocumented business rules embedded in the source files. Additionally, there are very few people with the skill set, expertise, patience, and sheer fortitude required to pursue subtle shades of meaning between attributes, understand the "points of view" implicit in the structure of the data, and communicate clearly the business implications of proliferating errors and assumptions into a new database environment.

DATA CONVERSION

Once the new, integrated data model has been designed, the source data must now be converted to populate the new target data structures. The actions that must be performed on each data element to populate the new data model is called data conversion. This is performed by data analysts for every field of every source file that populates the warehouse. The data conversion instructions are the program specifications used to write the conversion programs that load the data into the data warehouse.

Data conversion focuses on the content of the data by specifying how to alter the source data to fit into the integrated target data structure. The steps of the data conversion process are

- Map source file attributes to the data warehouse physical data structure
- Map source attribute allowable values to target value
- Specify default values
- Write conversion specifications

Producing conversion specifications involves mapping the source attributes, values, and default values to the data warehouse model. The instructions for mapping fields from source files to the target data warehouse are based on the understanding gained as a result of the analysis done in the consolidation phase. At this point the data analyst writes the conversion specifications and programmers write the programs to process the source data and load the data warehouse database. If a thorough job is done in the analysis phase, this should go quickly and smoothly. However, if the analysts and programmers get bogged down with lots of questions and clarifications and rework on the conversion specifications and programs, the project manager will have to determine the reason for it. It may be that there was insufficient time or a lack of experienced data analysts in the analysis phase.

Map Source File Attributes to the Data Warehouse Physical Data Structure. It is rare to find an organization that has consistently represented the same business fact across all of their operational systems. Many companies have as many as 40 different customer files, different product hierarchies, and organizational hierarchies within their organizations depending on which department you are talking to or which system you are sourcing from. These are some of the reasons data must undergo a conversion process to fit into the target integrated data structure.

Once all the source fields are analyzed and understood, they are then mapped against the target data warehouse model. In some cases this will be a straightforward move from one field to another. Often, however, it will require more complex processing to accurately convert the source data to fit into the warehouse structure because of the significant difference in the data structures, as described in Figure 8-4 example of customer addresses. The source to target maps represent newly created metadata about the information in the warehouse which describe the specific business rules being implemented in the data warehouse. These maps are extremely valuable and must be maintained in a metadata repository for access by future analysts and developers as well as business users of the warehouse to understand the nature of the information as it was consolidated and converted from the source system or external file into the data warehouse.

Map Source Attribute Allowable Values to Target Value. At the same time the attributes are being mapped to the target warehouse model, those attributes with a finite set of allowable values must be specifically identified so that the individual source file values can be correctly mapped to the target warehouse value. Usually this will generate a cross-reference table which is used to process the data as it is loaded into the warehouse.

Specify Default Values. Part of the conversion specification, in addition to the attribute and allowed value mappings, is documenting the rules for handling default values. During the domain analysis step in the analysis phase, the default values for the source file data were uncovered. This information is used to explicitly specify how to handle blanks, zeros, or values not available or not known as they are processed in the source files and translate them to the equivalent default values which have been defined and standardized for the data warehouse.

Write Conversion Specifications. Conversion specifications are the deliverable of the data conversion phase of the data integration process. The rules for populating the data warehouse tables and columns from the source data attributes are the conversion specifications. As a significant and persistent deliverable of the data integration process, there should be a review and sign-off by the key members of the data warehouse development team and the business sponsor. Once they are signed off, they are passed to the programmers to write the programs and they should be maintained under a change management system.

DATA POPULATION

The following summarizes the remaining steps of the data integration process that must be followed to physically load the data into the data warehouse. These steps are universally well understood since they are typically done regardless of whether the target system is a data warehouse or any system that requires data migration. Experienced develop-

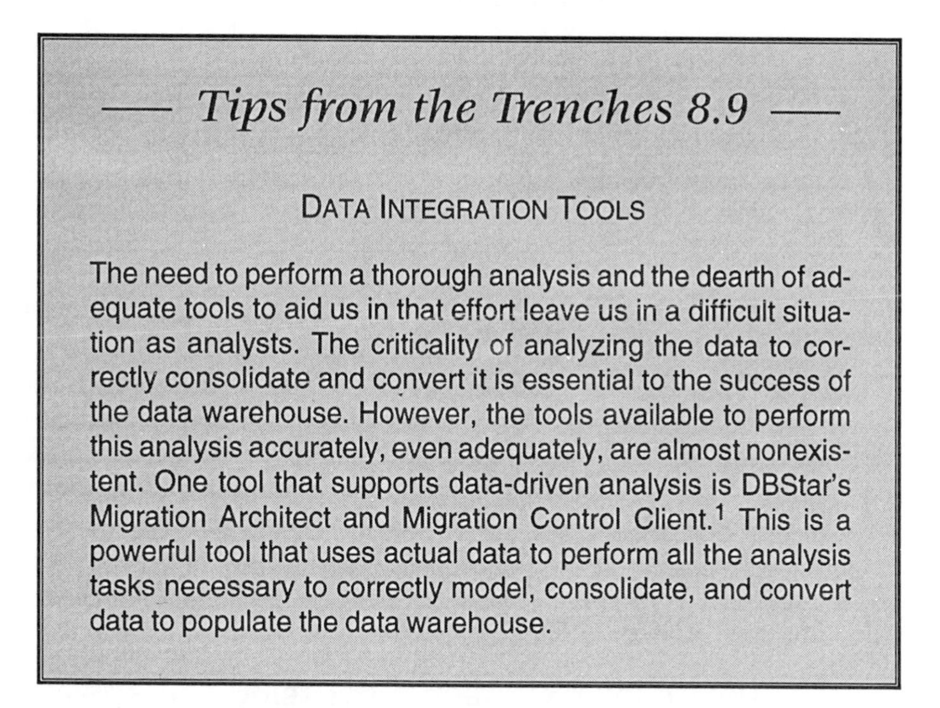

— *Tips from the Trenches 8.9* —

DATA INTEGRATION TOOLS

The need to perform a thorough analysis and the dearth of adequate tools to aid us in that effort leave us in a difficult situation as analysts. The criticality of analyzing the data to correctly consolidate and convert it is essential to the success of the data warehouse. However, the tools available to perform this analysis accurately, even adequately, are almost nonexistent. One tool that supports data-driven analysis is DBStar's Migration Architect and Migration Control Client.[1] This is a powerful tool that uses actual data to perform all the analysis tasks necessary to correctly model, consolidate, and convert data to populate the data warehouse.

[1]DBStar, Inc., 832 Folsom Street, 1000 San Francisco, CA 94107, (415) 512-0300.

ers are generally available to perform these tasks since they represent standard activities performed daily in every data center. The only difference in the data warehouse environment is that these steps are performed repeatedly for change requests to add or modify sources to populate the data warehouse.

Data population represents the steps that need to be performed to physically load the source data into the integrated target data structure. The deliverable is the conversion programs run to load the source data into the target database. These are the steps for data population:

- Write conversion programs
- Perform testing
- Determine exception processing
- Collect statistics
- Perform quality assurance
- Perform stress test

Write Conversion Programs. Once the conversion specifications have been signed off, developers are able to write the programs (or generate programs based on tool usage) that will load the target data warehouse. Once the programs have been completed, they should be signed off and put into change management under the same version number as the associated conversion specifications they were written against.

Perform Testing. Once unit testing is completed, it will be necessary to perform system testing by running the conversion programs to load data into the data warehouse test environment. Test plans and tools should be made available to review the data as it has been populated to determine if the business rules were written correctly. This is where you will discover the typical errors and exceptions to be wary of in the load process. The errors that occur may require the conversion specifications to be rewritten or may reveal "dirty data" that would require feedback to the person in the operational system area responsible for maintaining the source file.

Determine Exception Processing. When, for any reason, a record cannot be processed, the contents of the record will be written to an exception file with control information that describes the file it came from and the associated reason for the exception as well as a date and time stamp. This file should be reviewed as soon as possible and the information researched to determine the reason for the failure to process. This may result in modifications in the conversion specification or the conversion program or it could have been an error in constructing the file at the source. The reason must be identified, tracked, and resolved to support the ongoing delivery of data into and from the data warehouse.

The potential reasons for exceptions to occur should be analyzed to develop an exception strategy. This would specify when, under certain exception conditions, to write out an error message to an exception log and continue loading. In some cases, the exception error may affect a field which prohibits the continuation of the load process (i.e., if the field is used to perform a calculation or trying to load a null value in a primary key) which would require the program to abort the load and write out an exception report.

Collect Statistics. Generate log files to gather statistics regarding the load, for example, how many records processed, and start and end times.

Perform Quality Assurance. Use the conversion specifications as a basis to determine the accuracy of the data that has populated the data warehouse. Review the exception file and repeat the necessary steps in the data integration process as needed.

Perform Stress Tests. Test the data load processing against maximum volumes expected to be received to simulate the performance requirements and highlight any specific tuning that may need to be done to refine the data load strategy. Determine accurate processing estimates for the batch window. Write scripts to automate and schedule job pro-cessing.

Data Integration is the process of consolidating and converting data from disparate source systems, providing a consistent view of data across the organization. It is the cornerstone of any successful data warehouse implementation. Addressing the issues, problems, and challenges involved in the data integration process will substantially enhance and enrich the value of the content of the data warehouse.

SUMMARY

In this chapter you should have learned the following:

- Data and information are not interchangeable terms. The term "data" implies a collection of discrete elements such as a file. When data is merged, aggregated, derived, sorted, structured and displayed, it becomes "information."
- Data warehouses are developed to collect, integrate, and store data to perform actions with it that enrich and enhance the value of the data, and to transform the data into information.
- Data integration consists of distinct phases: determining the correct sources of data (data sourcing), consolidating the source files to an integrated target data warehouse data structure (data consolidation), converting the source data into the integrated target data warehouse data structure (data conversion) and loading the data into the data warehouse (data population).
- The data integration process can be thought of as the "pre-processing" of data that standardizes names and values, resolves discrepancies in representation of the data, merges together common values, resolves "equivalent" values of data from disparate sources that approximately represent the same business facts and establishes various access paths by identifying primary, alternate and nonunique keys.
- Data Sourcing focuses on the meaning of the data by identifying the source files that will support the business objectives and requirements of the target system. Taking a thorough inventory of available sources enables us to prioritize and scope the initial load of the data warehouse.
- Data consolidation is a data modeling activity. It is the process of analyzing and combining data from disparate sources or systems into a single, integrated data structure.
- Data consolidation is performed during the initial modeling of the data warehouse and every time a new source is added.
- The steps in the data consolidation process are:
  - Flatten out data into logical records
  - Perform domain analysis

  - Determine Primary Keys
  - Determine Foreign Keys
- The additional data analysis need for data consolidation includes:
  - Identifying overlapping data through subject area analysis and reconciling synonyms, homonyms, and analogs
  - Understanding business rules and nuances of meaning
  - Performing data-driven analysis
- Subject areas represent collections of data elements and files which are related to each other and, by definition, to a certain topic or area of concern within the organization. The most common subject areas chosen for data integration are customer, account, transaction or event, product, organization unit, person, and location
- The data modeler/analyst must identify the overlapping data from the various source files by determining the data elements that have common business meaning even though the names are different (synonyms).
- Additionally, it is just as important to distinguish the data elements across different sources that may have the same name but represent different business facts (homonyms).
- Analogs must also be reconciled. Analogous data often appears to be a synonym but has shades of differences in the meanings of the overlapping data elements which are significant to the business understanding of the data
- The failure to understand the importance of correctly identifying synonyms, homonyms and analogs in the source files will result in populating a warehouse with a disparate data that fails to provide the true integration points across files. The effect will be the propagation of the existing vertical view of the data, adding little additional value to the warehouse.
- Failing to distinguish the differences between synonyms, homonyms and analogs creates a falsely cohesive view of the data which delivers the wrong information.
- It is impossible to integrate data without having a "point of view." Data is created from the "point of view" of its usage in the source operational system.
- It is important to understand the "point of view" being taken by the data warehouse and realize that a successful data warehouse

implementation derives its "point of view" from the benefits the business sponsors and end users expect to realize by building it.

- Expect the analysis phase of the data integration process to be the longest; there are very few tools available to assist in the formidable task of analyzing data and uncovering the undocumented business rules embedded in the source files.
- Data conversion focuses on the content of the data by specifying how to alter the source data to fit into the integrated target data structure.
- The steps of the data conversion process are:
  - Map source file attributes to the data warehouse physical data structure
  - Map source attributes allowable values to target value
  - Specify Default Values
  - Write conversion specifications
- Data population represents the steps that need to be performed to physically load the source data into the integrated target data structure.
- The steps for Data Population are:
  - Write conversion programs
  - Test
  - Determin exception processing
  - Collect statistics
  - Perform quality assurance
  - Perform stress testing

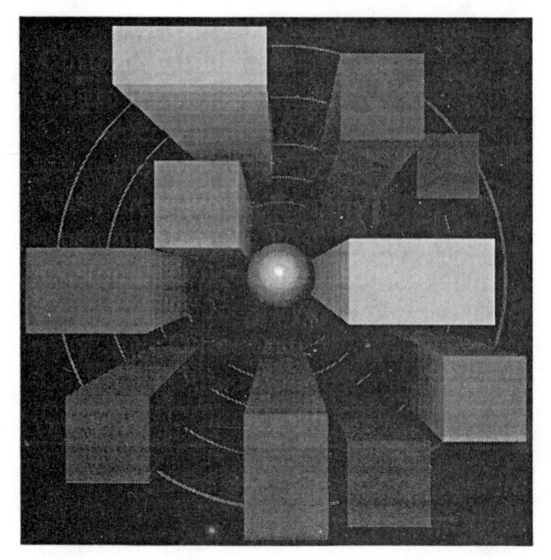

Chapter 9

DESIGNING THE DATABASE FOR A DATA WAREHOUSE

DECISION SUPPORT DATABASES

Decision support systems are designed to allow analysts to extract information quickly and easily. The data being analyzed are often historical in nature: daily, weekly, and yearly results. Examples of decision support systems include applications for analysis of sales revenue, marketing information, insurance claims, and customer profiling. These systems provide the information needed for business analysis and planning and are used to manage the business.

Decision support systems have the following characteristics:

- Understandable: Data structures must be readily understood by users, often requiring denormalization and prestored aggregations.
- Mostly static: Most changes to the database occur in a controlled manner when data is loaded according to a predefined schedule.
- Unpredictable and complex SQL queries: SQL query statements submitted against the database vary considerably and unpredictably from query to query. They can contain long, complex SQL SELECT statements that make comparisons or require sequential processing; these queries might reference many thousands or millions of records in a database.
- Advanced business measurements often require multiple SQL statements.
- Multiple/large/iterative result sets should be supported.
- Recoverable: Regular backups, or snapshots, of the static database ensure against data loss.

STAR SCHEMA DATABASE DESIGN

The goals of a decision support database are often achieved using a database design called a star schema. A star schema design is a simple structure with relatively few tables and well-defined join paths. This database design, in contrast to the normalized structure used for transaction-processing databases, provides fast query response time and a simple schema that is readily understood by the analysts and end users, even those who are not familiar with database structures.

The Benefits of Using a Star Schema

It is best to make the decision before beginning data modeling and physical database design to use a star schema or a more traditional relational database design. In both cases, you will optimize performance of the database by denormalizing and partitioning data. However, using a star schema provides some benefits that a regular relational structure cannot. The star schema is often used for data warehouse database design because it

- Creates a database design providing fast response times.
- Allows database optimizers to work with a more simple database design in order to yield better execution plans.
- Parallels, in the database design, how the end users customarily think of and use the data.
- Simplifies the understanding and navigation of metadata for both developers and end users.
- Broadens the choices of front-end data access tools, as some products require a star schema design.

Understanding Star Schema Design—Facts and Dimensions

A star schema contains two types of tables: fact tables and dimension tables. Fact tables, sometimes called major tables, contain the quantitative or factual data about a business—the information being queried. This information is often numerical measurements and can consist of many columns and millions of rows. Dimension tables, sometimes called minor tables, are smaller and hold descriptive data that reflects the dimensions of a business. SQL queries then use predefined and user-defined join paths between fact and dimension tables, with constraints on the data to return selected information.

For example, a fact table in a sales database might contain the sales revenue for the company products for each customer, in each geographic market, over a period of time. The dimension tables in this database define the customers, products, geographic markets, and time periods used in the fact table.

A well-thought out schema provides dimension tables that allow a user to browse a database to become familiar with the information in it.

The user can then write constraints for queries so that only the information that satisfies those constraints is returned from the database.

VARIETIES OF STAR SCHEMAS

How to Read the Diagrams

A series of figures is used throughout the rest of this chapter to illustrate specific schema concepts. The following conventions are used throughout:

- The items listed under each table heading indicate columns in the table.
- Primary and foreign key columns are boxed.
- The primary key columns in each table are shaded; however, foreign keys that are not part of the primary key are also shaded.
- Foreign key relationships are indicated by lines connecting tables. Notice that although the primary key value must be unique in each row of a dimension table, that value can occur multiple times in the foreign key in the fact table—a many-to-one relationship as represented by the crow's feet symbol on the connecting lines.
- Nonkey columns in a fact table are referred to as data columns; in a dimension table, as attributes.

The simplicity of the figures is intentional and used to explain concepts. An extensive and more realistic example will be diagrammed at the end of the chapter.

Simple Star Schemas

Each table must have a primary key, which is a column or group of columns (the key, the whole key, and nothing but the key) whose contents uniquely identify each row. In a simple star schema, the primary key for the fact table is composed of one or more foreign keys; a foreign key is a column in one table whose values are defined by the primary key in another table. When a database is created, the SQL state-

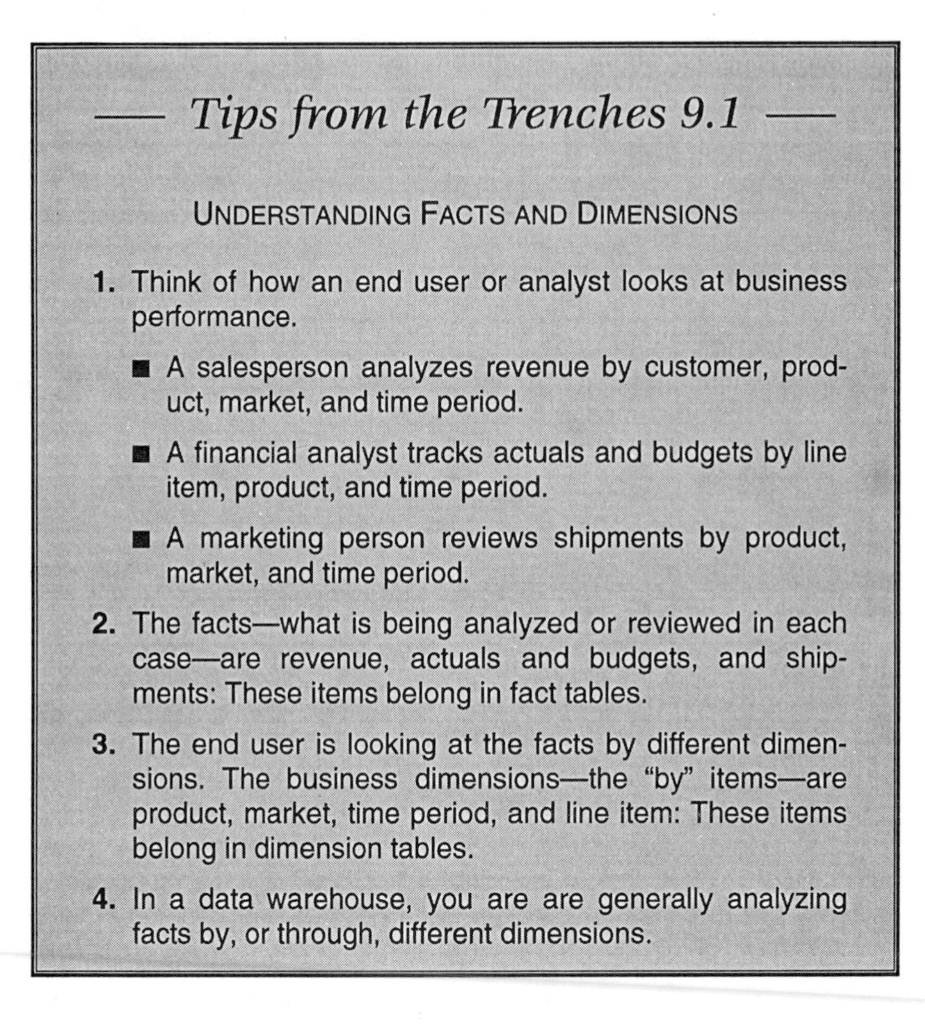

— *Tips from the Trenches 9.1* —

UNDERSTANDING FACTS AND DIMENSIONS

1. Think of how an end user or analyst looks at business performance.
   - A salesperson analyzes revenue by customer, product, market, and time period.
   - A financial analyst tracks actuals and budgets by line item, product, and time period.
   - A marketing person reviews shipments by product, market, and time period.
2. The facts—what is being analyzed or reviewed in each case—are revenue, actuals and budgets, and shipments: These items belong in fact tables.
3. The end user is looking at the facts by different dimensions. The business dimensions—the "by" items—are product, market, time period, and line item: These items belong in dimension tables.
4. In a data warehouse, you are are generally analyzing facts by, or through, different dimensions.

ments used to create the tables will designate the columns that are to form the primary and foreign keys.

Study Figure 9-1 which illustrates the relationship between fact and dimension tables. This figure has a single fact table and three dimension tables. The fact table has a primary key composed of three foreign keys: Key1, Key2, and Key3, each of which is the primary key of a dimension table.

Figure 9-2 illustrates a sales database designed as a simple star schema. In the fact table, the primary key is composed of three foreign keys Product_Id, Period_Id, and Market_Id. Each of these foreign keys references a primary key in one of the dimension tables.

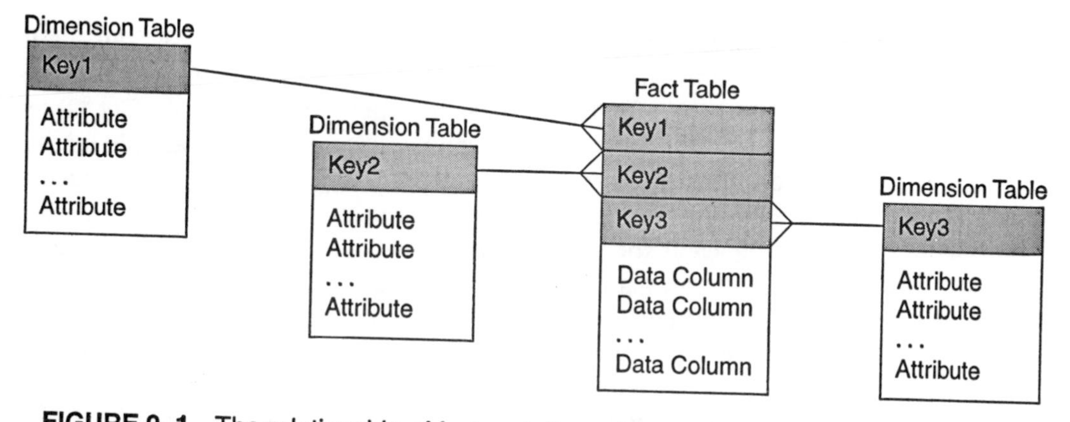

FIGURE 9–1 The relationship of fact and dimension tables in a simple star schema.

Notice the many-to-one relationships between the foreign keys in the fact table and the primary keys they reference in the dimension tables. For example, the product table defines the products. Each row in the product table represents a distinct product and has a unique product identifier. That product identifier can occur multiple times in the sales table representing sales of that particular product during each period and in each market.

Multiple Fact Tables

More sophisticated database implementations may require the use of multiple fact tables. In some cases, multiple fact tables exist because they contain unrelated facts or because periodicity of the load times dif-

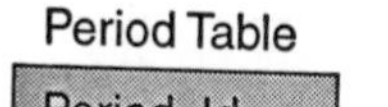
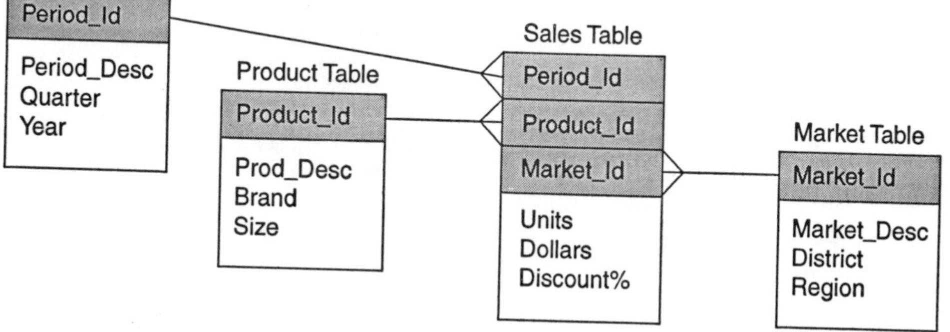

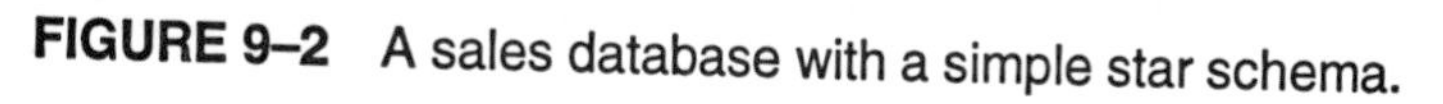
FIGURE 9–2 A sales database with a simple star schema.

fers. For example, internal shipment data is available weekly, but syndicated data is only provided every four weeks, so you may decide to create separate tables for these facts. In other cases, multiple fact tables exist because they improve performance. For example, multiple fact tables are often used to hold various levels of aggregated data, particularly when the amount of aggregation is large. An example of multiple fact tables being used for aggregation would be different tables for daily sales, monthly sales, and yearly sales. Creating different tables for different levels of aggregation is a common design technique for a data warehouse database so that any single request is against a table of reasonable size.

Figure 9-3 illustrates the sales database with an additional fact table for the previous year's sales.

Another use of a fact table is to define a many-to-many relationship between certain dimensions of the business; this type of table is typically known as an associative table. For example, in the sales database,

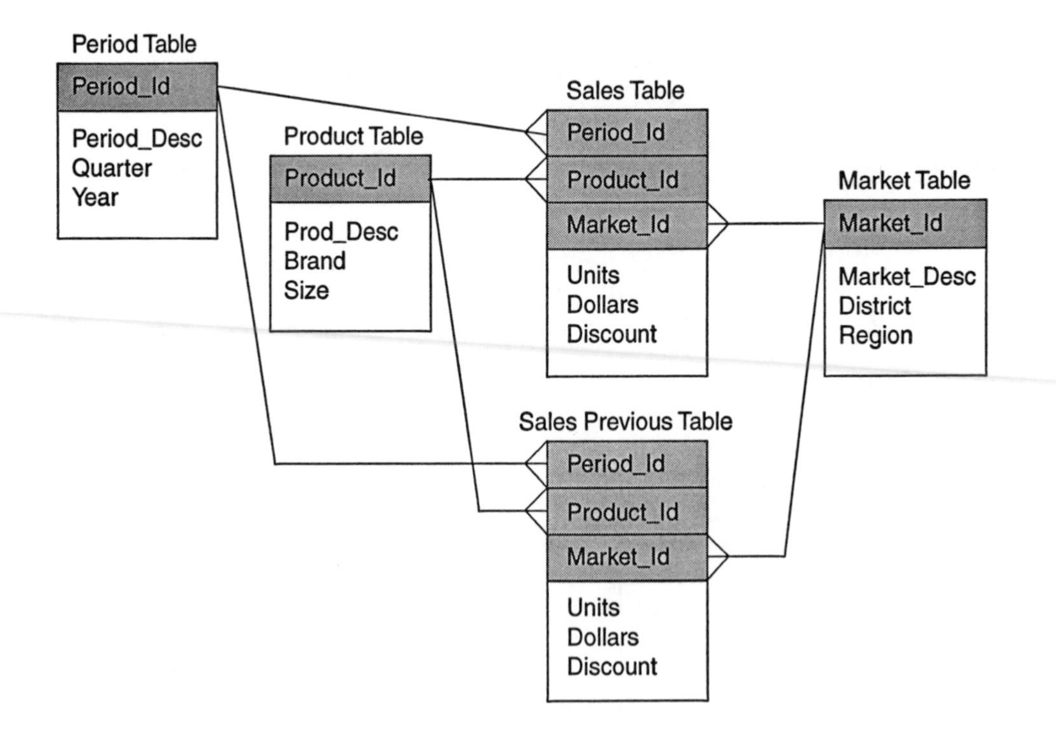

FIGURE 9–3 A sales database with an additional fact table for the previous year's sales.

each product belongs to one or more groups, and each group contains multiple products. A many-to-many relationship is modeled by establishing a fact table that defines the possible combinations of products and groups. To say it another way, a new fact table is being created to reconcile a many-to-many relationship between different dimensions as shown in Figure 9-4.

Outboard Tables

A dimension table can also contain a foreign key that references the primary key in another dimension table. The referenced dimension table is sometimes referred to as a secondary dimension table. Figure 9-5 includes two secondary dimension tables, District and Region, which define the ID codes used in the Market Table. Outboard tables may also be chained together to provide a hierarchy of dimension tables organized in a more normalized database design. A normalized design reduces the size of the dimension tables, but reduces the performance and usability advantages derived from a pure star schema design.

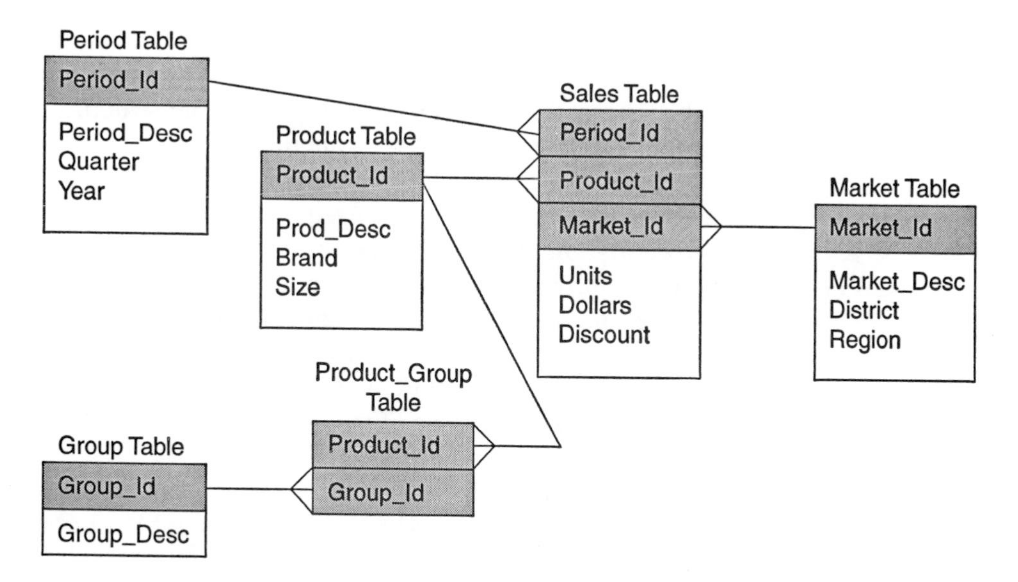

FIGURE 9–4 Another use of a fact table is as an associative table to resolve a many-to-many relationship between groups and products.

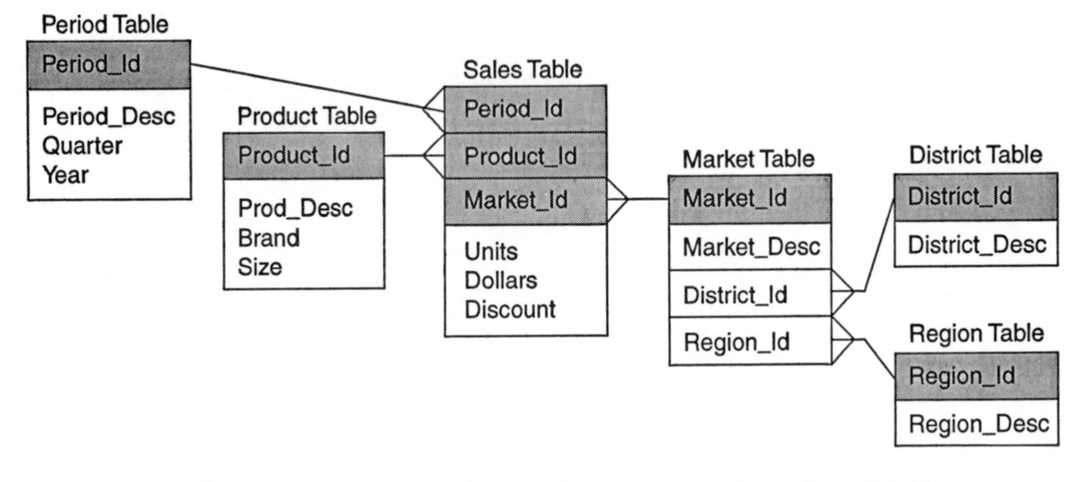

FIGURE 9–5 An example of secondary dimension (or outboard) tables.

Variations of a Star Schema

As data access tools mature, the distance between the end user and the physical database structures increases. (Data access tools are discussed in depth in Chapter 10). This provides for more flexibility in your physical design. One variation of a star structure is to store all dimensional information in third normal form, while keeping fact table structures the same. This type of star schema is sometimes referred to as a "snowflake" schema. While this sounds like a new concept, it is really a simple variation on the basic star schema that we have been talking about. The two common reasons for the interest in this variation are (1) the emergence of advanced decision support tools that can fully exploit this type of structure, and (2) that many Information Systems (IS) organizations feel more comfortable with a design in third normal form. Keep in mind that if your users will be working directly with the physical table structures, the total number of tables should be limited to minimize confusion.

Figure 9-6 shows the database structure from Figure 9-5 with completely denormalized dimension tables. In this example, there is a total of nine separate dimensional tables.

This is not an unreasonable structure. However, consider the ramifications of using a customer table with 200 different characteristics. It

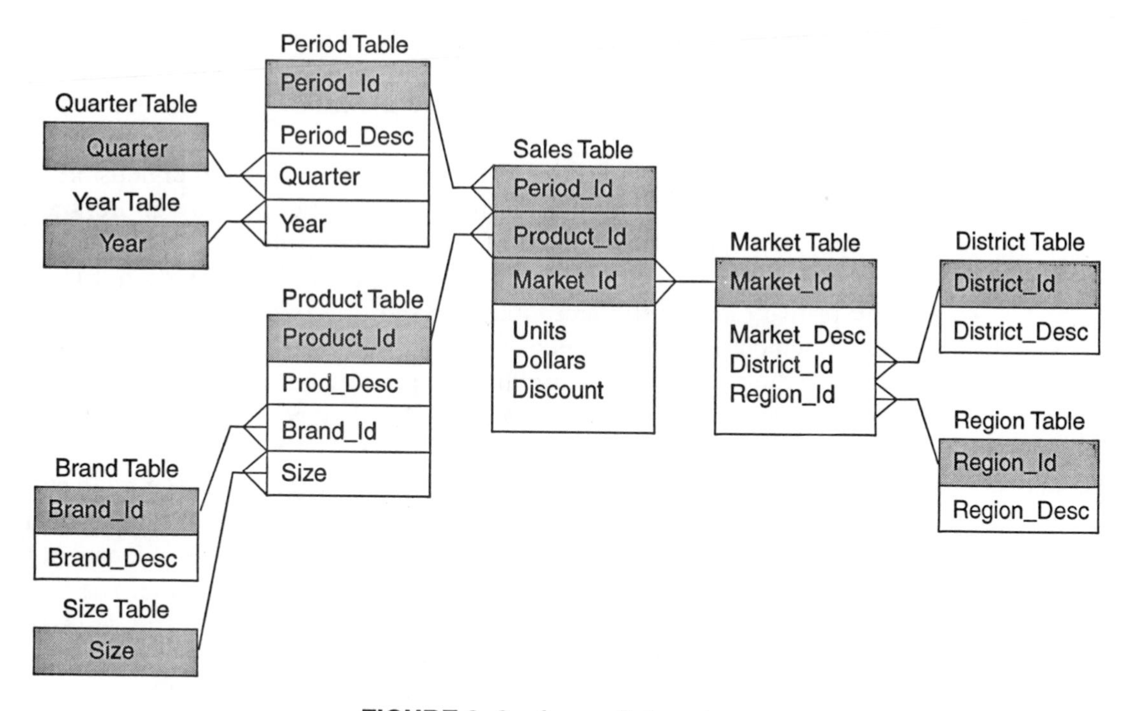

FIGURE 9–6 A snowflake schema.

is unreasonable to create 200 separate tables for the dimension to be in third normal form. While there are some proponents who advocate a pure approach from one end of the spectrum or the other, a more realistic situation is somewhere in between. A realistic example including denormalized dimensional tables is in Figure 9-17 at the end of this chapter.

Multistar Schemas

In a simple star schema, the primary key in the fact table is defined by the foreign key columns that relate to dimension tables in the database design. In some applications, however, the collection of foreign keys to the dimension tables might not provide a unique identifier for each row in the fact table. These applications require a multistar schema.

In a multistar schema, the fact table has both a set of foreign keys, which reference dimension tables, and a primary key, which is composed of one or more columns that provide a unique identifier for each row. The primary key and the foreign keys are not identical in a multi-star schema. This is what distinguishes a multistar schema from a single-star schema.

Figure 9-7 illustrates the relationship of the fact and dimension tables within a multi-star schema. In the fact table, the foreign keys are Fkey1, Fkey2, and Fkey3, each of which is the primary key in a dimension table. Unlike the simple star schema, these columns do not form the primary key in the fact table. Instead, the two columns Key1 and Key2, which do not reference any dimension tables, and Fkey1 are used to form the primary key. Note that the primary key can be composed of any combination of foreign key and other key columns in a multi-star schema.

Figure 9-8 illustrates a retail sales database designed as a multi-star schema with two secondary dimension tables. This multi-star schema was used because the foreign keys, Store_Id and SKU_Id are not enough to uniquely identify a row within the transaction table. The fact table records daily sales in a rolling seven-day database. The primary key for the fact table consists of the four columns Store_Id, Date, Receipt, and Line_item. These keys provide the unique identifier for each row. The foreign keys are the columns for Store_Id and SKU_Id, which reference the SKU (Stock Keeping Unit) and Store dimension tables. Two outboard tables, Class and Department, are also being referenced by the SKU dimension table.

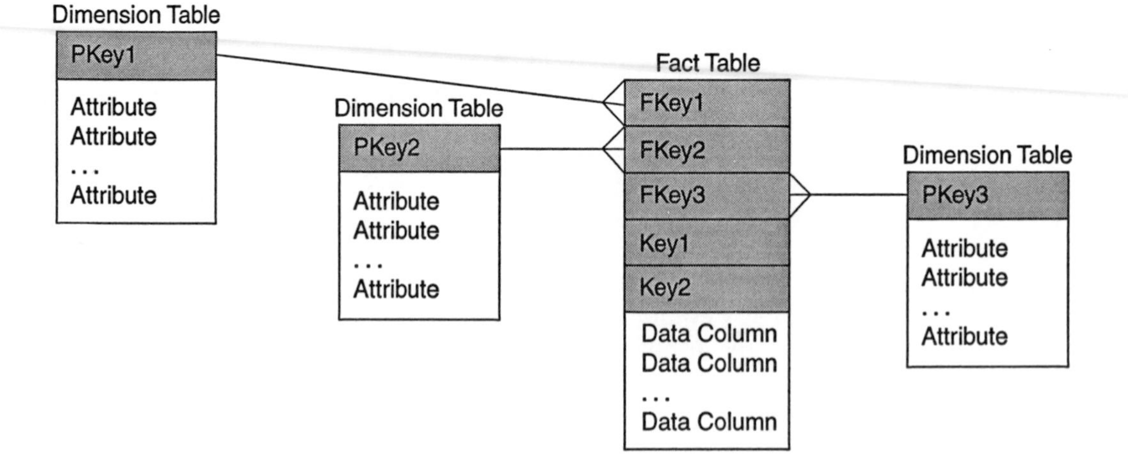

FIGURE 9–7 A multi-star schema design.

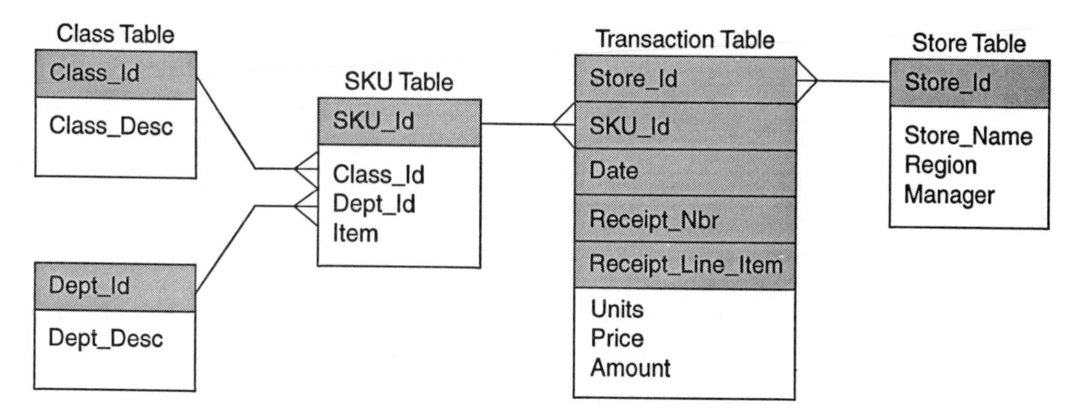

FIGURE 9–8 Retail sales database designed as a multi-star schema with two secondary dimension tables.

Notice that in a multi-star schema, unlike a simple star schema, the same value for the concatenated foreign key in the fact table can occur in multiple rows, so that the concatenated foreign key no longer uniquely identifies each row. For example, in this case the same store (Store_Id) might have multiple sales of the same item (SKU_Id) on the same day (Date). Instead, row identification is based on the primary key(s)—each row is uniquely identified by Date, Receipt, and Line_Item.

A SALAD DRESSING EXAMPLE

This example illustrates how the schema design affects both usability and usefulness of the database.

This database tracks the sales of salad dressing products in supermarkets at weekly intervals over a four-year period and is a typical consumer-goods marketing database.

- The salad dressing product category contains 14,000 items at the universal product code (UPC) level.
- Data is summarized for each of 120 geographic areas (markets) in the United States.
- Data is also summarized for each of 208 weekly time periods spanning four years.

The salad dressing database has one fact table, Sales, and three-dimension tables: Product, Period, and Market, as illustrated in Figure 9-9.

Each record in the Sales fact table contains a field for each of the three dimensions: product, period, and market. The columns in the Sales table containing these fields are the foreign keys whose concatenated values give each row in the Sales table a unique identifier. This is therefore a simple star schema. The Sales table also contains seven additional fields that contain values for measures of interest to market analysts.

Each dimension table describes a business dimension and contains one primary key and some attribute columns for that dimension.

Understanding the Available Data, Browsing the Dimension Tables

To write effective queries, a user needs to be familiar with the contents of the database. A convenient way to find the range of values for a specific dimension is to query the dimension table for that dimension. For example, to see what the markets are for the sales data, a user can request

```
SELECT market_desc FROM market
```

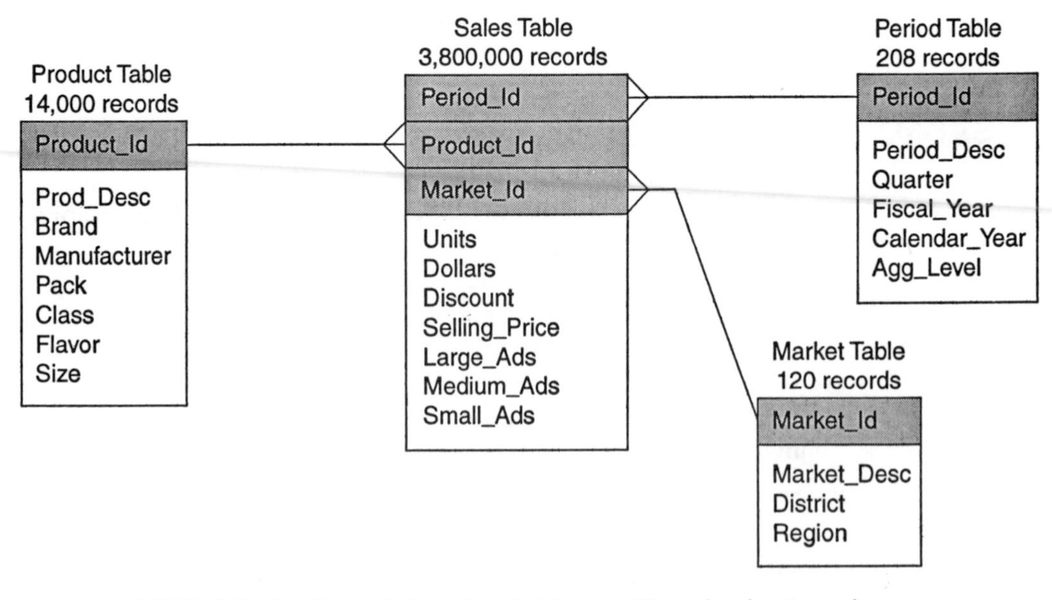

FIGURE 9–9 A salad dressing database with a simple star schema.

to display a list of all the markets, 120 in this case. Similar queries on the Product and Period tables provide the user with lists of the products and periods covered in the Sales Table.

WHERE clause expressions can be used to narrow down the browse list to specific items of interest. For example, if the user is interested only in dressings from Kraft, then a WHERE clause filter specifying manufacturer to be equal to Kraft will limit the browse list from the product table to the appropriate Kraft products. This creates a more workable subset of data by limiting the full 14,000 items of the table to the much smaller subset of Kraft products.

Browsing through the dimension tables is quicker than issuing a SELECT DISTINCT statement on a fact table, especially if the fact table contains millions of rows of data. Having tables of data that define each dimension of the star schema makes this type of browsing activity possible. Users can browse the dimensions of the database using the dimension tables to become familiar with the data contents.

After creating browse lists to understand which dimensions are being addressed in the database design, the user can review these lists to find which markets, products, and time periods in which they have a particular interest. The browse lists return the exact descriptions and spellings, making it easier to write the query constraints correctly.

Using Table Attributes

Nonkey columns in a dimension table are referred to as attributes. To see how attributes are used, consider the product table for the salad dressing database. It has 14,000 items that are identified by their universal product code (UPC), which provides the primary key (Product_Id). This identifier allows a user to retrieve a unique row. Usually, however, the user does not want data at the UPC level but is interested in higher-level categories such as brand or manufacturer. Additional attributes in the dimension tables permit commonly accessed subsets of an entire group to be differentiated.

For example, the brand attribute allows the 14,000 salad dressing products to be differentiated by brand so that a user can select only products with a specific brand name. Another attribute allows those same 14,000 products to be differentiated by manufacturer. A user analyzing the salad dressing sales could use the attributes Class, Flavor,

Size, and Manufacturer from the Product Table to select diet ranch salad dressings in 12-ounce bottles from major manufacturers.

Creating Attribute Hierarchies

Viewing data through different, but closely related, perspectives allows the end user to analyze data to the level of detail that is necessary to provide answers. Viewing data from a high level through different dimensions to a more detailed view of data is called drilling down. Viewing data from the detail level up to a summarized, or higher level, is called rolling up. Your database design and the granularity level of the data will determine your ability to drill down or roll up.

End users often wish to see different perspectives on the same data. For instance, you might view sales volume for a particular product across the country and then break up the country by region. Reviewing regional information may show a sales inconsistency that you would like more information on, so you drill down to sales territories that make up the regional data to see where sales may be slipping. Drilling down through the data this way allows you to get closer to a more detailed level of data.

A well-designed star schema will encompass these hierarchies within the dimension tables. Multiple hierarchies can also be represented in a single table. In a table recording information about geographic areas, for example, separate geographic hierarchies—one for physical geography and one for sales organization geography (they are often different)—can be represented in the same table. Any of these attributes can then form a basis for constraints. Figure 9-10 shows multiple attribute hierarchies within a dimension that are used for drill-downs and roll-ups of data.

A star schema design that contains complete, consistent, and well thought out attribute fields provides users with views of data they can inherently understand and use. A good star schema design helps users write queries that they intuitively understand and reduces the support burden on the organization responsible for database management.

AGGREGATION

Aggregation is the process of accumulating fact data along predefined attributes. For instance, you can create a summary of dollar sales by region and department by accumulating dollar sales from the store and

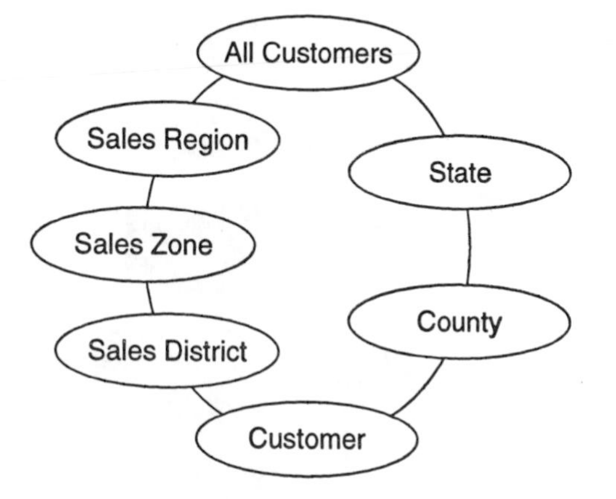

FIGURE 9–10 Multiple hierarchies within a dimension.

item level of detail. Within the context of database design, you must make decisions about creating aggregates during the data transformation process and loading the precalculated data into the data warehouse.

The primary driving factors for creating prestored aggregates are to

- Improve end-user query performance.
- Reduce the total number of CPU cycles used.

It does not make sense to prestore a specific aggregate that takes two hours to create if it is requested by one user once a year. On the other hand, if that same aggregate is requested by 300 users on a daily basis, this processing could adversely affect your operational systems. In this case, prestored aggregates would be warranted. You should create the prestored aggregate once during the data transformation process and load it into the database. Figure 9-11 shows prestored aggregate tables across both the geography and product dimensions.

It is not necessary to prestore aggregations on every combination of the attributes. To determine what to prestore in your data warehouse, you need to consider not only the frequency of end-user access but also the potential reduction in total number of rows. For example, in the tables shown in Figure 9-12, you may have a fact table that has 10,000,000 rows of data at the store and item level of detail. If you aggregate to the item region level of detail, you may end up with

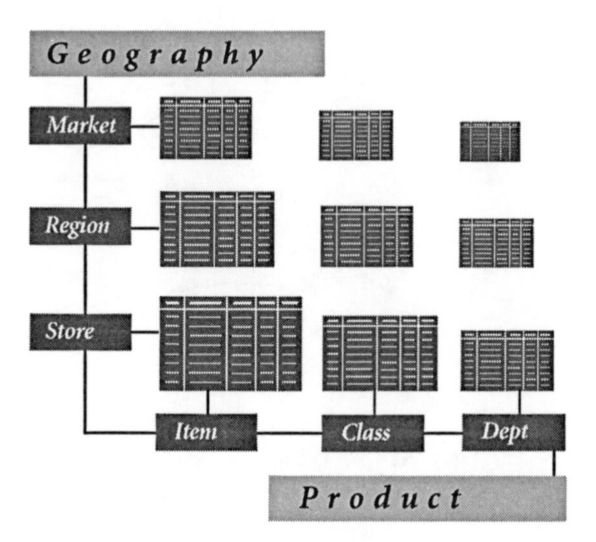

FIGURE 9–11 Prestored aggregate tables across both the geography and product dimensions. (Courtesy of Micro Strategy, Inc.)

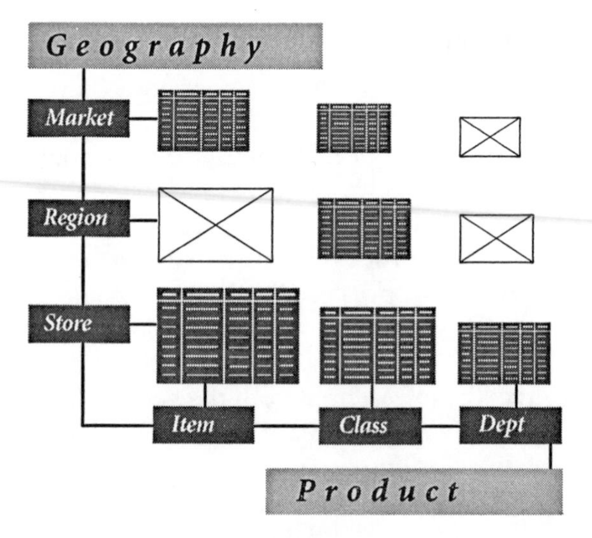

FIGURE 9–12 Sparse aggregation across both the geography and product dimensions.(Courtesy of Micro Strategy, Inc.)

9,000,000 rows of data. However, if you aggregate to the market and item level of detail, you have only 1,000,000 rows. In this case, do not store item region data, but keep the item market data. Summarizing data only at selected levels is referred to as sparse aggregation. The choice of summary tables will also be influenced by the access patterns requested from the end users. By selecting appropriate aggregation levels, optimization of both query performance and disk storage within data warehouse will take place.

One final concept to note is that when loading a data warehouse, you still need to use classic database techniques such as physical table partitioning. This becomes very important with data warehouses having hundreds of gigabytes of data. An example of how partitioning would be included in your aggregation strategy is shown in Figure 9-13, where only the largest aggregate fact tables are partitioned.

DENORMALIZATION

Denormalization is the process of combining tables in a careful and thoughtful manner to improve performance. This is really the process of breaking the rules for third normal form. The primary reasons to do this are

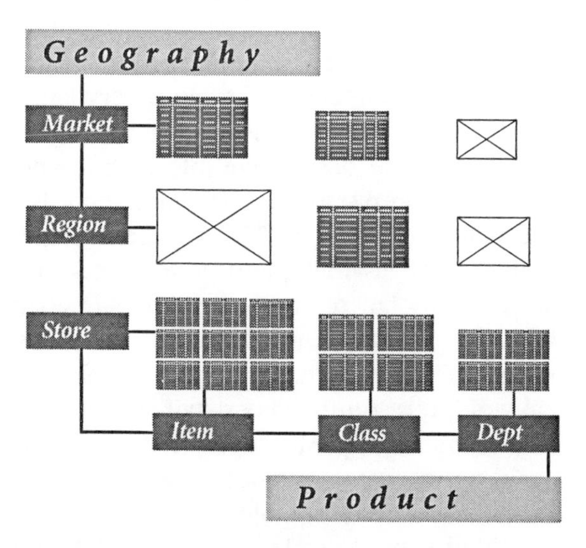

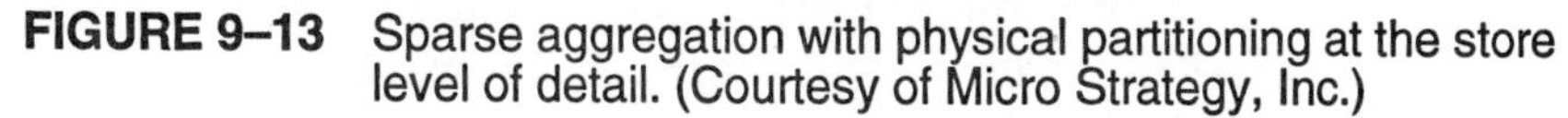
FIGURE 9–13 Sparse aggregation with physical partitioning at the store level of detail. (Courtesy of Micro Strategy, Inc.)

- To reduce the number of joins that must be processed in your average queries, thereby improving database performance.
- To map the physical database structure more closely to the user's dimensional business model. Again, structuring your tables along the lines of how users will ask questions will provide you with the opportunity to tune for common access paths which will again improve performance.

Over the last several years, data warehouse developers have fine-tuned denormalization techniques, resulting in the entire star schema approach.

LIMITATIONS OF THE STAR SCHEMA

It is critical to recognize that star schemas do not represent a panacea in data warehouse database design. While there are many decision support environments in which a star schema is very appropriate, there are also some cases where a star schema is not the best database design technique. The star schema approach was originally developed in the retail and consumer package goods industries for decision support databases. The star schema will almost always work well in these environments. This is because dimension tables such as Product, Period, and Market are very small compared to the Sales fact table in these industries.

When a dimensional table is very large in its number of rows and attributes, do not try to force a star schema design. We have seen databases in which descriptive information about customers has been denormalized into transactional detail records in an effort to adhere to the star schema approach. This can be a very big mistake in terms of the storage cost, usability, and performance of the database design. There are typically far too many customers in a large enterprise (with the exception of retail distribution) to effectively use star join query techniques. Denormalizing the large number of customer attributes typically of interest into every detail record will explode the size of the fact table substantially. Moreover, many questions will want to be directed against the customer without a desire to crawl through every detail record in a huge fact table.

You should not feel that the database design for your warehouse must fit into some predetermined formula. As mentioned in the Chapter on Critical Success Factors, the database design should be driven by the business considerations for a successful decision support environment rather than reliance upon technical panaceas. Do not be afraid to use variations on the star schema to best meet your business requirements. For example, the Reservations database design shown in Figure 9-14 uses a multi-star schema design in which the Frequent_Stayers, Actuals, and Bookings tables all provide major sources of facts for analysis. The customers identified in the Frequent_Stayers table should remain as a separate table even if there are a very large number of entries in this table because this will be a focal point for analysis in most decision support environments. Furthermore, combining the Actuals and Bookings tables for the sake of adherance to a simple star schema approach would be a big mistake because not all actuals have an associated booking, and vice-versa. Storage requirements, usability, and performance would all suffer by attempting to force fit into a simple star schema. An appropriate compromise between traditional database design techniques and dimensional database design must be arrived upon for a successful data warehouse deployment.

DATA WAREHOUSE DATABASE DESIGN EXAMPLES

A series of specific examples will show how the many different concepts discussed in this chapter are applied in the real world.

Reservation Database

Figure 9-14 illustrates a multistar schema, in which the primary and foreign keys are not composed of the same set of columns. This design also contains a family of fact tables: a Bookings table, an Actuals table, and a Promotion Schedule table.

This database tracks reservations (bookings) and actual accommodations rented for a chain of hotels, as well as various promotions. It also maintains information about customers, promotions, and each hotel in the chain.

Investment Database

Figure 9-15 is an example of a database that tracks sales of investment funds on a daily and monthly basis. It also maintains information about the client organizations, the investment funds, and various trading programs.

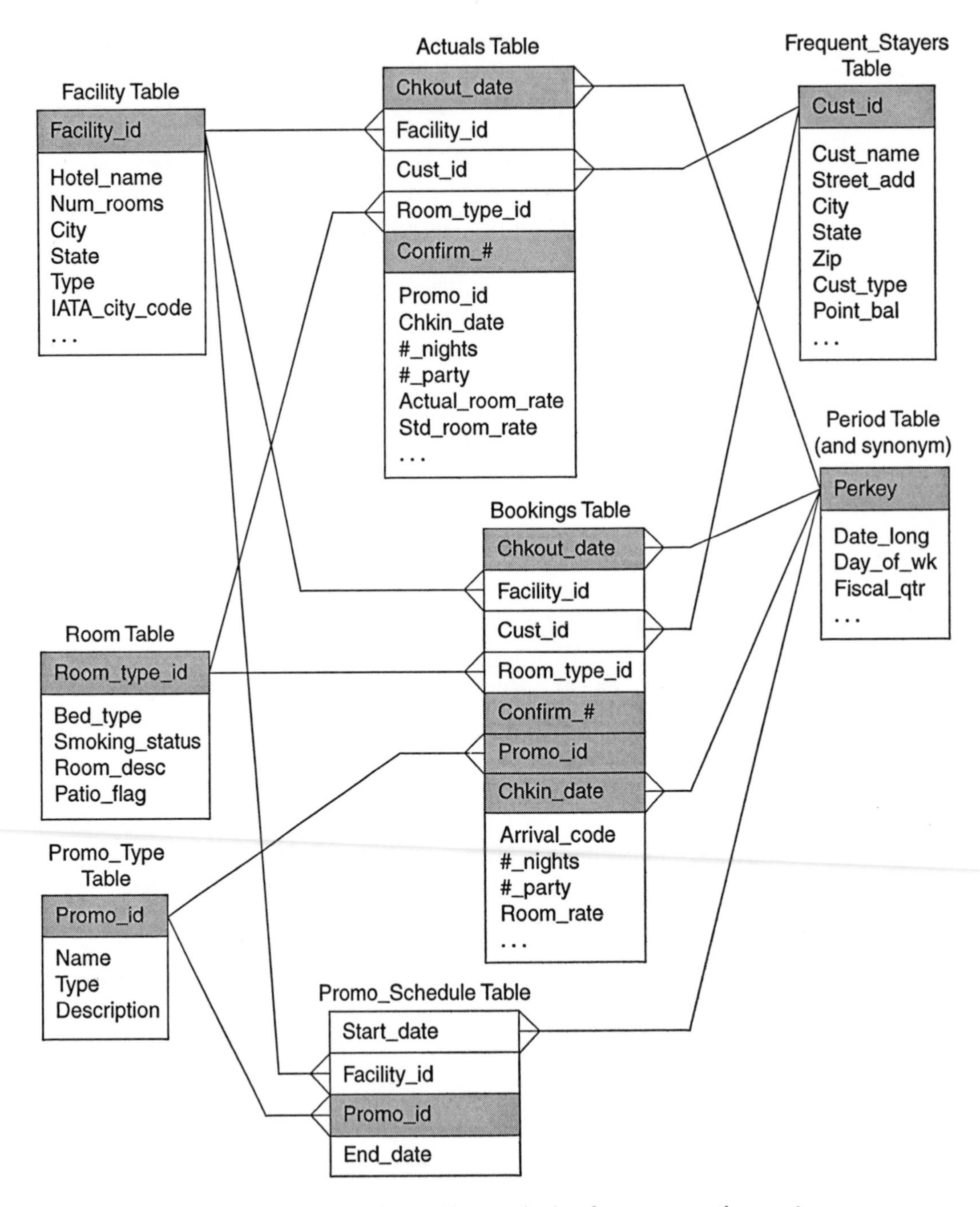

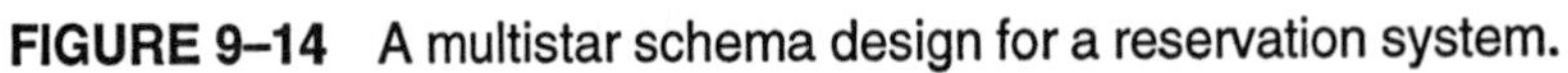
FIGURE 9–14 A multistar schema design for a reservation system.

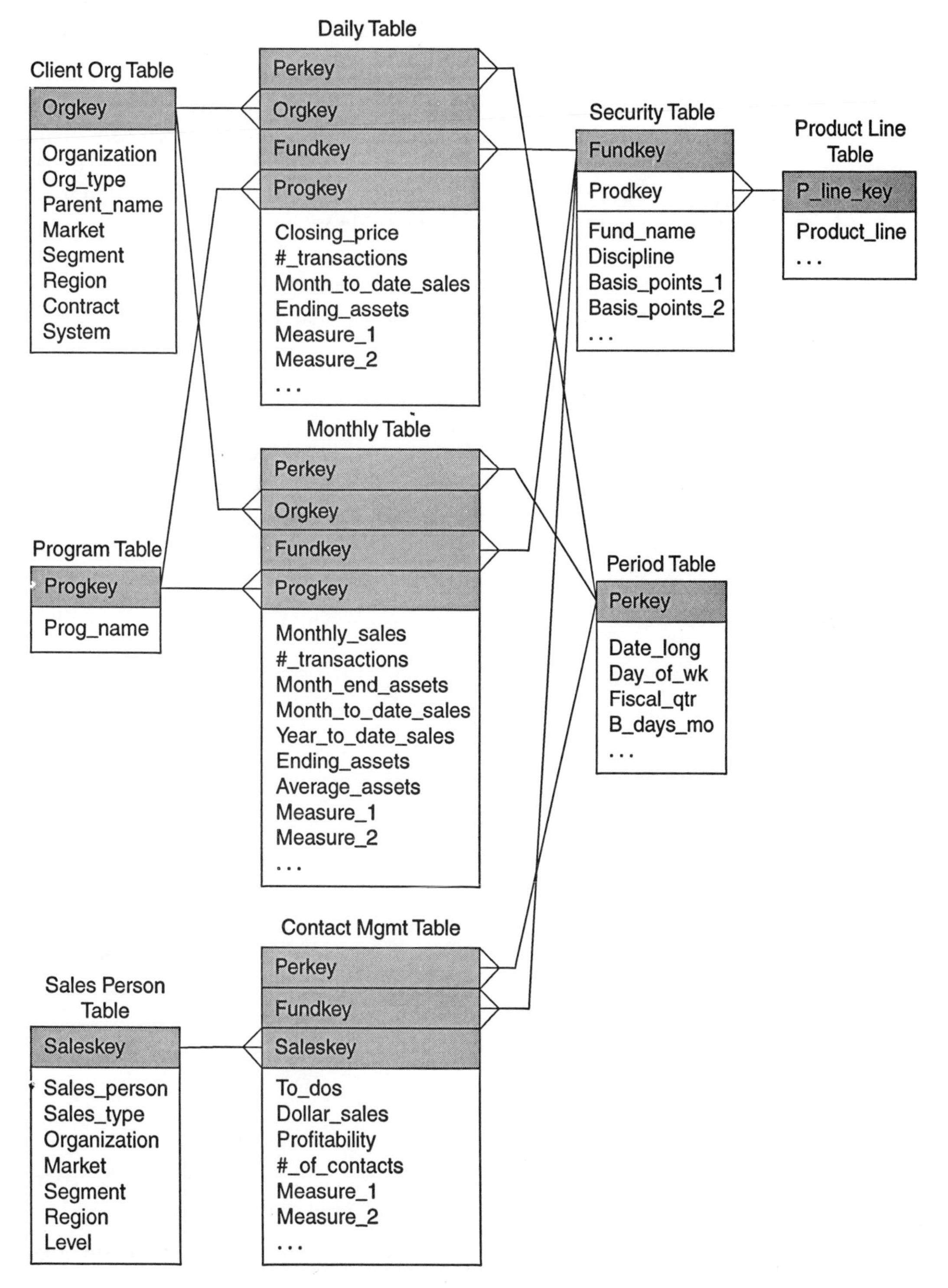

FIGURE 9–15 A simple star schema design for an investment system. Daily data is stored in one table and aggregated data is stored in another table.

This example illustrates a simple schema to handle aggregations. In this case, daily data are stored in one table and aggregated data in another, rather than combining both levels of aggregation in one table. The ratio of aggregated data to nonaggregated data and knowledge of the expected queries can help determine whether to combine various aggregation levels in a single database or use multiple tables. If aggregated and nonaggregated data are stored in the same table, each query must always specify the level of aggregation as a constraint.

Health Insurance Database

A simple star schema for a health care insurer used for claims analysis is illustrated in Figure 9-16. This database records policy sales and claims and maintains records of customers and their policies and claims against those policies.

Putting It All Together

Figure 9-17 displays a more realistic example of the many concepts that have been discussed throughout this chapter.

SUMMARY

In this chapter, you should have learned the following:

- The goals of a decision support system are often achieved by a database design called a star schema, a simple structure with relatively few tables and well-defined join paths.

The benefits of using star schema database design for a data warehouse include

- Creating a database design providing fast response times.
- Allows database optimizers to work with a more simple database design in order to yield better execution plans.
- Paralleling, in the database design, how the end users customarily think of and use the data.

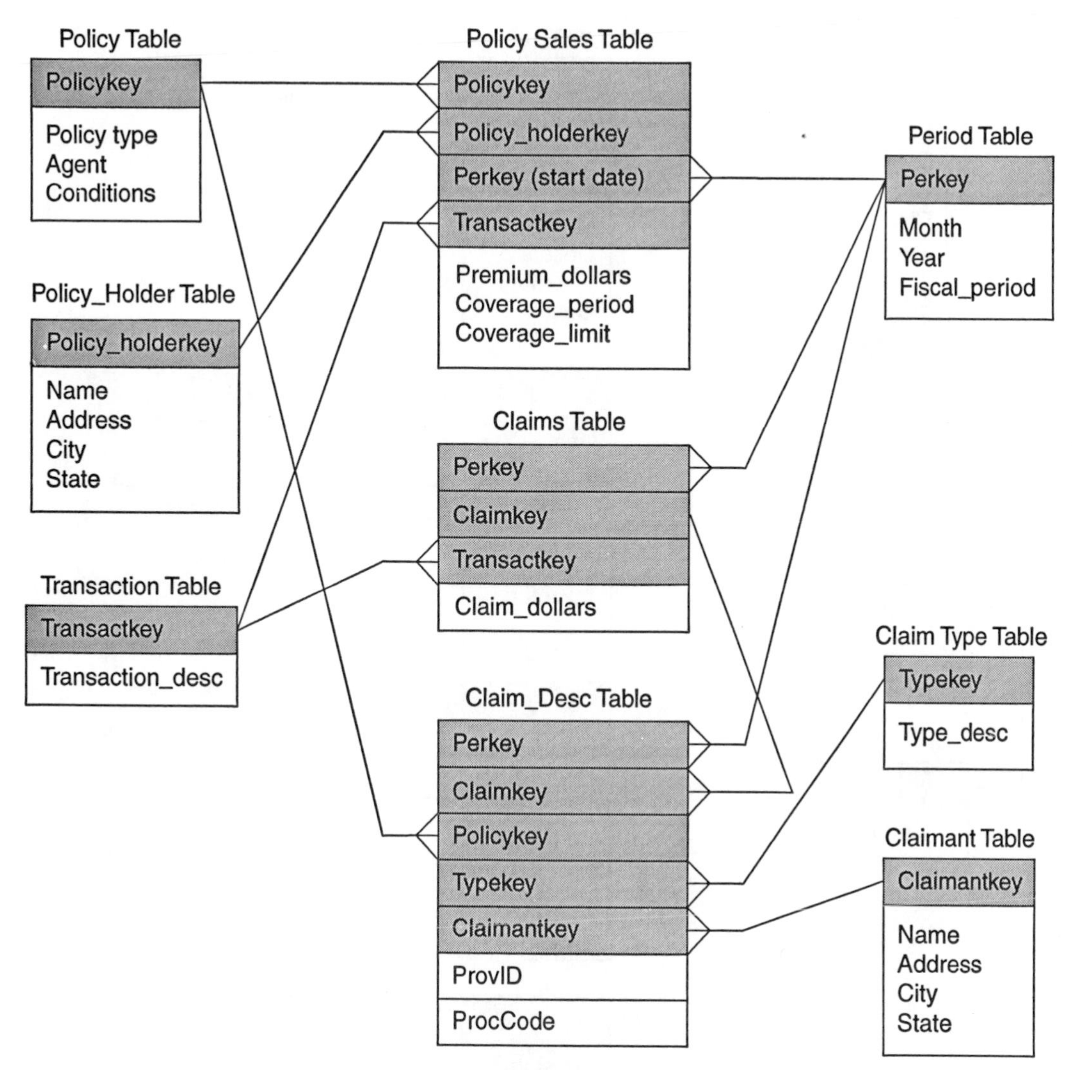

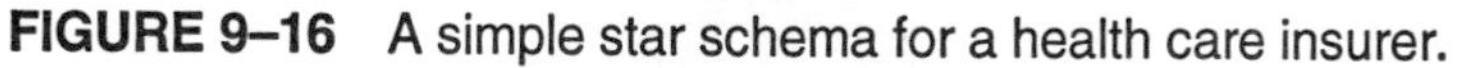
FIGURE 9–16 A simple star schema for a health care insurer.

- Simplifying the understanding and navigation of metadata for both developers and end users.
- Broadening the choices of front-end data access tools, as some products require a star schema design.
- A star schema contains two types of tables, fact tables and dimension tables.

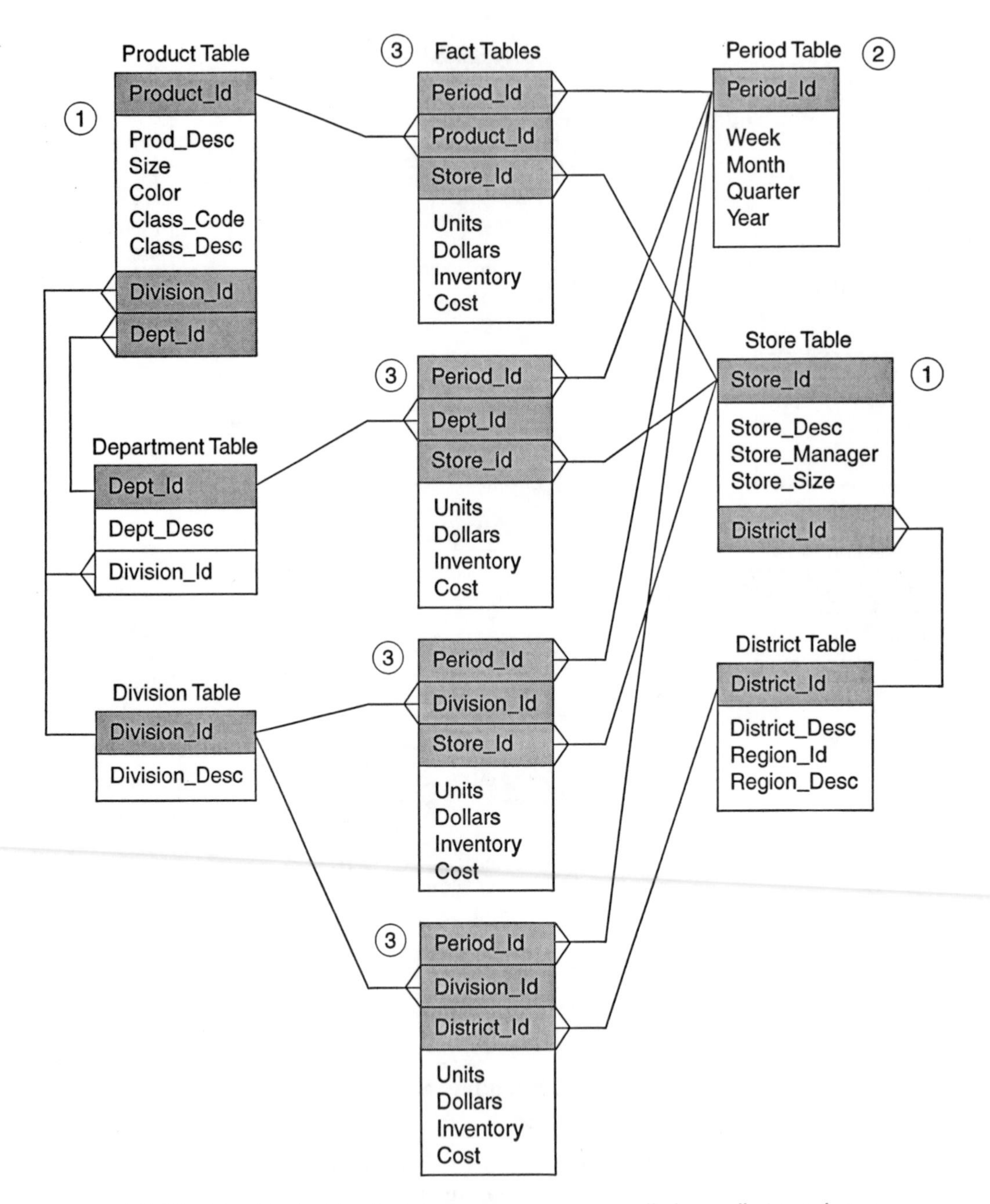

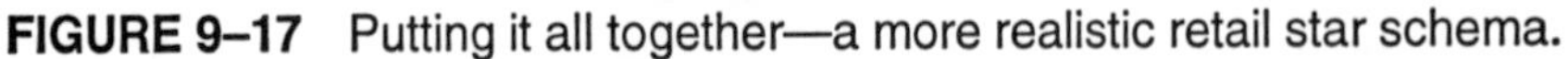
FIGURE 9–17 Putting it all together—a more realistic retail star schema.

- Fact tables contain quantitative or factual data about a business—the information being queried. Dimension tables hold descriptive data that reflects the dimensions of the business.
- In a simple star schema, the primary key for the fact table is composed of the foreign keys from the dimension tables.
- A star schema can, and often does, contain multiple fact tables.
- In schemas where the concatenated foreign keys from the dimension tables do not provide a unique identifier, a multi-star schema will be used. In a multi-star schema, the fact table has both a set of foreign keys referencing the dimensions, and a primary key to provide a unique identifier for each row.
- Dimensions often contain business hierarchies to allow users to drill up and down to the level of detail necessary to provide answers.
- Aggregation is accumulating fact data along predefined attributes. Aggregated data that is requested by users on a daily basis will often be precalculated and loaded into the data warehouse to improve end-user query performance and reduce the number of CPU cycles used.
- The determination of which aggregates should be prestored will be based on the frequency of end-user access, as well as the potential reduction in the total number of rows returned from a query.

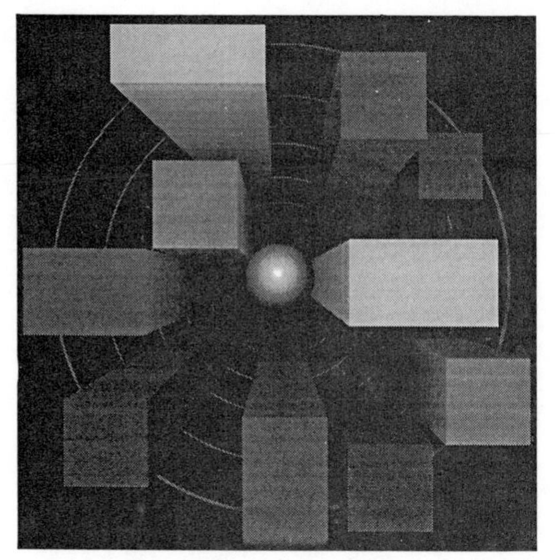

Chapter 10

Successful Data Access

GENERAL UNDERSTANDING OF DATA ACCESS

With a goal of providing information to users, front-end data access to your data warehouse becomes one of the most important aspects of building a decision support system (DSS). Experience shows that the tool or tools selected can make or break your data warehouse. Unfortunately, the selection of the front-end tool is often left until the warehouse is nearly complete. Information on what tools are available and what type of data warehouses they support is important to understand before you design your warehouse.

You need to think about setting up an environment to support data access and analysis rather than just selecting a front-end software package. This environment includes not only the software itself, but also the training, end-user support, and development of *predefined DSS applications.* It is important to realize that a DSS application is not the same thing as a COBOL program. A DSS application can, in general, be considered one or more predefined reports where users may or may not have the ability to provide input parameters.

As you begin to look at data access software that is on the market, do not underestimate the sophistication and complexity of this type of software. You need to make sure that you allow enough time and apply enough resources to really understand what you need and which tools can meet your requirements. In general, the selection of a tool can take several weeks, but keep in mind that the development of DSS applications will be much shorter than traditional application development.

WHAT ARE YOU REALLY TRYING TO DO?

You must review the overall goals for your data warehouse again when you begin your search for tools. You should step back and ask:

- What am I trying to do?
- Do I plan to be in the business of software development or am I trying to support the business?
- Am I planning to deliver reports electronically or am I planning to deliver analytical capabilities?
- Am I looking to replace the creation and delivery of all existing hard copy reports or are my users clamoring to have data they need at their fingertips to make better business decisions?

The in-house development of full data access software is not recommended. Even if you are able to develop an initial application quickly, the maintenance and enhancements to this application are usually extremely costly over time. Many software companies are dedicated to delivering this capability to the marketplace. These organizations are investing hundreds of person years into the development and maintenance of these tools, which have sophisticated analytical capabilities. Realistically, the effort to develop this type of tool will most likely exceed your schedule as well as your budget.

TYPES OF ACCESS

How do people receive information from the data warehouse? The most common ways are

- *Parameter-based ad hoc report:* Fixed report formats where the user can change the parameters. For example, the end user may be able to specify the time period or the products to be included in the report. The end user may also have the ability to further manipulate the results. Often, end users have the ability to copy an existing report to modify it for a specific purpose. While the user is really creating a new report, it is not from scratch, but rather from modifying existing reports.
- *Electronic access to predefined reports:* Predefined fixed format reports are generated and placed in a commonly accessible location for users to pull up for viewing as needed.
- *Full ad hoc analysis:* The user interacts directly with the tool to create a brand new analysis from scratch. This is also sometimes referred to as ad hoc reporting. It is important to make sure that everyone on your project team and within your targeted user base has a common definition of ad hoc. Since ad hoc has rather customized definitions, you should also clarify with external vendors or groups what their definition of ad hoc is.
- *Hard copy reports:* Predefined fixed format reports are generated, printed, and then delivered to the user.

There are a variety of ways that end users can navigate through the system to use it. The primary interface methods are

- *Executive information system:* Provides big-button navigation along predefined paths to access predefined analysis.
- *Structured decision support:* Provides big-button navigation along predefined paths to access predefined and ad hoc reports. The users have further analytical capabilities available once a report is retrieved.
- *Unstructured decision support:* Provides access to all predefined and ad hoc reports. The navigation to get to the specific reports is unstructured. The full range of tool capabilities is available to the user, including building new analyses from scratch.

LEVELS OF USERS

Not all business professionals have the same data and analytical requirements. Contrary to popular opinion, most business professionals will not develop their own reports. This is due to a combination of technical skill level and pure analytical requirements. Let's review the broad spectrum of users.

- *Executive User:* Wants easy-to-access status of the corporation. Needs predefined sets of reports that can be easily located through navigation of menus. Wants results displayed graphically, with support details as needed. Basic additional analysis may be desired, but often the next step would be to make a phone call or send an e-mail to the appropriate person or department.
- *Novice / Casual User:* Someone who needs access to information on an occasional basis. Will not be logged on daily, or in some cases even weekly. Due to the length of time between sessions, big-button navigation is also required here. Wants to step through predefined analyses. This type of user may also be interested in setting parameters to run any report at that moment. Prompting of choices will be critical for this user.
- *Business Analyst:* One of a large number of end users who use information daily but do not have (and don't necessarily want to have) the technical knowledge to build reports completely from scratch. This user may find predefined navigation paths helpful initially and may progress to wanting to go directly to the report of

choice. This user will regularly change parameters and look at the results in many different ways. He or she will want to modify existing reports to customize them to meet a specific need but will generally not want to start from scratch.

- *Power User:* The business professional who is very adept with technology. This type of user will want to change parameters and manipulate result sets and is comfortable starting with a clean slate and creating his or her own reports/analyses. Power users want to be able to write their own macros and often place result sets into end-user tools such as Excel for further manipulation. The power user often develops reports that can then be shared with others in the organization.
- *Application Developer:* Differences between a power user and application developer are often minor. Usually, the application developer's primary responsibilities are to support the business, rather than having actual business responsibilities. The application developer will be trained to not only create reports/analyses for use by others but will also be a driving force in setting standards, such as where and how reports will be named and located. The application developer will often be highly focused on performance optimization of the reports.

Every organization has some of the above types of users. You will find them across a continuum of experience and business units. The key here is to understand the characteristics of your target audience and relate these back to your choices in data access tools. Figure 10–1 summarizes the types of users and their warehouse usage.

WHAT IS A DSS APPLICATION?

If you build one, they will come.

This is one of the most common myths surrounding data warehouses, and it is not true. The idea that simply loading the data will allow your users to gain business knowledge is an unrealistic view of a data warehouse. Likewise, simply making a front-end access tool available will not ensure success.

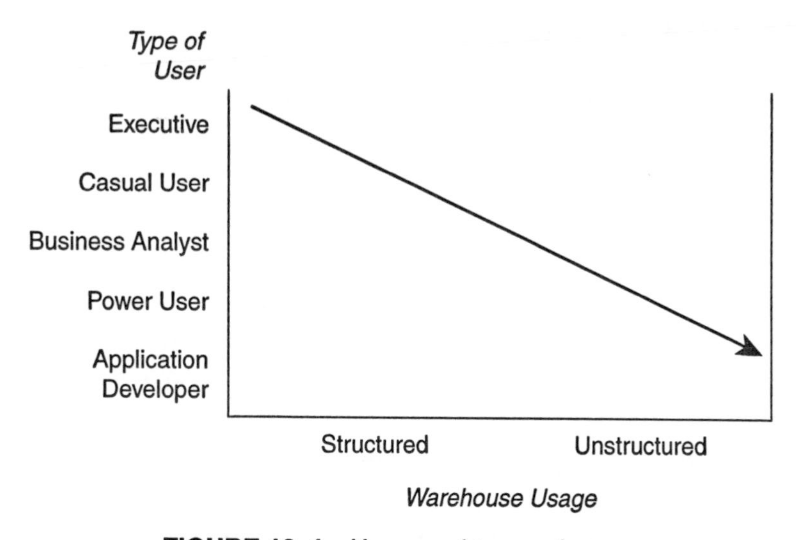

FIGURE 10–1 Users and types of access.

Data access tools are much too sophisticated for many business professionals to use right out of the box. Due to the complexity and breadth of the capabilities, even power users will have to progress along a rather steep learning curve. *Keep in mind that many of these tools are not designed to make easy tasks easier, but rather to make complex tasks doable.* The key to helping users along the learning curve is to provide structured or free-form navigation paths to a set of predefined reports and analyses. These predefined reports are considered the beginning of a DSS application.

We have established the need for many users in an organization to use prebuilt reports and analyses. Who develops these? How are they developed? The data warehouse project needs to accommodate both the time required and funding to support the development of these predefined reports. You must remember that this is a starter set. Do not spec out 100 reports. Define the top 10 to 12 analyses that will be required. Keep in mind that a single DSS "report" can yield hundreds of final reports by changing the constraints and/or level of aggregation or detail displayed.

Also, be aware that you will not necessarily be able to predetermine which reports will be the most valuable to your users. Take a first cut at it, and then work closely with the users. Looking at the core reports six months after initial development, you may not see any of the the original reports. This is evidence of a successful system at work.

DATA ACCESS CHARACTERISTICS

Before jumping right into a description of what you can buy today, we must provide a background explaining what capabilities are possible across a spectrum of software products. After you know what can be done, we will then review how different classes of software products address these capabilities.

How you access data follows several general steps. These fundamental functions will exist for all data access tools to some degree. In addition to data access, more advanced analytical capabilities also fall into several general categories. A description of each will be provided.

Visualization of the Data Warehouse

Users must be presented with the contents of the data warehouse. On the simple end, a list of tables and columns is all that is displayed. Advancing along the sophistication spectrum, presenting the tables and columns using business terms to providing full dimensional views of the database—where a user never interacts directly with table structures.

User Formulates Request

The full spectrum of capabilities ranges from manually writing SQL statements to drag and drop from a list of available tables and columns to complete multidimensional analysis where the user works completely with business terms, information is organized along business hierarchies, and drag and drop capabilities are used to create a request. A request is really comprised of two basics: what data you want (the constraints) and how you want to see it, including level of detail.

Viewing the Results

You need to be able to specify the general format of the returned data. Tabular or cross-tabular formats are most common. Business professionals think in terms of cross-tabular formats—rows and columns.

- The general row and column information needs to be specified. I want product information down the side and weeks across the top·

- The level of detail to look at is also important to specify. I want to see item detail by week.
- The specific facts or metrics also need to be selected.

There are several different types of metrics that may be supported by data access tools. Each type is discussed here.

Metrics and Calculated Metrics

Simple Metrics: The retrieval of columns of data that are physically stored in the data warehouse is the simplest type of metric. Common simple metrics are Sales Dollars and Units Sold.

Calculated Metrics: Metrics that are the result of performing standard mathematical calculations upon simple metrics are considered calculated or derived metrics. Examples include average retail price, which is Dollar Sales divided by Units Sold. Also a simple projection of a 15 percent increase in sales can be calculated as Dollar Sales multiplied by 1.15.

Advanced Metrics: This type of calculation requires data from multiple levels within the data hierarchies. For example, Brand Share of Category requires applying two sets of selection criteria—what brands and what is the associated category. The calculation is Brand Sales divided by Category Sales. Other common examples include penetration and contribution. *These calculations cannot be performed with a single SQL statement.*

Transformation Metrics: This type of metric requires that you pull information for one specified set of criteria and for a related criteria set to compare them. The most common example of a transformation metric is *time comparison analysis* such as comparing this year's versus last year's sales performance. The current period of sales is selected; then the related prior year is determined (the original date is transformed to the prior year). The prior year sales can then be retrieved. Finally, the variance between the two can be calculated. Another example is to compare store sales with other stores of a comparable background. This calculation also requires the transformation of a specific store into the related stores, so that the appropriate sales data can be retrieved. *These calculations cannot be performed with one SQL statement.*

Aggregation: How will the tool determine access to prestored aggregation and/or when to create the aggregate on the fly? It is also important to understand where the aggregation will occur—at the client workstation, the Relational Database Management System (RDBMS), or somewhere else? There are two types of aggregation that can occur:

- *Straight aggregation:* Accumulate information along the hierarchies and attributes within the data model. For example, items roll up to sizes, classes, and departments. This is usually the type of aggregate that is prestored in the database.
- *Custom aggregation:* Accumulate information along nonstandard paths. For example, aggregate all the items in a brand except for sample sizes, or aggregate to a specific list of markets that you have determined to use as test markets.

Row Math: Provide the same mathematical capabilities to perform calculations between rows in the database as is often seen with financial data. SQL does not support this type of calculation today. A common example of this requirement is when actual and budget information are stored in the same table as separate rows, distinguished by a Type Key. Most users want to see actual, budget, and variance information on the same report.

Nonaggregatable Data: How do you handle nonsummable measures? Or enable the analysis of stock metrics such as inventory levels, turnover, sell through, and reorder quantities? You must set up rules to handle this type of data; for instance, it does not make sense to aggregate the current inventory level over time periods.

Constraining a Request. Constraining a request specifies what slice of the data warehouse is to be selected. The ability to constrain should include

- Constraining a specific column to a value using basic operators (<, >, =, <>...).
- Specification of the time dimension. You can constrain upon specific dates that are stored in a lookup table, or you may need to use dynamic data definitions which are defined relative to a chang-

ing date. For example, return to me all the data for the last two weeks. This date calculation is between (today-2 weeks) and today. This type of constraint changes over time rather than being a hard-coded value.

- Constraints that may also be required against metrics. For example, return for me all the products where the difference between actual and planned sales is less than 0.
- Constraints for future use saved. Advanced tools allow you to combine collections of constraints using full set mathematics (intersection, union, not).
- The ability to automatically prompt a user for constraint values. You may want to prompt for only one or two variables (which region and which month) or you may want to prompt for all variables (which geography, customer, time period, and product).

How the Request Is Processed

Once a user has formulated a request, the tool must fulfill the request and return the appropriate answer set.

All tools that use precoded SQL pass the statement directly to the RDBMS (most tools use ODBC as a vehicle for communication; others may use different paths).

More sophisticated tools translate the end user's request to generate the appropriate SQL statement(s), and then pass the request along. You should understand how advanced metrics are being calculated. Are they created with multiple SQL statements or is there a programmatic process that operates on the base data themselves?

The multidimensional tools will translate the end-user request into the required language to retrieve the result set from the Multidimensional Database Management System (MDBMS).

Presentation of Results

Data returned from a request can be displayed in a wide variety of ways. All are designed to assist a user in gathering insights from the data. Samples of how information can be presented are illustrated in Figure 10-2.

Daily Sales Contribution

		Adjustable Wrench Set				Han...	
		Sales ($)	Contribution to Weekly Sales	Profit ($)	Contribution to Category Profit	Sales ($)	Contribu... to Week... Sales
Boston	5/1	360	13%	72	4%	192	
	5/2	360	13%	72	5%	72	
	5/3	320	12%	64	7%	72	
	5/4	320	12%	64	4%	72	
	5/5	479	18%	95	6%	408	
	5/6	320	12%	64	5%	408	
	5/7	559	21%	111	9%	144	
Boston		[illegible]	[illegible]	[illegible]	[illegible]	[illegible]	
	5/1	400	15%	80	5%	72	

Profitability Ranking (Top 10)

	Sales ($)	Profit	Avg Inventory	Sq Feet	Profit per Sq Foot	Rank
Power Drill (3/8")	476,523	138,471	58	4	34,618	1
Cordless Drill	300,532	90,029	81	5	18,636	2
Romex Wire (3 Strand)	99,384	66,256	64	4	15,492	3
Outlet Box (Single)	98,960	65,840	64	4	15,470	4
Garden Hose (75')	100,344	66,896	64	4	15,311	5
Delux Leaf Rake	98,784	65,856	64	4	15,073	6
Outlets (White)	99,000	66,000	65	4	15,000	7
Wall Switches (White)	96,192	64,128	58	5	14,178	8
Lawn Mower (3/4 hp)	96,312	64,208	65	5	14,100	9
Hammer (28oz.)	86,520	58,472	72	5	11,245	10

Actual/Plan Sales Comparison

	Sales ($)	Sales-Plan	Sales-Plan %Variation	LY Sales ($)	LY Plan Sales ($)	LY Sales-Plan %Variation
Power Drill (3/8")	125,123	2,212	2%	114,444	105,997	8%
Skill Saw	55,498	3,390	7%	50,102	51,738	3%
Electric Sander	33,017	1,249	4%	30,385	31,114	2%
Cordless Drill	78,111	2,011	3%	70,264	74,089	5%
Handi Screwdriver Set	26,715	1,050	4%	26,328	24,542	7%
Rachet Kit (74 Piece)	45,802	2,767	6%	45,236	39,920	13%
Adjustable Wrench Set	40,190	1,549	4%	38,927	35,714	9%
Hammer (28oz.)	19,704	1,875	9%	18,871	16,826	12%
Romex Wire (3 Strand)	21,696	1,275	6%	20,883	19,220	9%
Wall Switches (White)	21,744	1,414	7%	20,045	18,653	7%

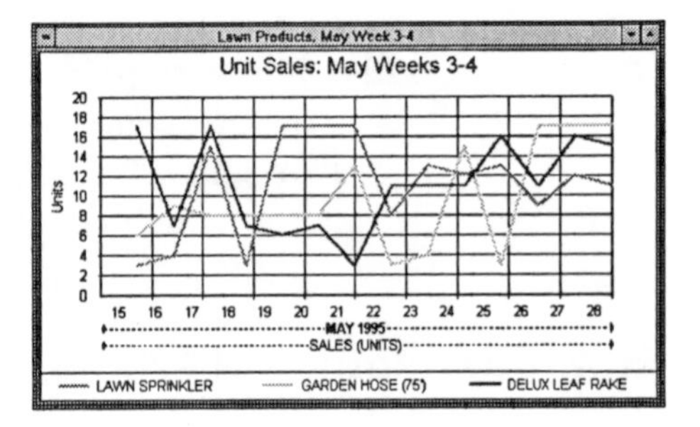

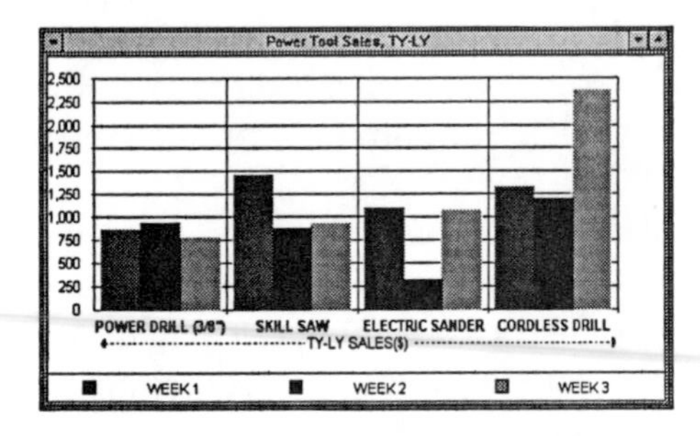

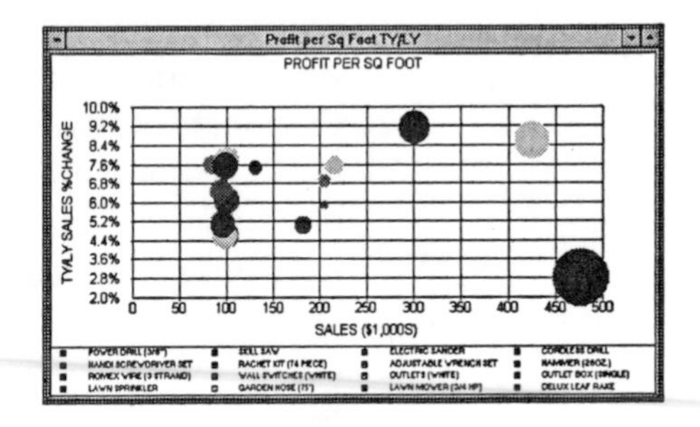

All Products : Figure 6

		Sales ($1,000s)				
		Week 1	Week 2	Week 3	Week 4	Week 5
New England	Standard	$12	$18	$13	$15	$5
	Wednesday Promo	$19	$14	$18	$14	$12
	Open Sundays	$17	$16	$16	$14	$6
	Two for One Special	$54	$54	$37	$49	$15
New England		[illegible]	[illegible]	[illegible]	[illegible]	[illegible]
Mid-Atlantic	Standard	$15	$15	$13	$14	$5
	Wednesday Promo	$14	$19	$14	$17	$8
	Open Sundays	$15	$15	$16	$16	$6
	Two for One Special	$55	$34	$54	$42	$24
Mid-Atlantic		[illegible]	[illegible]	[illegible]	[illegible]	[illegible]
	Standard	$17	$21	$19	$18	$7

94-95 Income Statement (Central Region)

	US Dollars ($1,000s)			
	94-95 Q1	94-95 Q2	94-95 Q3	94-95 Q4
Total Operating Revenues	643,810	636,333	628,153	596,169
Cost of Goods Sold	(469,962)	(464,523)	(458,552)	(435,204)
Selling, general, and admin. expenses	(90,133)	(89,087)	(87,941)	(83,464)
Depreciation	(25,752)	(25,453)	(25,126)	(23,847)
Operating income	51,505	50,907	50,252	47,694
Other income	6,438	6,363	6,282	5,962
Earnings before interest and taxes	64,381.04	63,633.27	62,815.33	59,616.92
Interest expense	(12,876)	(12,727)	(12,563)	(11,923)
Pretax income	51,505	50,907	50,252	47,694
Taxes	(25,752)	(25,453)	(25,126)	(23,847)
Net income	25,752	25,463	25,126	23,847

FIGURE 10–2 Various presentations of results. *(Courtesy of MicroStrategy, Inc.)*

Promotional Items Inventory Analysis

		Boston			
		Sales (Units)	Avg Inventory	Turnover (Days)	Sell Through
Power Tools	Skill Saw	181	62	19	80%
	Electric Sander	312	71	11	70%
	Cordless Drill	295	60	12	73%
Hand Tools	Handi Screwdriver Set	385	67	9	91%
	Rachet Kit (74 Piece)	264	66	13	40%
	Adjustable Wrench Set	355	68	10	85%
	Hammer (28oz.)	273	75	13	92%
Electrical	Romex Wire (3 Strand)	341	71	10	67%
	Wall Switches (White)	316	67	11	84%
	Outlets (White)	293	63	12	43%

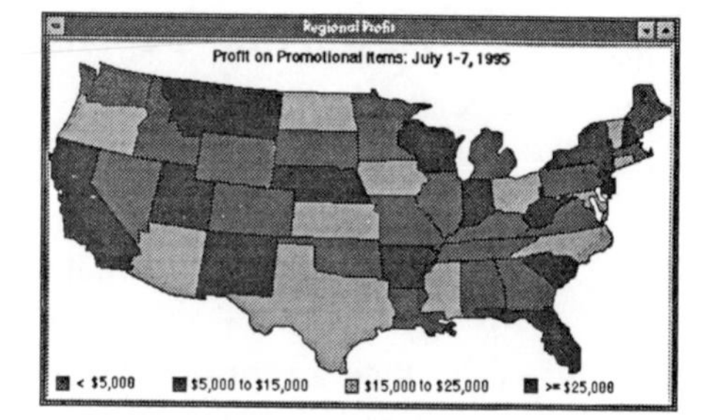

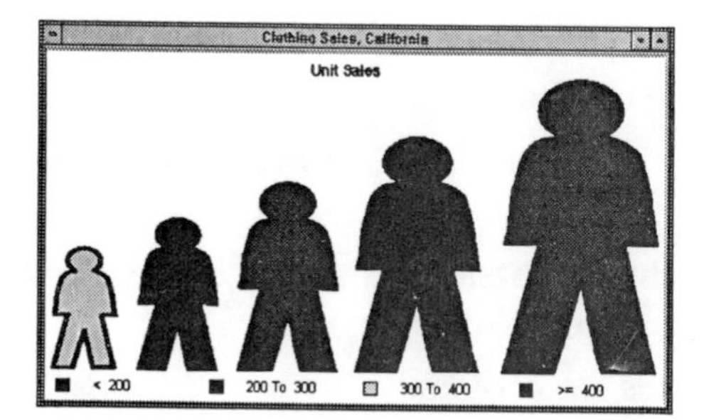

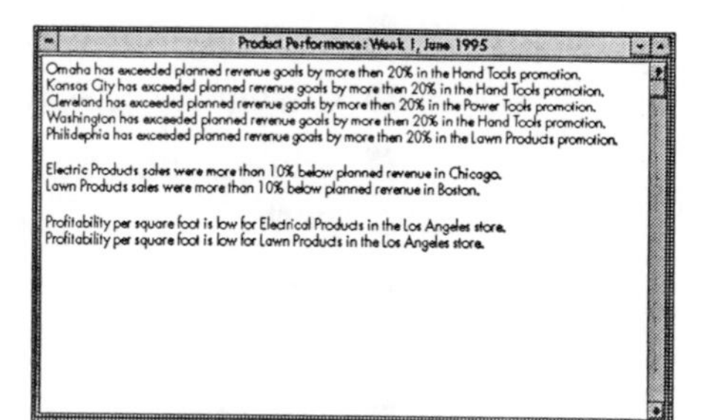

Product Performance: Week 1, June 1995

Omaha has exceeded planned revenue goals by more then 20% in the Hand Tools promotion.
Kansas City has exceeded planned revenue goals by more then 20% in the Hand Tools promotion.
Cleveland has exceeded planned revenue goals by more then 20% in the Power Tools promotion.
Washington has exceeded planned revenue goals by more then 20% in the Hand Tools promotion.
Philidephia has exceeded planned revenue goals by more then 20% in the Lawn Products promotion.

Electric Products sales were more than 10% below planned revenue in Chicago.
Lawn Products sales were more than 10% below planned revenue in Boston.

Profitability per square foot is low for Electrical Products in the Los Angeles store.
Profitability per square foot is low for Lawn Products in the Los Angeles store.

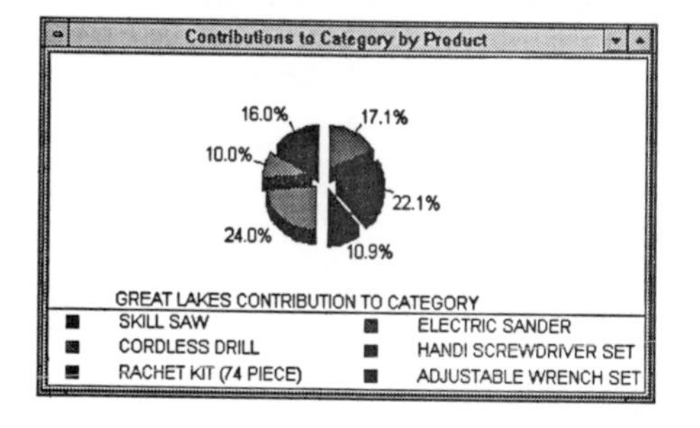

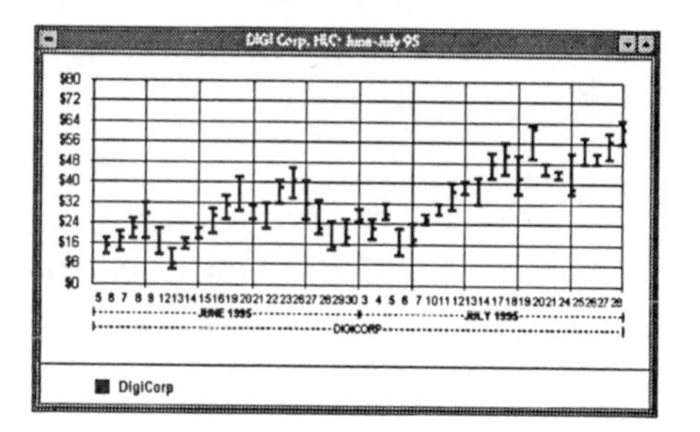

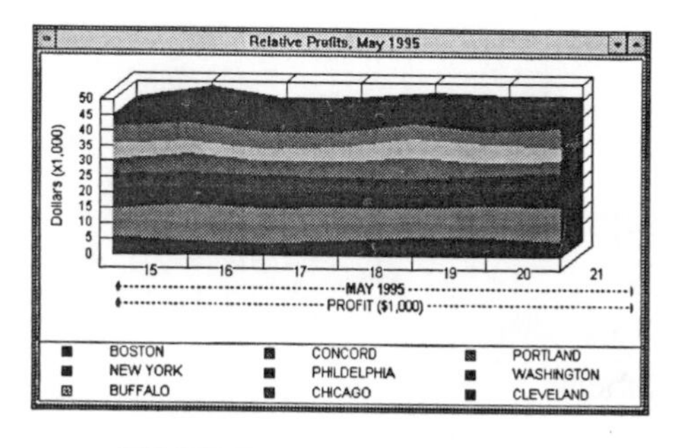

FIGURE 10–2 *(Continued)*

Reports. Reports can take two major forms:

- Columnar format (basic format returned directly from an SQL statement).
- Crosstab format supporting multidimensional views of the data.

Once a report is presented, a wide range of capabilities may allow modification of the display, including

- Changing the axis of the report (swap rows and columns).
- Changing the sort order of the results.
- Adding subtotals and grand totals at appropriate breaks in the reports.
- Creating stoplight-style thresholds (basic red, green, and yellow colors on the report to indicate ranges of values).
- Formatting of fonts, styles, sizes, and colors.

Graphs. Graphical display of information allows easy detection of trends and anomalies. A wide variety of graph types is often available, including

- Line
- Two- or three-dimensional bar
- Stacked bar
- Pie
- Scatter
- Bubble
- Tape
- Area

Within a graphical display, users may be able to change

- Graph type
- Axis labels
- Colors
- Titles

Maps. Mapping capabilities allow the presentation of information to expand beyond grids and graphs into the world of user-defined objects. Mapping provides a powerful method for displaying analyses that contain a geographic dimension. Both a high-level summary of the result set and the low-level details can readily be communicated through this pictorial format.

Communicate Findings

A DSS is not a stand-alone system. The results of any given analysis may be included in a formal presentation (slide show), e-mailed to management or appropriate team members, and otherwise shared throughout the company. No software tool lives on its own. The tool needs to interact with other personal productivity tools such as spreadsheet, word processing, and workgroup software.

Advanced Features

Advanced Analytics. Beyond these fundamental steps, there are some more advanced capabilities that many organizations require to support the full decision-making process. These may include

- Exception reporting: Alerts are messages that appear when user-defined conditions are not met or when there is a problem.
- Drill-down: Users have the freedom to "drive off" the existing report and retrieve information that may lie along, above, or below the current level of detail. Drill-down can be done from a report or a graph.
- Data surfing: You can keep the report layout constant but change the constraints. For example, a sales trend report for basketballs in the Northeast, changing to a sales trend report for shoes in the Far West. Data surfing also allows you to keep the constraints constant but vary the report. For example, continue to look at shoes in the Far West, but for an inventory status report instead of the sales trend.
- Ranking: Review information that is ranked on one or more columns.

- Automation: Mechanisms are in place to schedule recurring analysis at a specified time.

Batch Query Processing. Batch query processing is the offloading of query processing to free up the end user's workstation for other work. It is also beneficial to support recurring analysis. Users often run analyses on a weekly basis. For example, users may wish to create a group of Monday morning reports that have already run and are waiting for them when they arrive at work. This functionality is really providing the ability to offload and run now, or schedule a specific analysis to run at a specified date and time.

DSS Application Development

The development of a DSS application varies from actual programming to drag-and-drop construction. The fundamental questions to understand are

- How are reports or analyses shared between users?
- Is programming required or can you create reports and analyses without programming?
- Can you set up libraries of reports?
- How are reports upgraded when new versions are released?
- Do IS application developers use the same development tool as power users?
- How are structured navigation paths or big buttons created?
- Is there a query governor to limit the allowable elapsed time for a query to run or to limit the total number of rows that can be returned?
- Can workflow management be used to manage the query load against the database?
- Is there an ability to run a query during off-peak hours to save on costs?

CLASSES OF TOOLS

Now that you have an understanding of the types of things that you may be able to accomplish with a DSS tool, it is important to understand the classes of tools that are actively being marketed today. There are five major classifications of tools. An overview of each is provided.

Data Access/Query Tools

This class of tool provides a graphical user interface to the data warehouse. The user will interact directly with the table structures. Some of these tools may provide a layer of abstraction that allows you to assign business names to the different columns and tables. These tools primarily return data in tabular format and may provide manipulation of the result set.

Report Writers

This class of tool may also provide a layer of abstraction that allows you to assign business names to the different columns and tables. These tools primarily return data in tabular or cross-tabular format. These tools provide extensive formatting capabilities to allow you to recreate a report to look a specific way. Again, users tend to have to work closely with the physical table structures.

Multidimensional Database Management Systems (MDBMS)

This class of tool provides advanced metric support with extensive slice-and-dice capabilities. Multidimensional Database Management Systems (MDBMSs) require that data be loaded into the multidimensional databases. The data does not need to be resident in a data warehouse in order to be loaded into a MDBMS but can come directly from the operational systems. Access to data in a multidimensional database is accomplished via two primary paths. Many of the software packages provide Application Programming Interfaces (APIs) so that you can develop your own front end to tap into the MDBMS. Many MDBMS vendors also provide a suite of graphical data access software or a graphical user interface that can be used to develop end-user applications. Some of these tools can technically reach through the MDBMS into a data warehouse to provide further drill-down capabilities.

Advanced DSS Tools

A key differentiating characteristic of advanced decision support tools is the ability to provide multidimensional analysis directly against the data warehouse database. These tools are often driven off shared metadata (see the section on metadata later in this chapter). They support advanced metrics, extensive slice and dice of the data, and drilling capabilities. Many also offer batch query support. The architecture of many advanced DSS tools, as shown in Figure 10-3, can be applied to large data warehouses.

Executive Information Systems (EISs)

Historically, Executive Information Systems (EISs) were created by constructing predefined reports with a structured Graphical User Interface (GUI) for navigation. Often, the EIS was completely separate from any decision support system, often with its own database. Today, EIS is viewed more as an extension of a DSS, providing a higher-level view of the same information. The EIS of today is often created with the same tool as the DSS.

Tiered Architectures

When researching the more advanced tools, you may hear about multitiered architectures. Tools with multitiered architectures generally work as follows:

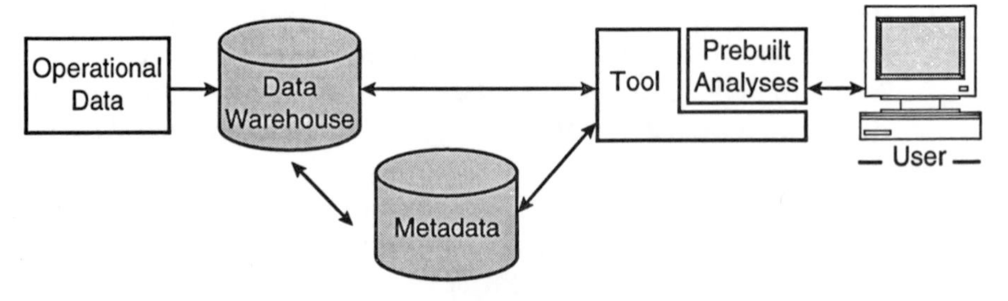

FIGURE 10–3 Advanced DSS tool architecture.

- One-tier: The client software and the database reside on the same physical machine.
- Two-tier: The client software and the database reside on two different machines.
- Three-tier: The client software and the database reside on two different machines. The third tier varies dramatically between vendors. The third tiers will be generally be used for one or more of the following:
  - *Computational engine:* The raw data are returned to the middle tier, advanced multidimensional calculations are performed, and the answer is sent back to the users.
  - *Resource manager:* Performs no additional analytical functions from the basic two-tier implementation but provides the ability to offload work from the client workstation to run in the background, at off-hours and at regularly scheduled times (for example, after new data have been loaded).
  - *Multidimensional database:* The multidimensional database itself can be considered a third tier. Data is loaded into the MDBMS from operational systems or the data warehouse and is made available to the end users.

SELECTING TOOLS FOR YOUR ORGANIZATION

One Tool Fits All?

Historically, no single tool has been able to provide all of the capabilities to span executive information systems through decision support systems through report writing. As each class of tools matures, the strict lines of delineation are beginning to blur. As you review the tool environment, you must determine what specific class of tool you require.

You will need to set up procedures and infrastructure to evaluate the different tools. In the optimal world, one tool would provide everything and all users would use it. Reality says that many organizations have different target audiences and may indeed consider acquiring multiple tools to meet a spectrum of data access requirements (see the earlier section on levels of users).

The Request for Proposal (RFP)

It is common practice to use a Request For Proposal (RFP) as a vehicle to learn about different products and to reduce the number of products to review in detail. There are some cases where the time and effort to develop and evaluate the results from an RFP can take longer than implementing the tool itself. If your corporate culture requires you to include the RFP as part of the selection process, make sure that you do the following:

- Educate yourself and your team prior to developing the RFP.
- Understand and target a specific class of tool.
- Predetermine the weighting factors for the characteristics.
- Predetermine how you will tabulate responses.
- Use relevant questions.
- Make your questions specific enough to determine tool differences.
- Give vendors enough time to do you justice (giving only a week to respond may not yield the best answers).
- Be prepared for the responses—don't be overwhelmed. If you send out a 25-page RFP to 15 vendors, you may see 100+ page responses—a total of 1,500 pages! Do you have procedures and the time to analyze 1,500 pages?

Key Considerations

You need to understand your corporate requirements and how potential tools address those requirements. The primary areas to make sure you understand include

- *General architecture requirements:* What infrastructures are currently in place? What are your corporation's future architecture plans?
- *Scalability requirements:* How big will your data be? How many users will you support? How soon will your warehouse reach those volumes?

- *Tool requirements:* Is a particular database schema required? Does the tool support prestored and/or on-the-fly aggregation? If so, how?
- *Implementation:* How do the internals of the tool work? What is set up for you? What do you need to set up? How difficult is it to perform the initial setup? What is required for initial installation?
- *Support:* How are DSS applications constructed? What will be required to support those applications over time?
- *Price:* Compare apples to apples and include all the component parts ("per client workstation" prices do not necessarily tell the whole story). Also consider potential volume discounts. What costs are constant regardless of tool (i.e., data preparation)? What do the development and support costs look like over time? What is the cost of the maintenance contract?

Overall, be sure to gain a realistic understanding of how the "magic"' occurs on the screen.

What Matters to You?

Make sure that you keep the big picture in mind when doing tool selection. If you are in a point-by-point, feature-by-feature battle between multiple tools, you must step back. Does it really matter if you have 10 versus 12 color graphs available to you? Keep a broad corporatewide perspective.

Many of the most visible components of a tool are the easiest to change. With today's advancements in GUI, you may find that the differences may only be who compiled using the latest VBX. So, while the interface is important, it is by no means the most important feature in selecting a tool.

A much more important consideration are the fundamental architecture issues. These are what differentiate the various products and will also be the hardest to change over time.

Selecting a Vendor, Not Just a Tool

As you begin to narrow down your list of possible tools, make sure that you take the time to understand the vendor's corporate vision and the future direction of that company. What are the product plans for the immediate, mid- and long term? What is the vendor's track record for delivering high-quality releases on schedule? How much do you want to be able to influence the next releases? How willing is the vendor to partner with you for design input?

If you have external consultants involved in your data warehouse development and tool selection, make sure you know their knowledge levels of the tools. You should also be aware of their vendor relationships, business alliances, and biases because these may substantially affect your options. You need to stay involved in the process too—someone from your organization should be speaking directly with the vendors. (Remember the game telephone as a child?) Additionally, be sure to ask for and call references from other companies that are actively using the product.

SUMMARY

In this chapter, you should have learned the following:

- An understanding of what tools are available and what types of data warehouses they support is important to understand before you design your warehouse.
- An environment for data access includes the data access software, training, support, and a starter set of applications to enable users to access information from your data warehouse.
- Do not underestimate the sophistication of tools currently on the market; these tools may have a long learning curve, so be prepared to support this.
- The in-house development of a front-end data access tool is not highly recommended; maintenance and enhancement costs could far exceed your schedule and budget.
- The levels of users should always be a major consideration in choosing a data access tool.
- The idea that simply loading the data will allow your users to gain business knowledge is an unrealistic view of a data warehouse. Likewise, simply making a front-end tool available will not ensure success.

- A DSS application is a "starter set" of predefined reports created in your front-end tool to accommodate the need for different levels of users to have prebuilt reports to begin their analysis.
- Different classes of tools are currently on the market: report writers, data access/query tools, advanced decision support tools, and multidimensional database management systems. These tools can have single or multitiered architectures.
- General data access characteristics are visualization of the data warehouse, formulation of the request, processing the request, and presentation of the results.

Case Study 4

Selecting a Front End to the Data Warehouse

by Debora Stranaghan, Implementation Services Manager, British Columbia Hydro

BRITISH COLUMBIA HYDRO BACKGROUND

British Columbia (B.C.) Hydro and Power Authority is the third largest utility in Canada, servicing more than 1.4 million customers in an area containing over 92 percent of British Columbia's population. B.C. Hydro generates between 45,000 and 50,000 gigawatt-hours of electricity annually, depending upon prevailing water levels. Electricity is delivered to customers through an interconnected system of over 70,000 kilometers of transmission and distribution lines. There are approximately 4,500 B.C. Hydro employees, located at headquarters in Vancouver and in regional offices all over the province.

About five years ago, B.C. Hydro initiated an effort to improve access to business data. Tools available in their existing mainframe environment required considerable technical knowledge to run even the simplest reports, and user demand for information was increasing rapidly. Fueling this effort was the fact that the company has been headed in new directions: The Canadian energy industry is facing rapid change, including the introduction of competition to a field that has essentially consisted of nationally protected monopolies. Availability of business information for timely business decision making would be a critical factor to future business success.

THE SEARCH DEFINED

In August 1995, a B.C. Hydro team developed a business case that outlined their problems and investigated ways to build a "real" data warehouse for financial information that would serve the entire organization. The team—which included Debora Stranaghan, implementation services manager; Peter DiGiulio, project manager for the development of the data warehouse; and Stewart Shum, manager of knowledge and information management—decided that front-end data access would be a key focus of their efforts. To deliver the variety of information users needed, the team determined that multidimensional analysis would be a requirement.

Since the business was changing, they needed more than a tool that could efficiently deliver today's information to the users—they wanted a tool to create systems that could grow and change with the company.

The B.C. Hydro team also determined that the users would require a tool that could handle two approaches: The new system must address the needs of "power users" who were comfortable with the existing environment and could write their own SQL queries, and so on, and it also needed to make information accessible to the large number of users without technical expertise who wanted a user-friendly interface. These users needed to be shielded from the complexity of the data but still had to be able to retrieve, analyze, and manipulate complex information.

By the end of December 1995, the team had looked at more than a dozen front-end products, using well-defined and specific criteria for reporting and results manipulation, which had undergone further refinement after a request for information was issued. B.C. Hydro's investigation was complicated by complex data hierarchies that are imbalanced, and they found that not many products could deal successfully with this issue. Their search was further narrowed in January 1996 to Arbor Software's Essbase, MicroStrategy's DSS, Oracle's Express Analyzer, Sinper's TM1, Kenan's Acumate, and Seagate Software's Seagate Holos® Business Intelligence software product—"a good cross-section of the market," noted Stranaghan.

BUSINESS INTELLIGENCE TRYOUTS

In mid-February 1996, after further comparisons, they were able to narrow the selection down to Seagate Holos and Oracle Express Analyzer for benchmarking. The B.C. Hydro team gave each company's representatives three days to produce a mock application, built to B.C. Hydro's specifications and using actual data. The mock applications were then turned over for two days of testing to 10 to 15 business analysts from B.C. Hydro's individual business units and users from the company's budget management group.

An interesting twist to this benchmarking effort was that it happened to fall during the company's planning cycle; thus, because the data used with these prototypes was actual, current data, the real-life applications were very welcome indeed. "The users weren't too happy when we took the products away," observed Shum.

B.C. Hydro started the benchmarking without any experience on Seagate Holos, which was the first to be benchmarked. Since the B.C. Hydro team knew the capabilities of Oracle Express Analyzer, many of the functions they asked Seagate Holos to execute were ones they knew Oracle Express Analyzer could do. Seagate Holos surpassed their expectations. "We really put Seagate Holos to work, and we were frankly surprised by what it could do," said Shum.

During their exploration of Seagate Holos and Oracle Express Analyzer, the B.C. Hydro team found that the more they saw of Seagate Holos, the more they appreciated its potential for developing their enterprisewide applications. Seagate Holos fulfilled these key conditions for B.C. Hydro:

- Simple storage requirements.
- Little time needed to develop models (B.C. Hydro had very little time to build their system, so the time factor was key to their purchase decision).
- Data refreshed quickly.
- Seamless integration with their relational database.
- Very thin client so that users could easily multitask.
- Reporting interface that provided a great deal of control and flexibility.
- Customizable user interface that could suit the needs of executives and nontechnical users, as well as those with technical expertise. "Many of our users just want data dropped on their desktops," said Shum. "They don't want to have to build it or wait for someone else to build it for them."

A DECISION REACHED

Once the benchmark tests were completed and the development team had compiled and compared the results, recommendations were made to the users at the end of February. Seagate Holos was the choice for the front end to B.C. Hydro's data warehouse, and the company began the purchasing process in mid-March 1996. Seagate Holos arrived in April, and by late July the first pilot application was rolled out to the user community.

ABOUT SEAGATE HOLOS

Seagate Holos is an application development environment for large-scale client-server business intelligence systems, combining OLAP (On-Line Analytical Processing) multidimensional data access and reporting with data analysis, data mining, and forecasting techniques. Seagate Holos offers tools both for the design and development of applications and for the ad hoc analysis and reporting needs of individual users. Seagate Holos has a wide range of options for storing and analyzing multidimensional data, techniques that are optimized across the spectrum of business intelligence applications Relational OLAP (ROLAP) to Multidimentional OLAP (MOLAP). This approach is sometimes called Hybrid OLAP.

The multitiered client-server architecture of Seagate Holos provides centralization of data storage and transparent access across client and server filestores, fault tolerance, easy maintainability and distribution of applications, and rapid accommodation of organizational changes. A single Seagate Holos client can connect to multiple servers concurrently. Seagate Holos reports can include tables, graphs, charts, text blocks, interactive database queries, multimedia objects, live buttons, report navigation facilities (such as "drill-down"), automatic plotting facilities, and live links to other applications. Two approaches to data mining are embedded in the current version of Seagate Holos, version 5.0—pattern matching and neural nets—along with intelligent agent technology.

THE SITUATION TODAY

Today, B.C. Hydro has a financial data warehouse running on an HP 9000 Model K460 using Informix Relational Database Management System (RDBMS) and Prism Warehouse Manager. Data is extracted, integrated, transformed, and summarized from the many different mainframe sources down to the HP platform, and Seagate Holos is the primary information delivery tool, providing access and multidimensional analysis of warehouse data.

All the Seagate Holos users at B.C. Hydro are looking at financial data for cost control; some are managing their own business units and some are monitoring the business of the entire company. The pilot application was initially deployed to approximately 20 financial and business unit analysts; the final application is likely to be used by approximately 100 users.

"Before we started using Seagate Holos, it would often take a business systems analyst several iterations, and even days, to generate the complex SQL queries needed to satisfy the nontechnical analyst's or manager's reporting requirements," said Shum. "Now a nontechnical analyst can produce that same report, manipulate the data, and format a report without additional technical involvement in a very short time. Users are surprised that there are so many ways to do different things."

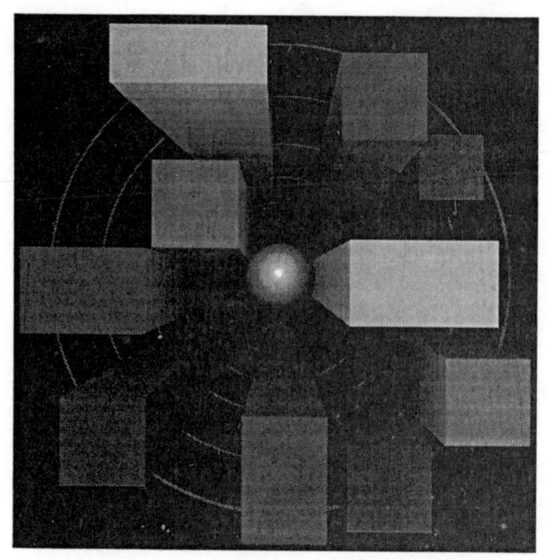

Chapter 11

TRAINING, SUPPORT, AND ROLLOUT

TRAINING

We cannot emphasize enough the importance of training for a successful data warehouse implementation. Consider the following:

- Your users are undoubtedly much more comfortable receiving reports, even if they have to go to five different reports for their information, than learning a whole new sophisticated system. The status quo will seem, and probably be, easier.
- Learning to think in a multidimensional, heuristic mode is a skill set that is learned and improved as it is used. It is quite different from a flat file or paper reporting mindset.
- Most users have no idea and cannot visualize the breadth of functionality that sophisticated decision support tools offer.
- Front-end data access tools are not simple to use. In fact, they can be relatively difficult.
- The data warehouse is not an operational system. In many cases, users don't *have* to use it; they can *choose* to use it to do their jobs. If you want your data warehouse to bring real value to the corporation, it has to be used.

The most successful data warehouse implementations create ongoing, well-designed, and implemented training programs for their user communities. Training should be focused on

- An introduction to data warehouse concepts.
- An introduction to your own data, where it is in the warehouse, and how it relates to reports or systems the user already knows.
- The mechanics of using the tool. It is important for people to understand basic navigation within the tool.
- The type of analysis that can be performed.
- Using the tool against your own data. What starter set of reports has been developed, how to use them, and how they are organized.

The optimal learning environment is usually a customized class created either internally or by a vendor, using a subset of your own data. This approach has the following advantages:

- Uses data that users know and can identify with.
- Provides custom training material and manuals.
- Provides formal exercises and materials to assist in training new personnel.

It is very important to understand that a multiple-day course at a vendor site is not enough training for the average user. These tools are extremely sophisticated. Often users get confused by the overload of information or forget the information before having a chance to use it. It is imperative that procedures and programs be implemented that can provide ongoing assistance and training on the data warehouse and the front-end tool of choice.

SUPPORT

In order to ensure success, you will need to develop a support structure and plan an approach. When people are using the system, the questions will flow. If you are not getting any questions, chances are that no one is using the system, and your development has been for naught. The questions will range across the board to include

- Questions about the validity of the data itself.
- How to use the data, what calculations make sense, and what levels of aggregation are valid.
- How to pick a report.
- How report measures were calculated.
- How to use the front-end application or toolset.
- How to change the front-end application or toolset.
- How to build your own application.
- How to navigate through the metadata.
- How to add new data or subject areas to the existing warehouse.

This first and most obvious method of support is to create and/or expand the help desk. This gives the client one place to call. The people at your help desk need to be skilled enough to work their way through a technical problem but also need to have an understanding of the business, the data that is in the warehouse, and how it can/should be used. This complete skill set may not reside with one single person, but you can set up a team that can cover the entire spectrum.

INTERNAL MARKETING OF THE DATA WAREHOUSE

Chances are pretty good that you have not been in the business of marketing the systems you have developed. This is one aspect of building a data warehouse that can be quite different from developing an operational system. You will need to spend time internally selling the data warehouse. The warehouse is a considerable investment for your organization and it is a new way to do business. Any change is not easy, and cultural changes are especially difficult. So what can you do? How do you get people to use the warehouse?

You must develop a strategy to encourage use, but you must keep in mind your goal—to excite interest in using the warehouse while simultaneously managing expectations. Make sure that people understand when their data will be available and what types of analyses they can perform with them. Some ideas on internally marketing your data warehouse follow.

DATA WAREHOUSE MARKETING IDEAS

Target Specific Groups

Identify two groups of people within the end-user community: the technically adept and key influencers in the business group. Target these two groups. The first group will have an interest in new technology and will be able to use the front-end tool fairly quickly. Early investments with this group will get them off and running. This group can feed success to management and colleagues.

The second group, the influencers, are important because they are the thought leaders; others watch what they do and follow. If you are lucky, these two characteristics may be found in the same group of people. If not, bring the influencers in early and have them help make decisions—perhaps in the priority of development. Have them on the project team. When you are rolling out to other users, they will then be in a position to explain to others the advantages of the system. Early success with key influencers will cause others to feel that they need to keep up which will make them more willing to invest time in learning. The more they learn, the more they will use the system. The more they use the system, the bigger the benefits and return to the corporation.

Get Clear and Visible Management Support

Other ways to get people to invest their time and energy in the data warehouse comes with clear and visible management support. This comes in a variety of flavors:

- Include use of DSS/data warehouse in annual performance goals.
- Provide visible management recognition when people use it.
- Have key executives request information from the warehouse or, when provided with information, respond positively. Sometimes a simple e-mail will motivate people to learn more.

Provide Visible Opportunities

Provide visible opportunities for people to share and learn from each other. Set up brown bag lunches or breakfast meetings once a month to display the capabilities of the system to users who are not yet using it. Set up a quorum of advanced decision support users, so they can share new analyses and ways to use the data.

Be Proactive

Another key to providing support is to be proactive. A help desk provides the foundation we all expect, but this is only reactive. It works when the user takes the time to try to use the system and then also takes the time to call. Often, many people don't even know where to begin and therefore, never even call for help. To reach this group of people, apply the same principles as management by wandering around. Place one or more people from the support team in the user work area. These people should be aware of general activity and be on hand to provide assistance and tutoring. Actively helping people over their initial fear of the new system and assisting in their learning curve is a proactive and usually successful way to get users to use the data warehouse.

Create a Publication

Start a newsletter, or get a column in an existing newsletter.

PLANNING A ROLLOUT: DEPLOYMENT

Phased Rollout Approach

Consider the ramifications of bringing hundreds of users on-line at the same time. The support load alone should be enough to scare those thoughts away. The most successful approach is to set up a schedule to bring new groups of people on-line every few weeks or so. This way, you can schedule people for training, then when they get back they will have the live application ready to use on their workstations.

You should plan for greater amounts of time between the first few groups. This will allow you to make any adjustments to the application and/or approach before the next group comes into training. After you work out the wrinkles, you can then run several classes a week. You should consider having two introductory classes a week initially. Then move to one intro class and one advanced class each week.

The phased rollout also provides you with the opportunity to track support requirements and add more staff if required.

Logistics of a Rollout

As you get closer to releasing your decision support system for production use, you need to plan how you intend to distribute the software and/or applications to the users. The cleanest implementations occur when the front-end software tool is separate from the database application. One of the key requirements for any large-scale deployment is the ability to share the fundamental objects of the application. Object sharing allows an organization to efficiently and effectively demand and deliver information without requiring hundreds of users to constantly "reinvent the wheel." Then, central modification of the reports can be shared by all users immediately. If you have elected not to use a meta-data-driven approach to your front-end data access, you need to develop a strategy for distributing new applications to the users. If you are distributing the application to remote users, you might consider using electronic software distribution tools.

SUMMARY

In this chapter, you should have learned the following:

- User training and support is one of the most important aspects of building a successful data warehouse.
- Learning to think and work in a multidimensional, heuristic mode is a skill set that is learned and improved over time.
- The data warehouse is not an operational system—in many cases the users do not have to use it. And if it is too difficult to use or appropriate levels of training and support are not supplied, they probably won't use it.
- You must be proactive in getting users to use and appreciate your data warehouse.
- For a successful data warehouse, plan your in-house marketing and support structures as part of your implementation. Several examples of in-house marketing were supplied in this chapter.

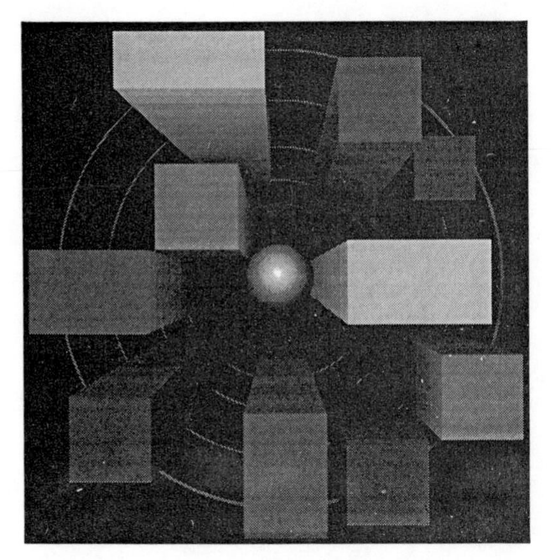

Chapter 12

METADATA

INTRODUCTION

There is no discussion of a data warehouse without a discussion of metadata. Vendors of data conversion tools, data access tools, and databases talk about metadata, your project manager wants to know how you are going to handle metadata, and any number of technical journals have articles about metadata. There is a great deal of confusion surrounding metadata and frankly, a good percentage of this confusion comes from the marketing of the many tools and products associated with the data warehouse environment.

To cut through this confusion, we will first provide you with an overview of using metadata for change management in a production decision support environment. Although this may not be the level of metadata management that your organization is ready to tackle, it will give you a vision of what your are working toward. Since this may be your first data warehouse and the infrastructure for metadata management may not be in place in your organization, we will simplify the concept of metadata by categorizing it into two different types, which will assist in breaking down the very large task of implementing metadata management into workable steps. We will then provide some ideas on how to approach metadata management on a short-term basis, so you can implement the metadata that is needed by your end users for your particular project.

Using Metadata for Change Management

Data warehousing places a greater emphasis on the quality, integration, and availability of data to provide information to support a variety of decision support requirements. Business users of the data warehouse often participate with the data interactively as they create queries to answer business questions. This greater degree of hands-on use usually generates a greater number of requests to add or modify the data in the warehouse as the business users become more familiar with the kinds of questions they want to answer.

This higher degree of user involvement results in a greater emphasis on change control processes and metadata management to support the volume of change requests that inevitably occur. The volatility of a production data warehouse environment demands a rapid development cycle requiring new roles, methods, tasks, and tools to manage metadata, versioning, and multiple test environments in a consistent and reliable manner. The need for these development environment functions is not always apparent until the data warehouse is in production.

Metadata and Data Administration

Data administration is really a misnomer. It is a familiar term freely used in corporate information resource management to describe the role of someone responsible for metadata. It should be called metadata administration because that is what is really occurring! The typical function of a data administrator is managing metadata. No wonder everyone is always confused about the difference between data and metadata! Even as data professionals we use our terms interchangeably and we are the pickiest people on earth when it comes to distinctions between terms and definitions.

Metadata management has traditionally been the province of the corporate data administrator. Many organizations that embraced CASE technology in the 1980s created a function to establish naming standards and business definitions for shared data used throughout the organization. The data warehouse could get a significant jump-start in integrating its data and beginning the process of metadata management if this function is already identified and established within the organization. Otherwise there will be a costly, time-consuming learning curve while the data warehouse sponsors and management discover the critical role of metadata management for the successful warehouse implementation. The companies that never placed an emphasis on data administration in the past are now scrambling to understand the issues surrounding metadata, identify roles, put procedures in place, and select tools to perform metadata management.

Rigorous documentation (or automated collection) of metadata and the ability to store, manage, and access metadata will provide a vehicle to maintain version control of individual objects and, additionally, associate all the related objects for a specific release. The ability to perform these tasks efficiently will have an impact on the timely delivery of data in the successful data warehouse environment.

Metadata Directory

What is a metadata directory? Simply put, it is the database that carries all the data describing the data warehouse. It will be used by business users who will view the data transformation metadata before querying the data in the data warehouse. It will be populated with metadata for data integration by the systems developers responsible for the creation and management of the data warehouse and it will be maintained by the data administrators responsible for maintaining the accuracy and currency of the metadata.

The contents of a metadata directory may consist of business-related information such as source applications, file and field names, usage descriptions, data owners, application owners, and application user names. The most common metadata found describes data types, lengths, null rules, default rules, valid values, and indexes because it is defined in the Entity Relationship Diagram (ERD) or Data Definition Language (DDL) generated using a modeling tool. Some of the most critical information, such as conversion, derivation, and aggregation rules, is often not captured consistently and therefore is not readily available. System content such as program names, data set names, DDL, log statistics, source and target system names, and file names and locations are usually recorded in a source code library or job scheduler and with a little work could be included in the metadata directory.

Even though we may grasp the significance of having a metadata directory, there are many obstacles. As we said earlier, metadata is a byproduct of one or more processes. Performing those processes is usually done with different tools. The tools each have proprietary methods of storing the metadata being generated and the purpose of the tool is to produce a specific deliverable that may be considered metadata or only a partial description of the metadata that is generated. The rest of the metadata are trapped in the data structures of the tool. There is a movement to establish a standard to be used by tool vendors that will simplify the gathering and integration of metadata into a metadata directory. Unfortunately the standards process is still in its infancy and at this writing most companies are faced with a significant amount of work to pull together the necessary metadata required to manage the data warehouse life cycle and support the information needs of the users and developers of the data warehouse.

Companies that recognize this problem and understand the value of taking on the collection and management of metadata have come up with a variety of solutions. Many simply publish a set of procedures establishing standard usage of each of the tools in the development environment to promote consistency. A "table of contents" or index is provided to users and developers to find the information they seek. Others have created their own database to collect the metadata and published it on the company intranet to make it available. These solutions are better than relying on "word of mouth" communication that occurs in most environments where you have to run around to find the *right* person to point you to the *right* location to find the *specific* information you need.

The anticipation that metadata will be passively updated after the fact is a futile expectation and should be recognized as such. The only real hope is in the active generation and usage of metadata throughout the development cycle to establish it as a necessary and viable component of the data warehouse architecture. This is rarely recognized up front as the architecture is being defined, the tools are being selected, and the environment is being put in place. It is typically a retrofit once the need is painfully exposed and the difficulty is now a hundredfold. The development process must change to accommodate the delivery and maintenance of the metadata along with the data itself. This typically is seen as a reduction in productivity and the resistance is likely to be significant.

Tips from the Trenches 12.1

A Cautionary Note

If you expect to hire an expert to establish a data administration function and implement a metadata directory, it must be recognized as a significant undertaking that requires the participation of the key members of your development team and business sponsors. This will inevitably cause a reduction of your current productivity just as the "nay-sayers" asserted. You have to pay that price up front to derive an environment and process that will actually be used so the true improvement in productivity will be realized and the success of the data warehouse will continue to derive benefit to the organization.

Metadata Administration in Practice

All of this talk about metadata administration, directories, management, proliferation, generation, and usage is a little theoretical without a framework for understanding how metadata fits into the data warehouse environment. A data warehouse project never ends. The process is the true deliverable. Continuous consolidation, conversion, and population of data both into and out of the data warehouse will be happening based on the continuous flow of change requests that will begin as soon as the data warehouse goes into production. Building the data warehouse is the easy part in one sense because you have a specific target. Once in production, you are in the uncharted seas of ever-changing sources and targets.

Growth is inevitable. Adding a new source to the warehouse, modifying an existing source in the warehouse, adding additional scope to the warehouse, adding a new distribution channel, modifying an existing distribution channel—all are examples of the kinds of requests that will be made as soon as the data warehouse is built. This requires continuous improvement of the analysis and conversion process along with highly skilled resources and tools to support the ongoing demand. Metadata is necessary to manage the change request process by providing the information to perform gap and impact analysis against the existing warehouse to assess time estimates and handle version control.

CHANGE MANAGEMENT

Change management is the cornerstone of a successful production data warehouse. Change management requires tracking all the components required to support the ongoing growth of the data warehouse.

Understanding Versions and Releases

It is extremely important to have systems in place for version control and release management. People often use the terms "version" and "release" interchangeably. It is important to distinguish the various definitions of these terms. In the application development environment version and release often have different connotations. A version is often referred to as a specific iteration of an object whether it is a model

(ERD), a program, or DDL. It is the current version or the latest version or the last version or the test version or the production version of a particular object or persistent deliverable within the application development process. A release, in this context, is the grouping of the current versions of all the objects that together make up the application or system. The first release of the system would consist of the specific version of each object required to run the system. When changes are requested to the system, each object must be analyzed for the impact of that change and they may go through various versions before they are ready for the next release. The versioning processes of the objects are independent of each other because the changes may require significant work on one object and little or no impact on another. Because these are important concepts to understand relative to the topic of metadata, I would like to clarify, for the purposes of this discussion, the definition of each term.

Version—When an object (data model, source code, physical database structure, etc.) is changed, the new state of the object, after the change is applied, is a new "version."

Release—Release, in the context of release management, refers to a related group of objects required to run an application. A release would be the current version of all the objects that are running to execute the application. In the data warehouse environment it would consist of the database, programs loading it, the definitions of the data structures, the scripts, Job Control Language (JCL), and control files used to execute the jobs.

Metrics for Change Management

Change management requires the coordination of impact analysis, change request overlaps, estimates, and implementation schedules. The availability of metadata and quantifiable metrics improves the accuracy of estimates. The usage of templates to quickly perform impact analysis of requested changes and a system to manage and report on change requests which provides view access to project members are essential to manage the service-level objectives of the data warehouse development.

The first template, Table 12-1, is a general impact analysis template for a change request. The second template, Table 12-2, represents the cross section of modifying the existing source and the development im-

Table 12–1 General Inpact Analysis Template

Change Management Metrics	Development impact	Complexity	Resource skill level	Resource availability	External org. resource dependency	Docu-mentation quality	New platform & training requirements
add new source							
modify existing source							
add new distribution							
modify existing distributiion							

Table 12–2 Modify Existing Source-Development Inpact Matrix

Modify existing source-development impact	Warehouse	Marts	Reports	Allowed Value Changes	Rules	Conversion Programs	End User Access Queries
key field							
nonkey							
nonkey-allowed values							
nonkey derived							
nonkey-foreign key (join)							

Table 12-3 Documentation Quality Matrix

Documentation Quality	Completeness	Depth	Accessibility	Currency	Consistency
system overview					
file & data element descriptions					
data type, lengths & default value definitions					
allowed value definitions					
file usage description					
control information					

- completeness—Every field in the files is documented.
- depth—Detailed information available.
- accessibility—Ease of access to documentation (electronic vs. hardcopy)
- currency—Up-to-date information.
- consistency—If there are multiple references to the same fields are they consistently represented.

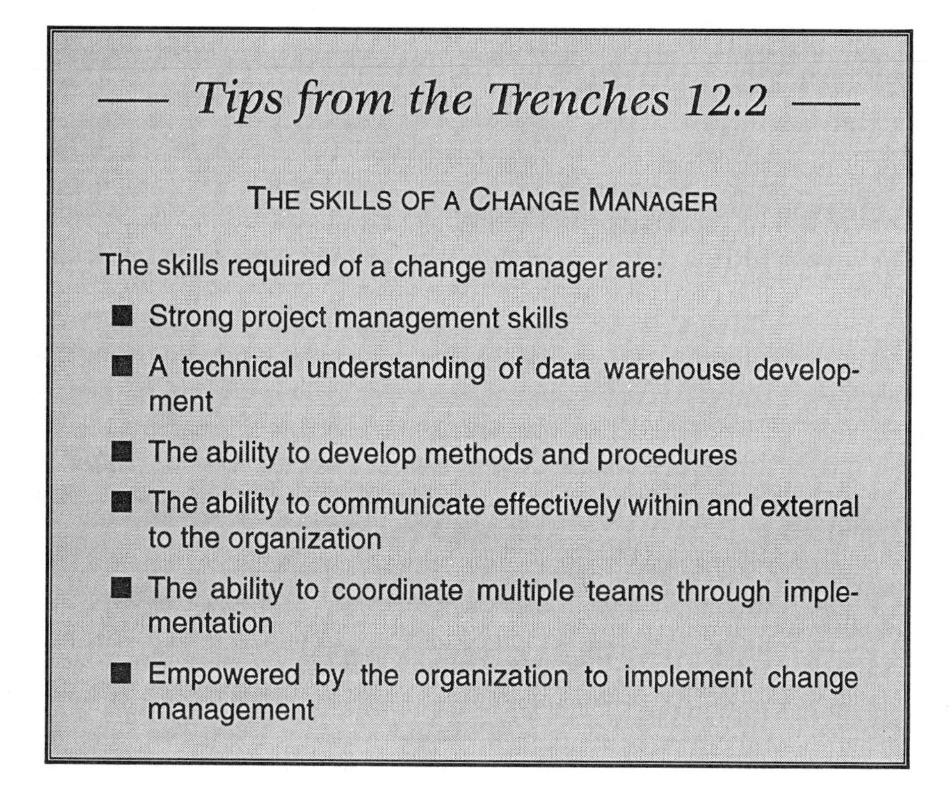

— *Tips from the Trenches 12.2* —

THE SKILLS OF A CHANGE MANAGER

The skills required of a change manager are:

- Strong project management skills
- A technical understanding of data warehouse development
- The ability to develop methods and procedures
- The ability to communicate effectively within and external to the organization
- The ability to coordinate multiple teams through implementation
- Empowered by the organization to implement change management

pact. The explosion of complexity is quickly evident as you drill down through these templates. A separate table should be created for each cross section of the general impact analysis template to accurately determine change request estimates. Tables 12-2 and 12-3 are examples of two cross sections from the general impact table: "development impact—modify existing source" and "documentation quality—add new source." These templates will aid developers and change managers to analyze all the components of the data warehousing development cycle they will have to consider to determine accurate estimates in response to change requests.

Table 12-3 provides an example to help understand the significance in not only capturing and documenting metadata, but also an appreciation in the difference in the quality of metadata. It will also demonstrate the impact of metadata on the ability to provide accurate estimates and specific enough information for business users and developers to determine the content of the data being analyzed.

A REALISTIC APPRAISAL OF METADATA MANAGEMENT WITHIN CORPORATIONS

As we described earlier, as more and more companies develop and deploy data warehouses, the lack of the policies, procedures, and organizational structures to manage metadata becomes increasingly apparent. It is the movement into the decision support arena, with its emphasis on accessible data for the end user, that is only now forcing companies to address the issues surrounding information resource management. In our experience, we find that it is quite common for infrastructures for metadata management to be almost nonexistent within corporations.

Hence, for many project teams building their first data warehouse, there are no legitimate structures to assist them in implementing metadata. It frequently becomes part of the initial data warehouse project team's task to try to begin building these infrastructures, often requiring the navigation of many political and organizational obstacles. If you are in a similar situation, you must budget for and request additional resources that can focus on analyzing and implementing a metadata solution for your project.

Often we will find that the metadata implementation portion of the data warehouse project was dropped somewhere back in the middle of the life cycle. This is when the illusion of how easy it is to develop a data warehouse crashes head to head with the reality. As project time lines tighten, finding a workable solution to metadata implementation is one of the first things that gets cut from the project plan. Although we can wholeheartedly empathize, this is really not a very good idea. If you must take on beginning the infrastructure development for metadata management and implementing a metadata solution within your project team, a better solution may be to

- Recognize and address this need during the planning stage of the life cycle.
- Dedicate a resource to the task.
- Set up a short-term solution based on your end users' need for metadata that can be later built upon and expanded.
- Begin lobbying heavily for a person or group within your organization to take on the responsibility for metadata management and associated infrastructure development.

UNDERSTANDING TYPES OF METADATA

Metadata is data about data. As we have described, metadata for a decision support system encompasses the data about data generated at every point throughout the full life cycle of development. To simplify your understanding of metadata and to bring clarity to any discussions of the topic, it will be helpful to differentiate between metadata for data integration and metadata for data transformation. Making the distinction between these two types of metadata will allow you to create a workable plan for managing metadata within your company by breaking this very large task into smaller more workable chunks, because each of these two types of metadata has a particular purpose. This distinction will also provide a good basis for conversation with any product or tool vendors you may encounter; when they say they handle metadata within their tool, you can question them to understand what parts of the data warehouse process the tool metadata is addressing.

Metadata for Data Integration

Metadata for data integration, in various forms; are produced at every point along the way as data goes through the process of moving from the source operational systems to populating the data warehouse. Examples of this type of metadata are the initial documentation that describes the source system data, the processing rules to convert the source data into the data warehouse, and the Data Definition Language (DDL) used to create a relational database. This is the type of information that enables an administrator or change manager to perform the analysis required to estimate the impact of change requests against the current warehouse implementation. The efficient management of a production data warehouse relies heavily on the collection and storage of metadata required for data integration.

Metadata for Data Transformation

Metadata for data transformation is produced at every point along the way as data goes through the process of moving from the data warehouse to arriving at the end user's desktop as the result of a query. Data transformation metadata is used during the process in which end users access data from the data warehouse and transform it into information. Metadata for data transformation will generally include the processing rules to derive and calculate data (if it was not done in the database load), the business definitions of tables and attributes, as well as default and allowed values associated with individual attributes or domains. It will also include the dimensions within your warehouse and the hierarchies within your dimensions that will be used with a multidimensional data access tool. The end user refers to this metadata to transform the data in the warehouse into usable, value-added information by formatting, summarizing, and viewing the data in specific ways.

HOW TO APPROACH A SHORT-TERM SOLUTION FOR YOUR PROJECT

To develop a short-term solution to your metadata needs, you must first look at what metadata you will really need. The first step is to develop a matrix of metadata needs based on the level of users within your company.

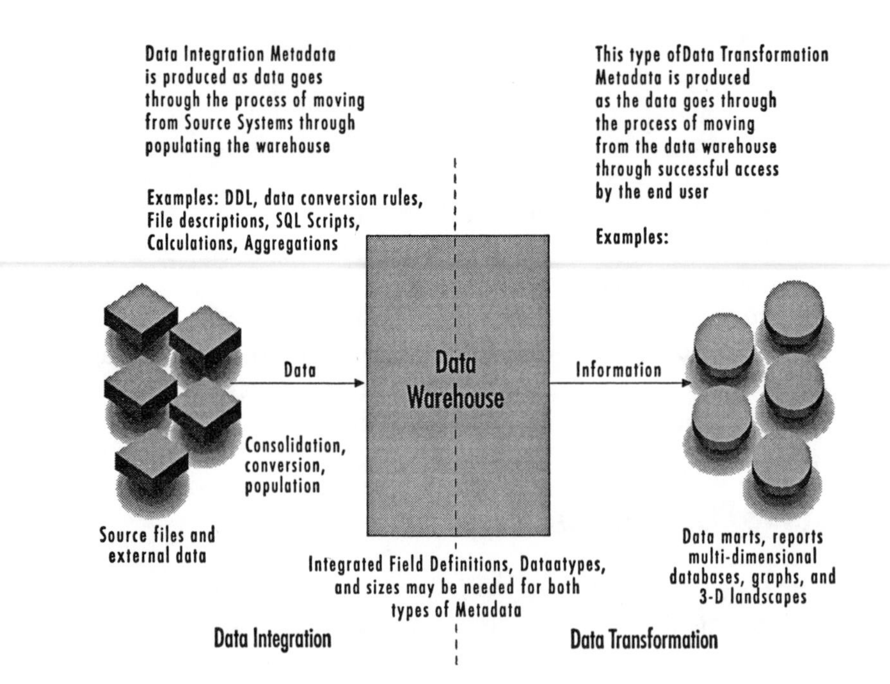

Figure 12–1 Data integration metadata and data tranformation metadata.

To review, levels of users (as described in Chapter 10) for a data warehouse are categorized as follows:

- Executive User
- Novice / Casual User
- Business Analyst
- Power User
- Application Developer

One method that companies have implemented that is a short-term and very workable solution for business analysts and casual and executive users is a simple help program allowing users to click on a specific field name to get a definition for that field. Included in these definitions would also be (especially for financial institutions) the calculations of the particular field, and any other pertinent information that would assist this level of user.

For power users and application developers, the full range of data integration and data transformation metadata is necessary. If you do not have the infrastructures to integrate all of this metadata into a manageable system, you may have to provide manual metadata or a simple database of metadata information to these users for the short term.

By looking at the matrix in Table 12-4, you can see that a great deal of the necessary metadata is data transformation metadata (business definitions, summary rules, dimensions and hierarchies, query descriptions) which are actually much easier to implement routinely than data integration metadata.

The good news about data transformation metadata is that many of the data access front-end tools, especially multidimensional tools, provide as part of their tools the functionality to view the data transformation metadata structures needed to access the data in the data warehouse. For the end user to be able to view their data through multiple dimensions, the front-end tool must be able to show the dimensions and hierarchies within the dimensions to the end user. For instance, if you are looking at sales within a specific region, over time, you are viewing a fact (sales) through the dimensions of geography and time. If you wish to view sales by additional dimensions, or change the time dimension from daily to monthly, the tool will provide the mechanism for you to make those choices. The tool does this

Table 12–4 Levels of Users and Metadata Needs

	Executive	Casual	Business Analyst	Power User	Application Developer
Business Definitions	x	x	x	x	x
Source to target Conversion rules					x
Source file Description					x
Target DDL, data Types, & defaults				x	x
Summarization Rules			x	x	x
Calculations			x	x	x
Dimensions and Hierarchies	x	x	x	x	x
Query definitions			x	x	x

by allowing you to see the structure of the metadata which makes up these dimensions. In this example, you can change your time dimension to monthly because the tool allows you to see the hierarchy of daily, weekly, monthly, quarterly, and yearly within the time dimension. What you are looking at is one very valuable type of data transformation metadata.

A well-designed Decision Support System (DSS) application (as defined in Chapter 10) using a front-end data access tool retrieves data from a database and translates it into meaningful data based on your dimensional business Model (see Chapters 7, 9, and 10 for additional information). To do this, the application must understand both the dimensional business model and the location and structure of the data warehouse. Data transformation metadata, the data about data, acts as the link from the warehouse and the conceptual business framework to the front-end application.

Other Uses of Data Transformation Metadata

Data transformation metadata provides a layer of abstraction between the data warehouse and the reports and analyses. As you change your physical database structure, you only have to update your metadata once and all the applications will use the new structures. The metadata layer prevents changes to the underlying warehouse from causing the reports and analyses to break down. As a result, evolutionary or architectural changes in the data warehouse can immediately be reflected in your decision support application. For example, if a corporation restructures to eliminate a layer of management, the DSS

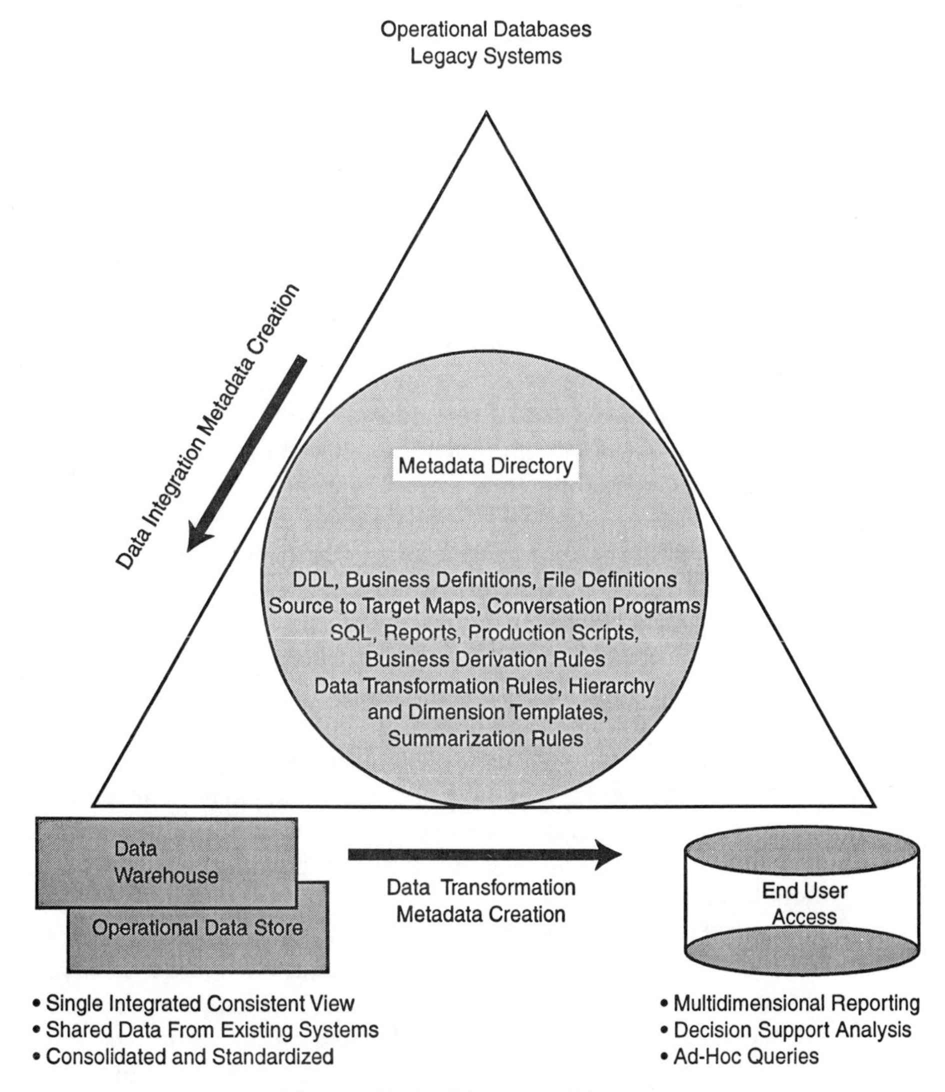

Figure 12–2 Metadata Directory.

application using a front-end tool should "reconfigure" itself using data transformation metadata to reflect the new organizational hierarchy as soon as the data corresponding to the new hierarchy is added to the warehouse.

The decision support tool provides the front-end user interface to manipulate the data transformation metadata and use it to build reports and analyses. This allows the Graphical User Interface (GUI) to drive off the metadata for both ad hoc analysis and prebuilt reports. This technique allows applications to be configured, not custom coded.

Using Data Transformation Metadata for Application Deployment

Data transformation metadata serves another purpose as well. In large-scale deployments, shared metadata can significantly reduce maintenance costs and update cycles. Applications can be rolled out onto thousands of desktops, with a layer of data transformation metadata serving as the link between the client application and the data warehouse. Therefore, when the structure of the warehouse is altered to reflect current business conditions, the shared data transformation metadata can be changed centrally by the warehouse administrators, and all the client applications will be updated automatically and transparently. If the warehouse is moved to another location, the data is distributed over multiple warehouses, or if the database software is replaced, the shared metadata allows the end users to carry on with business as usual with no maintenance and update interruptions.

As you can see, there are short-term solutions that are applicable to your particular project and decision support environment. Data integration metadata may be more difficult to implement for your first data warehouse; however, data transformation metadata management may not be as difficult. Understanding what your end user really wants and needs for metadata will take you fairly far down the path of short-term metadata management.

A full metadata management solution, including using metadata for change control in a production environment, is a substantial investment of time and money. Our recommendation is to empower a team working with a specialist in this field to assist you to set up the infrastructures, processes, methods, organizational structures, and metadata management system.

SUMMARY

In this chapter, you should have learned the following:

- Metadata is data about data. Metadata for a decision support system is the information generated at every point as the data moves from the source systems to the data warehouse and the data warehouse to the users' desktop.
- Metadata management is necessary in a successful data warehouse because the higher degree of user involvement with the data results in a greater need to establish procedures for change management to support the growth of the data warehouse.
- A metadata directory manages all the information about the objects that make up the data warehouse.
- Because of the short turnaround times expected by users in a data warehouse, it is essential to have a method to assess the impact of changes against the data warehouse as accurately as possible.
- These are two types of metadata. Metadata for data integration is the information about the data as it passes from the source systems into the data warehouse. Metadata for data transformation is the formation that describes the data as it is accessed from the data warehouse and delivered to the users' desktop.
- Data transformation metadata can be implemented relatively easily using some front-end access tools. It also provides a layer of abstraction between the data warehouse and the end user which will mitigate the impact of changes to the warehouse on the user.

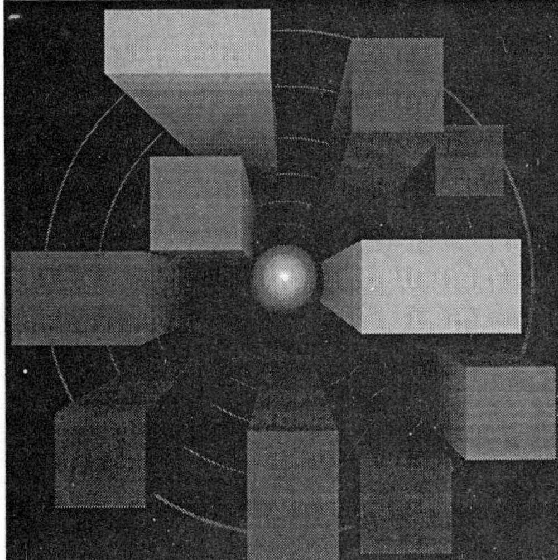

Appendix

CONSULTING COMPANIES ASSISTING IN THE DEVELOPMENT OF THIS BOOK

Vidette Poe is the founder and President of Strategic Business Solutions, Inc.

Strategic Business Solutions, Inc. is a consulting company specializing in the planning, design, development, and implementation of data warehouses and related technologies. Strategic Business Solutions, Inc. provides the following services:

- Data Warehouse Planning
- Gathering Requirements and Designing the Database for a Data Warehouse
- Enterprisewide Data Architecture & Strategies for Decision Support Systems
- Hands-on Project Management for Data Warehouse Development and Implementation
- Infrastructure Strategies to Support Data-Focused Decision Support Environments
- Corporate Readiness Assessments for Data Warehouse Development

For more information, contact Vidette Poe at warehs@aol.com

Patricia Klauer is the President of Design Data Systems, Inc.

Design Data Systems, Inc.
Design Data Systems, Inc. is a San Francisco based consulting firm providing services that specialize in designing the infrastructure, architecture, organizational structure and procedures for Information Services. Design Data Systems, Inc. has developed information architecture strategies for OLTP and DSS applications to support Year 2000, Risk Management, Market Analysis, Financial Instrument, and Client Relationship Management Systems for large financial institutions worldwide.

- Enterprise Management and Strategic Integration of Data
- Data Warehouse Design and Architecture
- Gathering Requirements and Data Modeling
- Training in Data Modeling, Data Integration, Requirements Gathering Techniques

- Data Management Practices to support Data Warehouses
- Enterprisewide Information Services Planning and Strategies

For more information, contact Patricia Klauer at pklauer@aol.com

Patricia Klauer is also one of the founders of Manage Data, Inc.

Manage Data, Inc.
Manage Data, Inc. provides software and strategic consulting for Internet and enterprisewide management, distribution, access, and storage of data. Manage Data's mission is to provide intelligent information management across platforms and storage devices providing cost-effective and efficient distribution and access to all types of media. Manage Data, Inc. has offices in Toronto and San Francisco. For more information contact patty@managedata.com.

Stephen Brobst is a Senior Consultant at Tanning Technology Corporation.

Tanning Technology Corporation
Tanning Technology Corporation is a premier systems integrator specializing in very large database (VLDB) and on-line transaction processing (OLTP) applications. The company prides itself in delivering three-tier open-based system solutions that are sufficiently flexible and scalable to meet both the current and future IT needs of its corporate clients, which include some of the largest users of information technology in the world today. This often includes an information warehouse that enables the owner to make essential business decisions about customers, products, operations, markets, and competitors in an organized, controlled-access environment. With offices in Denver and London, Tanning Technology can be contacted at www.tanning.com.

Stephen Brobst is also a founder and managing partner at Strategic Technologies & Systems.

Strategic Technologies & Systems
Strategic Technologies & Systems is a consulting and systems integration company focused on high-end database design and construction, specifically in the area of sophisticated data warehouse environ-

ments. The company was founded in 1983 as an MIT spinoff and since that time has implemented numerous data warehouse projects working with clients such as Fidelity Investments, L.L.Bean, Foster & Gallagher, Blue Cross, Blue Shield, John Alden Financial Corporation, J.P. Morgan, Hannaford Brothers Company, Amalgamated Banks of South Africa, Metro Cash n' Carry, and many others. Strategic Technologies & Systems (STS) is not wed to any specific technology solutions, but rather focuses on selection of the best combination of parallel hardware and relational database products to meet client requirements on a per project basis. Strategic Technologies & Systems is privately held with offices in Boston (headquarters) and Miami. You can reach STS by mailing to sts@strattech.com or by paper mail to Strategic Technologies & Systems, 186 Lincoln Street, Suite 611, Boston, MA 02111, (617) 422-0800.

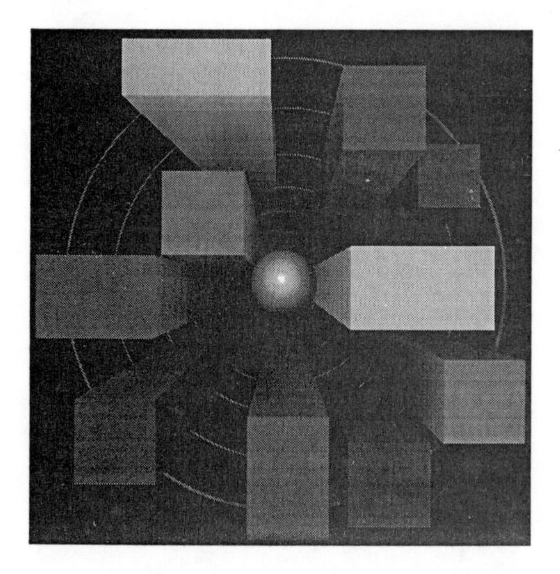

INDEX

T

U

V